What People Are Saying About John Wooden . . .

"When I think of John Wooden, I think of principles, discipline and organization."

—Phil Jackson
Los Angeles Lakers coach

"My favorite coach of all time is John Wooden, without question. I think he was a guy that coached the best way of anybody that I have ever heard talk about the game."

—Steve Spurrier
head football coach, University of South Carolina

"I admire Coach Wooden so greatly because of his core of integrity which leads to an honest, straightforward life. He has always thought about the purpose of his life, knew what he believed and then proceeded with that in mind."

—Bill Bradley
former basketball Olympian and U.S. Senator

"John Wooden set his rules and enforced them rigidly. There was no question about who was in charge. If you didn't live by Wooden's rules, it was see ya. Kids ended up doing it John's way and not even know it was happening."

—Keith Jackson
ABC-TV sports announcer

"He was a rare person who deserved the praise of greatness, but Coach Wooden also was a man of goodness. That's a rare combination that very few people attain—greatness and goodness. John Wooden is God's closest creation to the perfect man. Next to my Dad, John Wooden was the greatest influence in my life."

—Dick Enberg
TV sports announcer

"Twenty-nine years have passed since I left UCLA and it amazes me how smart Coach Wooden has become in those 29 years. I'm 50 years old now. We thought he was nuts. He was a walking antique. It wasn't until adversity hit us that I realized he was right."

—Bill Walton
former UCLA player and basketball legend

"John Wooden is a man of integrity and has always remained true to what he believes. He coached at a different time, but has never abandoned his life values."

—Bob Costas
TV sports announcer

"Coach Wooden believed in treating people with respect and he got respect back. He was a humble man who had great pride, but it never went to his head."

—Dick Vitale
basketball TV personality

"Very few people are great, but John Wooden is a superstar. Part of it is his accomplishments and the way he did it which commands people's respect. Years from now people will ask, 'How did Coach ever accomplish that?' He is a unique man."

—Jerry West
president and general manager, Memphis Grizzlies

"I admire Coach Wooden for the way he lived his life. He had a strong moral compass and had his priorities in order. Then he lived them out on a consistent basis."

—Kareem Abdul-Jabbar
former UCLA player and basketball legend

"John Wooden has morals, ethics and spiritual beliefs and as a result, he sees what life is really all about. Because John is so personable he makes you feel comfortable in his presence."

—Lute Olson
head basketball coach, University of Arizona

"Coach didn't just make up his pyramid. He is the pyramid. He believes those lessons, teaches them and lives them. John Wooden is an honest, sincere, competent man."

—Pat Riley
president and coach, Miami Heat

"John Wooden is the greatest coach of all time in any sport. He had the ability to teach, his values were strong and he knew how to get inside the heads of his players."

—Marv Levy
former head coach, Buffalo Bills

"At his age, Coach is still living every day to the utmost. That's what all of us should do."

—Baron Davis
NBA All-Star

"With Coach Wooden, it's not about the records. It was always about his people and getting them to do the best they were capable of doing. The feeling his former players have for him is truly amazing."

—Roy Williams
head basketball coach, University of North Carolina

"Coach Wooden gives you insights about humanity. At a time in history where we have so much noise, anger, hate and disenchantment, we need more John Woodens."

—Howard Schultz
CEO, Starbucks Coffee Company

How to Be Like Coach WOODEN

Life Lessons from Basketball's Greatest Leader

Pat Williams
with David Wimbish

Health Communications, Inc.
Deerfield Beach, Florida

www.hcibooks.com

Publisher: Health Communications, Inc.
        3201 S.W. 15th Street
        Deerfield Beach, FL 33442-8190

Cover design by Larissa Hise Henoch
Inside book formatting by Dawn Von Strolley Grove

I dedicate this book with love, respect and admiration to
John and Nell Wooden and their family—especially
their two children, Nancy and Jim, their seven grandchildren,
and thirteen great-grandchildren. What a legacy
the Wooden clan has left for all of us to model.
May this book inspire you to live your life
to the fullest and become all you are capable of becoming.

Contents

Foreword

By Bill Walton
Former UCLA & NBA Superstar

ANOTHER JOHN WOODEN BOOK? The man is ninety-five years old, has been retired for more than thirty years and has had so many books, movies and projects done about him that you have to wonder what more could possibly be said. At least that's what I thought when I learned that Pat Williams was turning his attention to Coach Wooden as the seventh subject in his *How to Be Like* series about significant people who deserve to have their stories told.

While John Wooden certainly is a worthy candidate for Pat Williams's unrelenting passion for spreading good news and hope, one must be aware that many of Coach Wooden's former players and the sportswriters who regularly covered his teams have already taken their turn at trying to re-create the brilliance of this master teacher. All of this is in addition to the seemingly endless stream of books that Coach Wooden has written himself. I've read them all and have written introductions for most of them.

So what makes this book different and therefore worthy of your time and mine, particularly because Pat never met The Coach until 2001?

I have read and studied the life and times of Pat Williams since I first met him while I was attending UCLA, playing for Coach Wooden on a team that set standards that have stood the test of time, just like Pat and Coach. This book is clearly the best of the best, as Pat has taken his craft to the highest level. While Pat has certainly taken on daunting tasks before, this current masterpiece has consumed his life. As Pat started this book, more than four years and at least eight hundred interviews ago, he, like the rest of us who have hitched a ride on Coach Wooden's bus, had no idea what he was getting into.

Pat Williams is a man who for decades has perfectly embodied all the human characteristics and personal attributes that are the guiding

principles of Coach Wooden's life—and none more so than the cornerstones of the Pyramid of Success: industriousness and enthusiasm. But the
more work Pat did on *How to Be Like Coach Wooden*—from the trips to
Martinsville, Indiana, where he spent a day in Poe's Cafeteria with more
than fifty of Coach's hometown friends, to VIPs Restaurant in Los Angeles
where Coach eats breakfast every day, to the visits with the two living teammates of Coach Purdue's teams, to the time spent with the two surviving
members of Coach Wooden's first-ever team under his supervision
(Kentucky's Dayton High School)—the more he realized all that was still
left undone.

John Wooden is an intergalactic treasure who has selflessly lived his life
for the betterment of others. The same can be said about Pat Williams. This
collaboration between two of the most dynamic and creative forces that I
have ever encountered has resulted in a unique trip through the heart, soul
and mind of The Coach, a man I thought I knew until I read Pat's book.
This is the first book about The Coach from the outside, and it provides an
incredible amount of never-before-told information about a truly remarkable human being.

One of the amazing aspects of Coach Wooden's life is his accessibility.
Every day the mail brings overwhelming amounts of unsolicited correspon-
dence to the Mansion on Margate. At ninety-five, The Coach lives alone
and has no assistant, no cell phone, no computer and no fax machine. He
starts every day at his office desk and meticulously answers, in perfect long-
hand on unlined paper that would make his English and penmanship
teacher so proud, *every* query about solving the world's problems that are
heaped on his ever-more-frail shoulders. Then The Coach gets in his car,
drives to the post office and stands in line to buy the postage necessary to
send his reply, often including a small piece of his own memorabilia.

Coach Wooden is the most available and approachable person in the
world. He's like a church, always there for everyone. Even for Coach, there
are limits of time and space, and now it has taken someone so remarkably like
The Coach himself, Pat Williams, to bring the man and his reality to you.

How to Be Like Coach Wooden is the perfect textbook for you to find your
way into Coach's inner sanctum. Pat Williams takes you on a scintillating
journey that will make you feel a part of The Coach's extended family. This

ride will take you into his den, his office, his home, in the locker room and onto the team plane. Along the way you will learn many things that you will not fully understand or absorb the first time through. My advice: The Coach calmly teaches faith and patience.

As you will learn in this epic work by Pat Williams, Coach Wooden is a teacher preparing others for their life's work. Coach Wooden used to begin every pregame speech with these simple and understated words: "Men, I've done my job, the rest is up to you." That is what Pat Williams has done for us in this book.

This morning I told Coach how much fun I was having reading this fabulous book and how many new stories I was learning about him. The Coach, in his infinite wisdom, clarity and humility, told me in the quietest of voices: "You know, I'm just an English teacher. Shouldn't I be the one writing a book about Pat Williams?"

I Tried to Be Like Coach

cֵֶ᷿᷿֓

By Swen Nater
Former UCLA Center
Under John Wooden

I met a man, my coach, one yesterday,
His ways and peace of mind, they caught my eye.
And like an adolescent bird, I took the sky,
And then commenced to live a better way.

Though called "The champion's Champion," soberly,
He spoke with zeal of family, faith and friends,
As if the trophies were just odds and ends,
And trivial in contrast to those three.

As oceans discard refuse to the coast,
What mattered least, he gladly cast away,
And shelved those precious hours every day,
Reserving them for things that mattered most.

For all the blessed days I was a son,
I never saw one wasted, idle hour;
In daylight all the work, he would devour,
But evenings he was with his dearest one.

Like me, imprisoned in my quest for gold,
Magnetically, the curious ones drew near,
Who lost, or never learned, what should be dear,
But he so naturally lived, and wore and told.

I've tried to live a life beyond reproach—
A life that majors on what matters most.
Though blemishes have caused me not to boast,
I still am glad I tried to be like Coach.

A Word of Tribute

⊱✦⊰

By Charlie Moir

IN 1972, MY GREATEST TEAM in thirty-six years as a coach took me to the NCAA College Division National Championship. One of the most memorable events that came my way as a result was sharing the head table at the annual National Association of Basketball Coaches Convention in Los Angeles with John Wooden. Coach Wooden was on the eve of capturing his eighth National Championship, and I will never forget the honor of receiving a National Coach of the Year Award with him.

I had already known Coach Wooden as he and my brother Sam had become very good friends working the summer camp circuit in the sixties. Sam was the head coach at Catawba College in North Carolina, and he recalls that Coach Wooden always made you feel like you were the greatest coach in the world, as if he were the one trying to learn from you. The very fact that a man of Coach Wooden's stature traveled across the country annually to do a youth camp is a phenomenal statement about him and his desire to give something back to the game of basketball.

I know of no instance during my time as a college basketball coach that Coach Wooden let anyone down or set a bad example. He modeled decent, proper behavior 24 hours a day, 365 days a year. For example, at the annual NABC convention, just watching the way he treated Nell was a wonderful example to other men of how to be a good husband. When some people in the media took shots at him, he took the high road and never answered in kind. He never "big-timed" people, but he always had time for you and was always ready to answer your questions. It is well documented that he was never driven by a desire for money. On the bench, he didn't stomp and scream. He stressed that championships are won on the practice court and said that the game was the players' opportunity to shine, not the coach's.

Coach Wooden was an innovator as well. His Pyramid of Success is a foundation anyone can use in building a sound team, business or community. His books, *They Call Me Coach* and *Wooden*, are tremendous tools for any person trying to build a better life.

Coaches leave legacies, and Coach's legacy is that a lot of us are better people because he passed our way.

> —*From 1964 to 1968, Charlie Moir was head basketball coach at Tulane University, Virginia Tech and Roanoke College.*

Introduction:
Sometimes, Nice Guys Finish First

꧁ꙮ꧂

*John Wooden is a man of integrity and has
always remained true to what he believes.*
—*Broadcaster Bob Costas*

THE LATE LEO DUROCHER always insisted he was misquoted. He never really said, "Nice guys finish last."

But whether or not he was misquoted, Durocher's statement has become widely regarded as fact. People think nice guys can't win—in life, sports, school or in a career. In this era, when Donald Trump has become a television star and "You're fired" has become a catch phrase, most people believe you can't get to the top unless you're tough and ruthless—willing to push others out of the way so you can be the first one up the ladder.

But what they say is a lie.

Nice guys *can* and *do* finish first. How do I know? Two words:

John Wooden.

From 1966 to 1973, John Wooden's UCLA basketball teams captured seven national championships in a row. From 1964 to 1975, UCLA won ten NCAA crowns in twelve years. From 1971 to 1974, the Bruins won eighty-eight games without a loss. You can talk about Coach K, Bobby Knight or Dean Smith, but the simple fact is that John Wooden was the most successful college basketball coach ever. Period.

He did it with an honest program. And he did it as a nice guy. Oh, he was tough but not nasty. He was competitive but never had an attitude of "win at all costs." He treated his players as if they were human beings. He didn't yell at his assistant coaches and call them names. He wasn't one to rant and rave at the referees. He didn't stomp out of postgame press conferences or tell reporters they were "stupid." I can't imagine John Wooden throwing a chair onto the court.

Steve Bisheff, who has been a sportswriter for nearly forty years, says, "John Wooden is the most remarkable man I have met in this business."

What John Wooden accomplished on the basketball court is truly amazing.

What he has accomplished as a teacher and builder of young lives is even more amazing.

If you're reading this book because you want to be like Coach, congratulations! You've chosen a great role model. Over the next two hundred pages or so, we're going to take an up-close look at this remarkable man and see if we can't discover the qualities of character that helped make him so successful as a coach—and as a human being. My own life has improved through my efforts to follow Coach Wooden's footsteps, and I believe the same will be true for you—no matter how "together" your life may already be.

PART ONE

BUILD ON A SOLID FOUNDATION

꩜

When the whirlwind passes by,
the wicked is no more.
But the righteous has an everlasting foundation.

—Proverbs 10:25

Chapter One

⋯⁂⋯

If You Want to Be Like Coach: Be a Person of Character

It was his life that changed my life.
—Swen Nater, coached by Coach Wooden at UCLA

I HAVE A PROBLEM. How do I even begin to sum up a giant of a man like John Wooden?

That's the question that gnawed at me as I began working on this book.

How do I sort through thousands of wonderful stories about John Wooden and decide which ones don't make the final cut?

How do I even begin to tell you about the impact this incredible man has had on just about everyone who has had the privilege of knowing him?

Well . . . I could begin by telling you that John Wooden is one of only three people ever to be inducted into the Basketball Hall of Fame as a player and a coach. (The other two are Lenny Wilkens and Bill Sharman.)

I could mention that he was a first-team All-American for three straight seasons at Purdue University in the early 1930s—the first college basketball player ever to receive such an honor.

I could start by telling you that he was the NCAA College Basketball Coach of the Year six times!

But instead I think I'll start back in 1948.

That was the year a young coach by the name of Wooden had put together a pretty good basketball team at Indiana State University. That team included a young man by the name of Clarence Walker. Walker wasn't one of the starting five, but he came off the bench to help Indiana State win an invitation to the NAIA basketball tournament in Kansas City. Thirty-two teams were invited, and one of them would emerge as the small-college national champion.

But there was a problem.

Walker was black.

Remember that this was just the year after Jackie Robinson joined the Brooklyn Dodgers and was subjected to death threats and verbal abuse for breaking the "color barrier" in Major League Baseball. Racism was rampant in Indiana and most of the rest of the nation.

Tournament officials called Wooden and told him that his team was invited, but Walker wasn't. "We've never had a black person play on the Kansas City Municipal Auditorium floor," they said—only they didn't say "black person."

Now that tournament was a big deal, especially to a young man just starting out in his coaching career. But John Wooden didn't even have to think about it.

"If I can't bring Clarence, we're not coming," he said.

Fine. Indiana State was disinvited from the tournament. That's where the story might have ended, except for the fact that the national newswires got wind of the story. An article appeared in the *New York Times*, and it came to the attention of officials at Manhattan College, the consensus pick to win the tournament that year. (Manhattan still has a fine basketball program, as was shown by their first-round upset of Florida in the 2004 NCAA tournament.) Manhattan's coach called the NAIA offices and said, "If Indiana State can't come with that young man, we're not coming either."

Faced with the loss of their biggest draw, tournament officials backed down, and Clarence Walker became the first black to play basketball on the floor of Kansas City's Municipal Auditorium.

Stan Jacobs, who played on that Indiana State team with Walker, says he will never forget his coach's courage. He remembers that Walker wasn't one of the stars on that team. "But Coach's decision wasn't based on how the outcome would affect him. His action was motivated by only one thing—his own personal character and his decision to do the right thing."

John Wooden is a man of impeccable character. He has always followed his own advice to "be more concerned with your character than with your reputation, because your character is what you really are, while your reputation is merely what others think you are." I love the way Wooden's former star center Bill Walton put it:

John Wooden represents the conquest of substance over hype, the triumph of achievement over erratic flailing, the conquest of discipline over gambling, and the triumph of executing an organized plan over hoping that you'll be lucky, hot or in the zone. John Wooden also represents the conquest of sacrifice, hard work and commitment to achievement over the pipe dream that someone will just give you something or that you can take a pill or turn a key to get what you want.

As Coach always said, "The true athlete should have character, not be a character." What is character? Coach says, "It's how you react to things—sensibly, without getting carried away by yourself or your circumstances. A person of character is trustworthy and honest, and for a dollar, he or she will give you a dollar." He also said, "I believe ability can get you to the top, but it takes character to keep you there."

* * *

You're not supposed to put a halo on anyone . . . but if I were to put a halo on anyone's head, it would be John Wooden.
—Former Angels pitcher Dean Chance

* * *

Lorenzo Romar, head coach at the University of Washington, smiles as he remembers something that happened when he was head coach at Pepperdine in the early 1990s. "I took the whole staff to visit Coach Wooden at his condo," Romar recalls. "We spent four hours with him. He called me the next day and said, 'One of your coaches had seventy-five cents slip out of his pocket into my sofa. I want to get it back to him.'"

Seventy-five cents? That wouldn't be a big deal to anybody—except a man of absolute character like John Wooden.

Dozens of others who've known Coach over the years can tell you similar stories: Those who played for him, those who coached against him, those who've known him as friend or teacher—most can give you one example after another of John Wooden's honorable character.

Tony Luftman, UCLA student manager in 1984–85, said, "John Wooden is a genuine person in an era of self-promotion and hype. He remains a humble man who doesn't seek attention and doesn't promote himself. He proves that nice guys can finish first." Luftman pauses for a moment and then adds, "People should try to be like Coach. Some famous people aren't really worthy of emulation, but Coach is."

Joe Wootten, basketball coach at Bishop O'Connell High School in Arlington, Virginia, is the son of legendary prep coach Morgan Wootten. Because of his father's long involvement in the game of basketball, the younger Wootten has known John Wooden since he was a boy. When I asked him for his thoughts about Coach, he told me, "His life refutes the argument that to be successful in life you have to look the other way and cut corners. He has achieved the ultimate level of success in his career, and he never compromised his values to get there." He told me that whenever he's around Coach, he feels "surrounded by goodness. He gives you a great sense of peace and calmness."

As I write this, Coach Wooden is ninety-five years old. He's getting up there by anyone's standards. He tires out quickly and doesn't get around so well. Yet at a book signing a few weeks ago, he signed autographs for three hours straight. Afterward, he was exhausted, and his hand and shoulder were killing him. Someone asked why he hadn't just cut the session short. Coach looked surprised that anyone would even ask a question like that. The answer was simple: He didn't want to disappoint anyone. That's the kind of man he is.

AN INDIANA BOY

John Wooden was born in tiny Hall, Indiana, on October 14, 1910. If you know anything about Indiana, it won't surprise you to learn that John

Wooden began playing basketball at a young age. Whenever someone mentions Indiana, the first things I think of are small-town gymnasiums packed to the rafters on Friday or Saturday nights in the winter—rocking with the noise of crowds that are larger than their hometown's entire populations. Perhaps basketball was invented in Massachusetts, but I'm positive that no state has had a more passionate love affair with the game than has Indiana.

Coach remembers that when he was about eight years old (in 1918, when basketball was still a relatively young game), his father made a hoop out of an old basket and nailed it to the wall at one end of the hay loft in the barn. He and his brothers used a basketball made out of rags stuffed into a pair of their mother's hose. From that time on, John Wooden's plans for the future involved basketball.

Despite the fact that Joshua Wooden made it possible for his boys to play basketball, and encouraged them in the sport, he never gave them any particular advice about the game itself. He didn't teach his sons how to make a set shot. He never talked to them about their dribbling or passing skills. He didn't spend any time with them showing them how to hit a layup or a swisher from the free-throw line.

John says of his father, "He seldom attended games and was only slightly interested in results. His concern and guidance were deeper."

Coach was eleven when he first began playing basketball for Centerton Elementary School, under the guidance of Coach Earl Warriner, who also served as principal of the school. The court they played on wasn't much by today's standards. It was outdoors, with a hard-packed dirt floor, and even though it was swept clear of branches, leaves and rocks before every game, there were still many occasions when the basketball took "a bad hop" off some obstacle or another. Coach remembers that in the late fall, it would sometimes begin to snow during the middle of a game. Never mind. The game continued until the snow got too deep to dribble the ball.

Basketballs in the 1920s weren't easy to dribble anyway. For one thing, they were heavier leather balls that rarely held their round shape. A ball would often go flat during a game—and sometimes it would go flat two or three times. When that happened, the players would have to remove the laces, inflate the ball by blowing into it (this being before the day of bicycle pumps and air needles) and then retie the laces. Coach laughs when he recalls how, when he was starring for Purdue, "I received considerable attention for my dribbling skills. Learning with a lopsided basketball on a dirt court with potholes and patches may have been why I became a pretty fair dribbler."

Whatever the reason, he became such a good player that Coach Warriner began talking about the possibility of Wooden playing college basketball. Coach now recalls that in those days, he didn't even know what "college" was. But if there was a way to keep playing one of the games he loved, that was fine with him. (Baseball was his other passion, and Coach was so good that he was the starting shortstop for the town team at the age of fourteen.)

He will tell you proudly that when he was growing up, there was no question that Indiana's high school basketball teams were the best in the country. He remembers, "There were dozens of high school gymnasiums in the state that seated more than any college gymnasium in the country. There was a time that Amos Alonzo Stagg held a national high school tournament, but they wouldn't let Indiana high school teams in." They were too good!

CHARACTER CAME EARLY

If I were writing a book on John Wooden, I would call it Old School Is a Good School. *He was an old-school guy and believed in old-fashioned ideals—treat elders like they should be treated, be thoughtful of others, go to class and make something of yourself.*
—Sports announcer Jim Karvellas

Beginning when he was a small boy, John Wooden's parents taught him to be honest, fair and hardworking. He spent much of his childhood on a small farm, where he and his brothers, Billy, Daniel and Maurice, were kept busy milking cows, cleaning out horses' stalls, weeding crops, picking tomatoes and doing whatever else needed doing. None of the boys complained that it wasn't fair for them to do all that work while attending school. Their father led by example. In addition to working the farm, he had a second job as a rural mail carrier.

When John graduated from grade school, his father gave him a piece of paper, on which he had written these words to live by:

1) Be true to yourself.
2) Make each day your masterpiece.
3) Help others.
4) Drink deeply from good books, especially the Bible.
5) Make friendship a fine art.
6) Build a shelter against a rainy day.
7) Pray for guidance, count and give thanks for your blessings every day.

Coach says he carried that piece of paper in his wallet for years, until it began to wear out. Before his father's words became too faded to read, he made copies for himself and others. He says he has always done his best to live by his dad's creed.

As Coach's old friend Larry Rubin said, "John Wooden has always been guided by strong principles, a deep religious philosophy that has always been more important to him than any immediate gain."

In preparation for writing this book, I conducted hundreds of interviews with Coach's friends and former players and asked what they admired most in the man. Over and over again, I heard, "Coach was a man of character." When I asked, "What do you mean by that?" I got answers like the following:

1) COACH ALWAYS TRIES TO DO THE RIGHT THING.

A leader's most powerful ally is his or her own example. Leaders don't just talk about doing something; they do it. Swen Nater told me once, "Coach, you walked the walk." He meant that I led by example.
                                                                    —John Wooden

During his third year as a high school basketball coach, John Wooden was forced to suspend his team's best players and cocaptains when they failed to show up for a game. The boys both claimed they had been sick and in bed, but several people reported seeing them having fun at a dance the night of the game.

Coach told them, "It sounds to me like that dance was more important to you than the game or the team." Then he informed them that they were off the team—for the rest of the season. The boys didn't take the news well. In fact, one of them threatened that his father—the school's vice-principal—would have Wooden fired. Coach listened calmly and said that even if it cost him his job, he wasn't going to change his mind. Far from firing him, the vice-principal later thanked Coach Wooden for taking a tough stand. "That was the best thing that ever happened to that headstrong son of mine," he said.

Looking back on that tough situation and the hard decision he had to make, Coach says, "The incident gave me confidence in standing up for my beliefs. I was trying to do more than build a winning team; I was trying to build character. And building character is always the right thing to do."

In a late-season game at Notre Dame in 1973, Coach became upset by the play of Irish All-American John Shumate. Wooden thought Shumate was roughing up his center, Bill Walton, so he stormed down to the Notre Dame bench and told Coach Digger Phelps how he felt about it. "If he doesn't knock it off, I'll send Swen Nater in for Walton and he won't take that."

Phelps shot back, "It's a two-way street."

A few days later, after Wooden had a chance to think about things, he wrote Phelps a note:

Dear Digger,

I owe you and John Shumate an apology and I hope you will accept it in the spirit it is offered. I acted hastily without thinking clearly and taking all things into consideration and, as usual, actions from emotion are seldom with reason.

John Wooden

P.S. Please convey my feeling to John. He is a fine young man and an outstanding basketball player and I did him an injustice.

That heartfelt apology is typical of John Wooden's determination to do the right thing at all times. When he was coaching at UCLA, he sometimes lost his cool. He complained when a close call didn't go his way. But when he realized he'd made a mistake, he was quick to admit it. When an apology was necessary, he gave it.

2) Coach measures his words carefully.

If anyone is never at fault in what he says, he is a perfect man, able to keep the whole body in check.

—James 3:2

Coach remembers that one of the worst whippings he ever got was for swearing at his brother—who had just thrown a shovelful of horse manure in his face as the two of them worked in their father's barn. The brother was punished, too, but to this day, Coach still thinks he got the worst of it. Perhaps that's why no one I know has ever heard him say anything stronger than "Goodness gracious sakes alive." And he won't say that unless he's really upset.

Stan Jacobs, whom I quoted earlier, said, "John Wooden never uttered a curse word in his life." Jacobs says, "John Wooden has the highest degree of character and value structure of anyone who has ever crossed my path." Jacobs relates that he grew up in a "tumultuous" family. "The good family memories I have, frankly, were when I went to John Wooden's home," he says. "You know, I'm not a Christian, but I have Christian values—and I certainly got them there."

Former University of Virginia coach Terry Holland recalls that during his days as a college player he attended summer basketball camps at Campbell College in North Carolina. "I was most impressed with the consistency of his character," Holland says. "While the other coaches were drinking and playing cards, Coach would come out in his pajamas and just watch. Press Maravich would be cussing up a storm, and Coach would say, 'Now, Press, you shouldn't be talking like that.' He wasn't judgmental about it, but genuinely concerned. Coach was always the same and didn't alter his behavior based on who he was with or what he was doing."

Dutch Fehring, who played with Wooden at Purdue, and then went on to become line coach for the UCLA football team, told me: "John Wooden always had empathy for other people. I have never heard him bad-mouth anyone. He always had respect for his teammates and his opponents."

That's another thing he learned, at a very early age, from his father. "My dad was a wonderful person," Coach says. "I never heard him speak an ill word of anybody, never blamed anybody for anything. I never heard him use a word of profanity."

He remembers, "Dad would read to us every night from the Scriptures and poetry, and I think that created a love of poetry, which I've always had. I can still close my eyes and hear him reading 'Hiawatha.'

"I think that his reading to us caused all four sons to get through college, though he had no financial means to help and there were no athletic scholarships. All four sons graduated from college, all majored or minored in English, and all got advanced degrees. I think Dad had a lot to do with that."

3) Coach is a Man of Absolute Integrity.

John Wooden had his own value system and didn't let anything affect him. He was always consistent to his values and lived his life with conviction. He was a man of total honesty.

                                        —Jack Arnold

John Wooden says he learned about the importance of integrity from a frosty bottle of cream soda: He and his grade-school chum Freddy Gooch had walked to Breedlove's general store on a hot, sticky summer day. By the time they got there, they were *so* thirsty, and Freddy charged a nickel bottle of pop to his parents' account. John knew he didn't have permission to do anything like that, and he also knew his parents couldn't afford to waste a nickel. But it was so very hot! And Freddy's soda looked so cold and refreshing.

Unable to resist temptation, young Wooden gave in and got a bottle of pop for himself—and it sure tasted good. But even as the last gulp was making its way down his throat, he began to regret what he had done. He remembers that he was overcome with guilt—and fear of a hard whipping from his father. He slowly made his way home and confessed what he had done, prepared for the worst possible consequences.

"But Dad and Mother understood my being tempted, and they just explained firmly why my actions were wrong. Believe me, that made a big impression on me, and I never did anything like that again."

Coach's deep integrity is illustrated by how he came to be head coach at UCLA. It seems that he didn't really want to move to Los Angeles at all. He was a midwesterner by birth and by heart, and he preferred to stay there. In addition to applying for the coaching vacancy in Westwood, he had also interviewed for the head coaching job at the University of Minnesota.

Both schools were supposed to call him on the same day to tell him whether or not they were going to offer him a job. Minnesota was supposed to call first, and UCLA an hour later. Coach had set it up that way, because it would allow him to accept the Minnesota position if it were offered, and then say, "Thanks, but no thanks," to UCLA. Only Minnesota's telephone call didn't come as scheduled. Thus, when UCLA contacted him and made an offer, Coach accepted. He remembers, "About an hour later, I got a call from Minnesota." University officials told him they hadn't been able to get through because an "unseasonable" snowstorm had interrupted telephone service. "I said, 'I'm sorry, I've committed myself. I can't back out now.'"

In a world where contracts are loaded with fine print and legalese that no mere mortal can understand, John Wooden has always been a man of his word. He is a "promise keeper" of the highest order.

Ken Weiner, senior associate athletic director at UCLA, tells this wonderful story that illustrates Coach's commitment to integrity: "During the 1970s, an administrator for the athletic department issued a stern reminder that telephones were for official use only. When Coach went through his own telephone bills, he found three personal calls out of the dozens he had made. He dutifully wrote out a check for $1.50 to cover the cost of those calls, saying that he wanted to 'clear his ledger.' Can you imagine a person of Coach's stature being concerned about a dollar and a half? That's integrity!"

Former UCLA student manager George Morgan told me, "The John Wooden at practice was the same John Wooden in the locker room. The John Wooden in the locker room was the same John Wooden on the campus. The John Wooden on the campus was the same John Wooden at home. There was only one of them." That's as good an example of integrity as I've ever come across.

His nephew and niece, Ron and Judy Sherbert, told me, "You can always trust that John Wooden will be the same person. Always! He's never in a bad mood or displays an attitude. When he talks with you, he looks right in your eyes. We believe he can see your inner person." They also wrote that one of the important things they have learned from their Uncle John is that "What counts is how you act, not how you react. We have never seen him react—let himself be provoked."

Vaughan Hoffman, who played basketball under Coach Wooden from 1961 to 1965, had two serious knee injuries in high school. During his junior year, he had to have cartilage removed from the knee and underwent a lengthy rehabilitation period. Then, the following spring—just prior to graduation, and after accepting a scholarship to play basketball at UCLA the following season—he injured the knee again and had to have a second surgery.

Hoffman told me, "Coach Wooden came to see me in the hospital and said, 'Vaughan, if you can still play, you have your scholarship—and if you can't play, well, then you can be our student manager.'"

"He's a treasure," Hoffman says, "because he always sticks with his values." He adds that he and his teammates learned as much about life from Coach as they did basketball. "We learned lessons about discipline, honesty, trustworthiness and being smart. He taught us to stick with our convictions and that life is about the journey as much as it is about the destination.

"He is a unique human being."

4) COACH STRIVES TO BE A MAN OF HUMILITY.

Years ago, I wrote a major magazine piece on John Wooden. I spent seven or eight long sessions with him, and when I finished, I was in a deep depression. I thought, I can't go back because I have enough material, but I miss the man. *John Wooden makes you want to be a better man. He's a breath of fresh air.*
—Sportswriter Bill Dwyre

John Wooden is justifiably proud of what his UCLA basketball teams accomplished. But he is quick to share the credit, pointing out that it was his players who won all those games and championships, not him.

Columnist Adrian Wojnarowski, writing in *Basketball Times*, tells of a visit to Coach's apartment in Encino, California:

> *To insist to Wooden what most sensible sports minds consider fact—that he's history's greatest coach—invites a disapproving grimace, an understanding that he isn't interested in contributing to such a consensus. Wooden rises to his feet and instructs a visitor to walk with him to a mantle, insisting, "I want to show you something." He grabs a small wooden box, flips back the lid and cups a bronzed medallion in his hands. An award the Big Ten delivered him as a Purdue graduating senior in 1932, representative of the top student-athlete in the conference.*
>
> *"It's my most prized accomplishment," Wooden says, "because only I was responsible for it. All the coaching awards, I had just a small part in them. Those belonged to my players. . . . This, though, I was responsible for earning."*

Coach has always believed in sharing the credit. He says, "If a player scored off a pass, I wanted him to point to the man giving the assist until they made eye contact in a gesture of thanks and acknowledgment. I started that with my high school teams. I also wanted a gesture of thanks done for a good pick-up, for help on defense or for any other good play."

Former University of North Carolina Coach Dean Smith says that when he heard about the "pointing rule" from Coach, he instituted it at Chapel Hill. "We even had the Bobby Jones Rule. One game back in the early seventies, Bobby missed a layup after a beautiful pass from George Karl. Bobby still pointed to him. To this day, the Carolina players point to the passer even after a missed layup."

In 1995, when a reporter called Wooden "a legend," he replied, "I'm no legend, and I'm embarrassed by that." He went on to say, "I don't like false modesty. I'm proud of the fact that I was fortunate to have a lot of wonderful players who brought about national championships and that I'm a part of that. But I'm also realistic, and I know that without those players it wouldn't have happened."

On another occasion, after a particularly flowery introduction, Coach said, "I hope the good Lord will forgive my introducer for over-praising me, and me for enjoying it so much."

Longtime college basketball coach Bob Burke told me a story that speaks volumes about Coach's humble spirit: "Back in the 1960s, I was working on the staff at the Campbell University summer camp. On the first day, I went out early to get oriented, and there was John Wooden, championship coach, sweeping the floor all by himself."

5) COACH HAS HIS PRIORITIES STRAIGHT.

John Wooden was noted for his honesty and fairness to people. He never bent the rules to win an extra game or two. There was never anything under the table. The more UCLA won, the more Wooden went under the microscope. The closer you looked, the better John showed up.

—Dutch Fehring, former
UCLA assistant football coach

During the late 1960s, when the UCLA basketball program was at the height of its success, Jack Kent Cooke tried to hire John Wooden to coach his Los Angeles Lakers.

Coach went to Cooke's house at the invitation of Lakers' general manager Fred Schaus, where he found Cooke sitting behind a huge desk in his study. They sat in silence, just looking at each other, for several minutes before Cooke finally said, "Why do you want to coach the Lakers?" Wooden replied simply that he didn't want to coach the Lakers. He had come to Cooke's house because Schaus had asked him to.

Cooke was incredulous. "Anyone would want to coach the Lakers." The Lakers' owner thrust an offer sheet in Coach's direction. "What do you think of that?"

"Nobody's worth that kind of money," Coach said. But he still wouldn't take the offer.

"Well, then, how much do you want?"

Coach tried to explain that it wasn't about money. He didn't want to coach the Lakers because he didn't want to spend that much time on the road away from his wife, Nellie, and their children, Nan and Jim. Besides, he liked coaching and teaching on the college level. For John Wooden, coaching basketball had never been about money and never would be. Wooden left Jack Kent Cooke shaking his head in anger. Cooke simply couldn't understand why anyone wouldn't jump at the chance to take one of the most glamorous and highest-paid jobs in all of basketball.

When Coach was asked what his top priorities are, he replied, "Faith, family and friends." Then he smiled and added, "Sometimes I put family first. That's not really the proper order, but I think the Lord understands."

Are you surprised that basketball didn't make the list? It's not among the top three because Coach always tried to maintain an "eternal perspective," to see the bigger picture of what life is really about. That's why it didn't surprise me when Seattle Supersonics owner Howard Schultz told me, "Coach told us he once passed on a top high school recruit because he heard the boy speak to his mother in a disrespectful manner." John Wooden has always felt some things were more important than basketball-like respect for others.

Regarding his eternal perspective, Coach said, "I often think of Socrates, who was unjustly imprisoned and facing imminent death. The jailers couldn't understand his serenity, and they asked, 'Why aren't you preparing for death?' He answered them, 'I've been preparing for death all my life by the life I've led.' There is something beyond here that's more meaningful."

6) COACH NEVER JUDGED ANYONE BY SUPERFICIAL CHARACTERISTICS SUCH AS THE COLOR OF THEIR SKIN.

[John Wooden's] awareness of, sensitivity to and rebellion against racism is his most heroic but least known contribution to sport, indeed America and the world.

—Neville L. Johnson,
Wooden biographer

John Wooden received many important "life lessons" from his father's hands—lessons that helped shape him into the man of character he is. In his book, *They Call Me Coach*, he wrote, "My dad did love his fellow man sincerely. He was honest to the nth degree and had a great trust and faith in the Lord. And he taught us many lessons in integrity and honesty which we never forgot."

One lesson Coach learned from his dad was especially important: don't judge people by the color of their skin. Joshua Wooden was not a racist—and that's saying a mouthful for southern Indiana in the 1920s. In 1924, one out of every twelve residents of Indiana claimed membership in the Ku Klux Klan. In Morgan County, where Coach lived, the number was even higher, with more than one out of every four white male adults belonging to the Klan. Coach says simply that his father taught him and his brothers "that no one is better than anyone else."

Indiana high school basketball standout Davage Minor remembers that Coach had two black players on his South Bend Central High School team in 1951—a most unusual thing at the time. "It was very hard to be black in the thirties and forties in Indiana," Minor says. "Wooden was just completely nonprejudiced in any way, shape or form, and that was a rare thing to see."

Lucius Allen, who starred for Wooden at UCLA, is another who salutes Wooden for his unbiased attitude:

> He was remarkable for his color blindness, especially because it was kind of a new thing. Mike Warren and I, when I was a freshman, were supposed to be pretty good jump shooters, but Coach Wooden would bless us with his presence on the court and challenge us to a shooting game. Mike and I had heard that Coach would take the guards out and just let them know that, you know, "You guys might be pretty good players but old Coach here is still the best shooter out of anybody that ever blessed the halls of UCLA." So Mike and I, we vowed that we were going to retire him. Needless to say . . . he just whipped us.

A few years ago, when someone asked Coach Wooden to recall some of his proudest memories, he mentioned the time when a newspaper reporter asked one of his players, Curtis Rowe, if there were racial problems on the team. Rowe shook his head and said, "You don't know our coach, do you? He doesn't see color, he sees ballplayers." Then he turned and walked away. "That's what I'm proud of," said Wooden.

Legendary black coach R. L. "Bobby" Vaughan, who won more than five hundred basketball games at Elizabeth City State University in North Carolina, told me about attending a coaches' convention in Louisville in 1962. "I remember it vividly," he said. "Those were the days before full integration, and the Brown Hotel refused to let the black coaches stay or eat there. Coach Wooden stepped forward and said that if we couldn't eat there, neither would he. He skipped the banquet and ate with us at a 'colored' restaurant. It was a true act of character. The truth of Coach Wooden's words, the genuineness of his life, the unselfishness of his actions—all of these things have been so valuable to me."

The legendary "Big O," Hall of Famer Oscar Robertson, told me, "John Wooden got the cream of the crop of black athletes way before the other West Coast schools. These players were accepted at UCLA, and it paid off for John Wooden because he started winning championships."

7) Coach Tries to Live by the Golden Rule.

Coach was a great coach because he was a great humanitarian. You'd run through a wall for him because you believed in him.

—Ed Ehlers

Ed Ehlers played basketball for John Wooden at Central High School in South Bend, Indiana. He recalls that, "Every Christmas, John Wooden saw that each player on his team got a Christmas gift." He'd also take the team out to dinner after every home game—at his own expense.

"One game I broke my nose," Ehlers says. "There was no medical insurance in those days. But Coach Wooden sent a doctor over to my house to check on me." When that doctor determined that an operation was necessary, Coach paid for it.

Ask any of Wooden's former players what he was like as a coach and you'll probably hear the exact same thing. He was tough. He worked his players hard. He expected them to be ready when game day rolled around, and to work hard the entire game. At UCLA, he felt that opposing teams weren't supposed to be able to match the stamina of his Bruins for forty minutes, and most of them couldn't.

It wasn't a piece of cake playing for Coach. But as tough as he was, he also tried to be kind and supportive. He was never a "get-in-your-face" coach, swearing at his players and belittling them for their mistakes, even if those mistakes took place at crucial moments in important games.

His daughter, Nancy Muelhausen, says, "I see acts of kindness from Daddy every time we've gone out and people approach him. He's very kind, very interested and patient. It's because of the way he is. I don't see it as any particular, 'I think I'll do an act of kindness,' kind of thing. It's just the way he lives his life. He's just kind to people and considerate."

My longtime friend Mary Garber was America's first nationally known female sportswriter. An excellent journalist based in Winston-Salem, North Carolina, she often covered the summer basketball camps at nearby Campbell College. She says, "The big name coaches would rotate every ten minutes to talk to the media. For some reason, I didn't get to talk to Coach before he moved on to the next station. He said, 'Let's sit together at lunch.'" Garber said okay, although she didn't think he really meant it. But, "As I was walking to lunch, he called me by name and insisted that we eat together. He answered questions the whole time. I marvel at that experience."

Former college coach Marv Harshman said, "John Wooden never put anyone down and always looked for a way to compliment you. At the NCAA Final Four he might be in a coffee shop by himself when a high school coach would come by. John would invite him to sit down and then spend quality time with him. He was always so accommodating."

Looking back on his career, Coach once said, "There are coaches out there who have won championships with a dictator approach, among them Vince Lombardi and Bobby Knight. I had a different philosophy. I didn't want to be a dictator to my players or assistant coaches or managers. For me, concern, compassion and consideration were always priorities of the highest order."

8) Coach has an attitude of service.

Coach Wooden's two life heroes are Abraham Lincoln and Mother Teresa. I asked him why and he said, "Because of their consideration for others."

—College coach Dustin Kearns

John Wooden was one of two coaches who came from the Midwest to join the UCLA staff in 1958. The other was Dutch Fehring, who left Oklahoma State to become an assistant football coach for the Bruins. Fehring stayed at a hotel during his first few weeks in Los Angeles, until his family was able to come from Oklahoma to join him.

In 2003, Fehring, now in his nineties, recalled the day his family arrived at Los Angeles International Airport—at 4 A.M. "John Wooden got up with me to meet them at the airport. Now how many guys would do that for you?"

Don Landry, who is now retired from coaching, remembers an encounter he had with John Wooden at the Final Four in 1964. Landry was then an assistant coach under Scotty Robertson at Louisiana Tech. Tech had always been a relatively short team that tried to win by outrunning and outgunning opponents. But three seven-footers had been recruited to play for Tech starting with the 1964–65 season.

UCLA was on its way to winning a national championship with a seven-foot freshman center by the name of Lew Alcindor (who would later become Kareem Abdul-Jabbar). So Landry and Robertson approached Coach and asked him for some advice on how to best utilize their new big men. Coach gave them more than a little advice. He spent ninety minutes discussing strategy with them in the lobby of the Shoreham Hotel in Washington. "At that point," Landry says, "John Wooden became my hero." He was surprised by the fact that Wooden, who by this time was already a national celebrity, would spend so much time to help out two relative strangers—strangers who were, after all, his rivals.

Landry says, "I went on to be the head coach at Nicholls State, and after I retired from coaching I wrote John Wooden a letter and told him what he meant to me. I just thanked him for the kind of man he was and how he conducted his life. I got a beautiful letter back from him saying how touched he was and how appreciative. I have that letter in a safe deposit box, and my youngest son has already claimed it in the will."

John Moon, a high school coach from North Carolina, had a similar experience. "I worked the UCLA basketball camp for eight years and got to visit with John Wooden at his apartment. The first time I met him we spent four hours together. In fact, I missed my flight back home. When I left

John, I felt I was a better person for having met him. I had the same feeling as when I leave church on a Sunday morning. I was so happy to see his compassion, kindness, sense of humor and mental excellence."

Fred Hessler, who was UCLA's radio announcer for years, once said, "John Wooden tried harder than any man I have ever met to be like Jesus Christ."

9) Coach Wooden is a hard worker.

It's so easy to relax, to cut corners, to let down after you've reached your goal, and begin thinking you can just "turn it on" automatically, without proper preparation. It takes real character to keep working as hard or even harder once you're there.

—John Wooden

Author Neville L. Johnson, put it this way:

John Wooden is no enigma; there's nothing mysterious about who he is and how he got to where he wanted to go. He worked hard to climb his mountains, which were the highest peaks around, doing so with an organized plan and a great joie de vivre, leading a happy and fulfilled life.

Bill Walton added that his college basketball coach is "an incredibly fiery competitor who really wants to win, to be on top, to do it the right way, and he just works nonstop. He loves the competition—and he taught us how to win, how to rise to the occasion."

Coach remembers that when he was a child, "You had to work hard. Dad felt there was time for play, but always after the chores and the studies were done."

He feels that his work ethic was what helped him become an All-American at Purdue, where he was known as "The Indiana Rubber Man." Explaining that nickname, he says, "I always bounced off the floor if I went down."

"I couldn't do much about my height, but I could do something about my condition. I always wanted to be in the best possible condition, and I hoped that others wouldn't work as hard at it as I did." Most didn't.

Former UCLA student manager George Morgan said Coach carried that work ethic with him into game preparation at UCLA. "Practices were focused," he said. "He had his teams as well prepared as anybody. His teams were so well prepared that it was hard for them to lose. It was the emphasis on fundamentals and doing simple things right all the time." Dick Lynn, who played for Coach from 1964 to 1968, told me, "Coach taught us to prepare to do our best and then to give our maximum effort. He also taught us to be gracious when we won and not to blame others when we lost."

Eddie Sheldrake, who played for Wooden during Coach's first three years at UCLA, describes him as "a tenacious, tough, hard-nosed, vicious competitor." Sheldrake quickly adds, "He's a gentleman—he's honest, straight, he's not going to do anything to cheat you, but he's going to do everything he can to beat you. . . . Let him guard you for a game, and you'd wish you never went on the basketball court. And that's the truth."

10) COACH PAYS ATTENTION TO THE SMALL DETAILS.

Good character is not given to us. We have to build it piece by piece.

—John Luther, author

You know how the story goes. "For lack of a nail, the shoe was lost . . . for lack of a shoe, the horse was lost . . . for lack of a horse, the battle was lost . . . and so on." The idea is that small things really do matter. As Jesus said, "Whoever can be trusted with very little can also be trusted with much, and whoever is dishonest with very little will also be dishonest with much" (Luke 16:10). As a coach, John Wooden always made sure that his players could be trusted with small things—like putting on their socks the right way.

He wrote, "I believe in the basics: attention to, and perfection of, tiny details that might commonly be overlooked. They may seem trivial, perhaps even laughable to those who don't understand, but they aren't. They are fundamental to your progress in basketball, business and life. They are the difference between champions and near-champions."

Then Coach added, "There are *little* details in everything you do, and if you get away from any one of the *little* details, you're not teaching the thing as a whole. For it is the little things, which, taken together, make the whole."

Even socks?

Yes, and here's why:

"Wrinkles, folds and creases can cause blisters. Blisters interfere with performance during practice and games. Since there was a way to reduce blisters, something the player and I could control, it was our responsibility to do it. Otherwise, we would not be doing everything possible to prepare in the best way."

He said, "When a player came to UCLA, I didn't ask him what size shoe he wore. We measured his foot. Why? Because when children are growing up, parents buy shoes bigger than their feet, knowing they are growing fast. The youngster might think he's a size fourteen when he's actually a size thirteen. Shoes that are a little too big let the foot slide around. This can cause a blister, especially if there's also a fold in the player's sock. I wanted the socks to lie smooth and the shoes to fit correctly."

Says Coach, "Little details are what make big things happen." Or, as I've often heard it said, "If you take care of the little things, the big things will take care of themselves." In other words, if you don't tell little lies, you won't have to tell bigger ones later on. If you learn to resist even the smallest temptations, you'll be able to resist the big ones when they come your way.

Now, it could be that as you've read this chapter you've been thinking of times when you've fallen short of who and what you really want to be. All of us have many regrets in life. That's why, as we move on from the subject of *character*, I want to leave you with these words of wisdom from author Carl Bard: "Though no one can go back and make a brand-new start, anyone can start from now and make a brand-new ending."

Chapter Two

⁕

If You Want to Be Like Coach: Love God

Build a shelter against a rainy day. This is not necessarily a material shelter. Your faith, whatever it may be, is the greatest shelter of all.

—John Wooden

JOHN WOODEN REMEMBERS his parents as "good, Christian people" who took him and his brothers to church every Sunday. His father read to his sons almost every night, interspersing classic poems and literature with passages from the Bible. Joshua Wooden taught his sons to thank God for their blessings and pray for guidance every day, something Coach says he has always tried to do.

Tony Spino, for many years a trainer at UCLA, once said of Coach: "The John Wooden we see today is the direct result of his upbringing. Those Indiana roots and the values he learned there have kept him humble. His values are threefold: faith, family and friends. He has never strayed from them. He has always stayed focused on being a common person. Instead of being a world-famous basketball coach, he would have been just as happy as a schoolteacher."

Coach was baptized at the age of seventeen, but looking back on that occasion, he says it wasn't because of a commitment to Christ, but rather because his parents wanted him to be baptized. "I didn't really accept Christ then," he says, "and when I did, I can't say. It wasn't a sudden, overnight thing. It was gradual. I've heard of people saying that one thing happened and it changed. There wasn't any one thing with me."

In 1942, shortly after the United States had declared war on Japan, Coach joined the navy and went off to fight in World War II. He took with him a small metal cross, given to him by the minister of the church he attended. Just as he was about to ship out to the South Pacific aboard the USS *Franklin*, he experienced sudden, severe stomach pains. Medics rushed him to a hospital, where an emergency appendectomy was performed, and another sailor took his place. While Wooden was still recuperating from his surgery, the other sailor died in battle.

"I've had other strange things like that happen to me," Coach says. "I wouldn't necessarily call them 'spiritual' things, but something like that really makes you stop and think. I suppose it just wasn't my time."

After the war, Coach continued to keep the small metal cross in his pocket, in both good times and bad. It was a comfort to him when he lost his house in Indiana to foreclosure. And it helped to keep him grounded during his record-setting winning streaks and national championships at UCLA. He had it with him during every one of the games he coached for the Bruins, and his wife, Nellie, kept a similar cross in her purse. Coach says he didn't carry the cross because he was superstitious about it. He didn't expect it to bring him good luck or victories. It served, instead, as a reminder of his faith, to keep him centered and as peaceful as possible in high-pressure situations.

Discussing the calming effect that little cross had on him, Coach said, "If I am able to control myself, perhaps it will help my boys to control their emotions and play up to their true potential. I know that I have faltered at times, but I also know that the cross has been helpful. It gives me a certain peace . . . a serenity."

In his book, *They Call Me Coach*, he wrote, "It is most difficult, in my mind, to separate any success, whether it be in your profession, your family, or as in my case, basketball, from religion."

Coach always kept a small brown New Testament on his desk in his office at UCLA. It was worn and wrinkled from constant use. He said,

"Once in a while, one of my new players would pick it up when he came in and found me busy on the phone. Some of them used to be startled when they opened it, but many of them would read a bit while I completed my call."

Coach also regularly read devotionals such as *Daily Word* and *The Upper Room*, and he kept a little pamphlet in his wallet titled, *Where to Look in the Bible*. "It points out specific references that will be of help in time of need—when desiring inward peace, when things look blue, when tempted to do wrong, and so forth."

John Wooden's faith has never been showy or preachy. He is quiet and firm in his convictions, a "friend of God" comfortable and secure in his relationship with his heavenly Father. Bobby Hussey, a former assistant basketball coach at Clemson, recalls: "I was with Coach Wooden at the old Campbell College summer camp in the 1960s. I'd walk with him every morning, and he'd always end up by praying. He did it without fail."

Coach comments: "It is my belief that in one way or another we are all seeking success. And success is peace of mind, a direct result of self-satisfaction in knowing that you did your best to become the best that you are capable of becoming, and not just in a physical way. 'Seek ye first His kingdom and His righteousness and all these things will be yours as well,'" he adds, quoting Matthew 6:33.

Coach explains his faith this way:

> *God is either in control or he isn't. I believe he is. But I also believe he delegates certain responsibilities to us. Earning his favor isn't one of them. So I can't work my way into his good graces. But I do have some responsibility in the successful development of my faith. Faith without works is dead, but works without faith are also worthless.*
>
> *I've trusted Christ and I've tried to live as he would have me live. I've studied his Word, and I've prayed a great deal. I have faith that he will do what he's promised. I'm ready to meet him, and I'm anxious to see Nellie, but all in due time. I don't want to outlive my children or my grandchildren, but neither am I anxious to leave my family. Actually, I've put all that into God's hands.*

Coach says he wasn't the type to talk openly about his faith to try to get everyone else to see things exactly as he did—but that he tried to show his faith through his example, and he succeeded marvelously. As Bud Furillo, longtime Los Angeles sportswriter, put it, "John Wooden proves that Christian ideals must work. They do in his life." Furillo added.

* * *

John Wooden's strength came from putting God first in his life. He is a very nice, kind human being who never let his ego get in the way.

—Gale Catlett, former head coach
at University of West Virginia

* * *

Coach says, "There are many things that are essential to arriving at true peace of mind, and one of the most important is faith, which cannot be acquired without prayer."

For John Wooden, prayer comes as naturally and easily as breathing. Faith has always been a positive force, motivating him to "do to others as you would have them do to you" (Luke 6:31). He has always done his best to obey Christ's admonition, "Do not judge, or you too will be judged" (Matthew 7:1). Eddie Merrins, who was golf coach at UCLA for fifteen years, says, "Coach doesn't wear his faith on his sleeve, but everything he does in life is designed to please God."

College coach Dustin Kearns says he once asked John Wooden what he thought about the downward spiral in American society. "He disputed me on that and said that 90 to 95 percent of the people in the United States are good people. He said it's a very small percentage of the population who are doing the wrong things."

It has been said that if you want to know what a man really believes, pay more attention to what he does than what he says. John Wooden's actions speak volumes.

Ask him what "success" means, and he'll tell you: "With Mr. Webster, it's defined as something like material possessions or positions of prestige, or something like that." Then he gives his version. "These are worthy accomplishments, but I don't think they necessarily indicate success. They very well might, but not necessarily. My dad had said while I was in grade school, 'Never try to be better than somebody else. Always learn from others because you'll never know a thing that you don't learn from someone else one way or another. And, most of all, strive to be the best you can be in whatever you're doing, because that's under your control. The other things aren't under your control.'"

Larry Maxwell, who spent years refereeing high school basketball in Indiana, probably said it best: "John Wooden's faith is shown in his actions. He lives his Christian values. He doesn't go out and pound his chest and tell the world."

John Wooden is someone who understands that all of the success in the world doesn't really mean a thing if you don't have a proper relationship with God. When he was asked by *New Man* magazine how his personal faith has guided him through life, Coach Wooden replied, "It has given me certain peace and tranquility that has enabled me to accept the ups and downs of life. It has kept me from permitting the mountains to become too high or the valleys too deep. It gives you the serenity that you need." Again:

**If you want to be like Coach,
make God a top priority in your life.**

As Coach says:

I always tried to make it clear that basketball is not the ultimate. It is of small importance in comparison to the total life we live. There is only one kind of a life that truly wins, and that is the one that places faith in the hands of the Savior. Until that is done, we are on an aimless course that runs in circles and goes nowhere. Material possessions, winning scores and great reputations are meaningless in the eyes of the Lord, because he knows what we really are, and that is all that matters.

Chapter Three

❦

If You Want to Be Like Coach: Love Your Family

Next to faith, I wanted to put my family first.

—John Wooden

During his years at UCLA, John Wooden saw to it that his wife, Nell, spent as much time with him as possible. "Nellie always went to games with me," he said, "and I wouldn't leave her to go scouting or anything of that sort, unless she could go with me."

He also says that he "tried not to bring basketball home with me." Nell often said that she could never tell, by John's demeanor at home, how things were going with the team. "I couldn't tell if he had a good practice, a bad practice or if there were any problems at all," she said. Coach's response: "Maybe she stretched the truth a little bit there, but I certainly tried not to bring any problems home with me. I wanted to put my family before my career."

Nell's words may have been slightly exaggerated, but not by much. Former college coach George Terzian told me that he was in attendance at a conference game UCLA lost because their opponent held the ball. "After Coach met with his team he came out onto the floor to greet his family and friends. I was amazed at his countenance, and the real joy he showed as he hugged and even tossed his grandchildren in the air. You could never tell he

31

had just lost an important conference game under intense and exasperating circumstances."

By Final Four time in 1984, Nell Wooden's health was failing. Even so, she made the trip to Seattle with her husband, who pushed her around in her wheelchair. Every night, the two of them spent time in the lobby of the Hilton hotel, talking to old friends. Author John Feinstein remembers, "One night, after all the greetings, Coach started pushing Nell toward the elevator to go to bed. One person started to clap—and the next thing you know the entire lobby just sort of opened up a pathway and everyone gave the Woodens a standing ovation. It was one of the most powerful experiences I have ever had in sports." He adds, "There weren't too many dry eyes in the Hilton lobby that night."

John Wooden has always been the prototypical family man. He married his high school sweetheart and stayed married to her for fifty-three years. Fact is, she was the only girl he ever dated. As Jay Carty, a former assistant at UCLA, said, "He has been a one-woman man and never strayed. No slips."

The depth of Coach's love for and commitment to his wife was illustrated by a comment he made at a UCLA summer camp in 2001. Ron Steinschriber, a former student manager for UCLA who now coaches high school basketball in St. Louis, told me that Coach was taking questions from the campers when one young man asked what he considered to be his greatest accomplishment. "Wooden didn't hesitate for a second," Steinschriber said. "He didn't mention any of the championships that he won, or any of the All-Americans he coached, or even his playing days at Purdue. He responded that his greatest accomplishment had come when he asked a beautiful young woman to be his wife and she said yes. Here he was, widely considered the greatest basketball coach ever, and all of his basketball accomplishments paled in the face of his love of his family."

Despite the fifty-three years they spent together, John and Nell's relationship did not get off to the best start. Coach remembers that he was so shy when he was a boy that he had to summon up all his courage just to tell his future bride "Hello." Once, when she was a teenager, Nell and some other girls who lived in the town of Martinsville drove out to John's farm for a visit. They found him out in the field, taking care of some plowing for his father.

The girls waved at John, and giggled among themselves, trying to get his attention, but he didn't even look in their direction. Instead, he kept his eyes focused on the ground in front of him. Nellie thought John was stuck up, a basketball star who wouldn't even give her the time of day. But the truth was that John was too shy to go over and talk to her and so insecure that when he heard the girls giggling, he thought they must be laughing at him.

The incident led to a misunderstanding that John later said was "the closest I ever came" to losing Nellie. "I was just very ill at ease with girls." Fortunately, their relationship made it over this early bump in the road and blossomed.

John and Nell made plans to be married on August 8, 1932. He had managed to save up just over nine hundred dollars, enough to get the young couple off to a decent start in life. But immediately prior to the wedding date, the First Bank and Trust Company closed its doors forever and the money was lost.

A local businessman, whose daughter Mary was Nellie's best friend, came to the couple's rescue by offering a two-hundred-dollar loan to be paid back whenever possible. In his book, *They Call Me Coach*, John wrote, "Though it was and still is against my principles to borrow from anyone, we did accept the loan. My brother Cat and his wife-to-be drove us to Indianapolis and stood up for us."

The next morning, John left Nell back in Martinsville and headed off for Vincennes, in another part of the state, where he would earn twenty-five dollars for coaching a weeklong basketball clinic. So it was that John and Nellie Wooden spent their first week of marriage apart. But from that time on, Coach did his best to stay at home with his family, despite a career that took him away from home for many weeks every year.

During John's first basketball game for Martinsville High School, he and Nellie began a ritual that continued throughout his coaching career. Before the center jump for that first game, Wooden looked over to the band section, where Nellie was playing the cornet, and winked at her. She smiled back and gave him the "okay" sign with her thumb and forefinger.

* * *

Coach has influenced me as a Christian and as a husband. He always made Nell number one. His eyes would light up whenever she walked in the room.

—Chris Smith, Coach Wooden's
former camp coordinator

* * *

When John became a college coach, it was always important for him to know that Nellie was in the stands and ready to cheer his team on to victory. He would wave a rolled-up program in Nellie's direction, and she would wave back. Sometimes, he had a hard time finding his wife in the crowd, but he wouldn't give up until he'd spotted her. At the NCAA championships at the Astrodome in 1971, "Nellie had to stand up and wave her arms like a navy signalman before I could see her," he chuckles.

The Woodens' granddaughter, Cathleen Trapani, says her grandparents "had such a special marriage. They just really trusted and loved each other, and they were well suited for each other, even though they were so different."

Different? "She was just very feisty, and he was so calm," she explains. She remembers that, "My grandmother, when she was watching the games, would get irritated. I've seen my grandmother mad. I remember my grandfather telling her, 'Oh, Nellie, calm down. It's okay. Nellie, it's okay,' and patting her constantly. She'd say, 'Oh, that just makes me so mad!' And he would tell her it was her Irish temper."

Coach's daughter, Nancy Muehlhausen, agrees that her mother sometimes seemed to have a harder time than her father did dealing with losses on the basketball court. "There were times when my mother would be angry—if UCLA lost a game and she didn't feel we got a fair shake [from the referees]. Daddy never felt that way."

* * *

My grandfather's views on life have had a powerful influence on our family. He's never judgmental and doesn't give you his opinion. He wants to make you think out the answer for yourself. He has always been there for me. I can go to him about anything, and he'll help me.

—Coach's granddaughter Caryn Berstein

* * *

John and Nellie Wooden had a terrific marriage for many reasons. One of those reasons is their understanding of a truth articulated by Dr. Joyce Brothers: "Marriage is not just spiritual communion and passionate embraces. Marriage is also three meals a day and remembering to carry out the trash."

I've heard it said that the hardest job in the world is that of a pastor's wife. That's because the pastor's wife is always under a microscope. She has to have an even temperament, be musically inclined, know the Bible backwards and forwards, never spend too much on her hair or nails but look like a million dollars just the same, and so on. But if that's true, the second-most difficult job in the world must be that of being a coach's wife. The most avid sports fans never seem to be satisfied. They are ready to pounce on any mistake, or any perceived mistake, like a pride of lions on an injured gazelle.

Coach was usually able to shrug off such criticism. At least, that's the message he gave off through his calm, never-ruffled exterior. On the inside, his emotions may have been churning up and down like an ant on Lance Armstrong's racing shoe. But he never let it show.

Nell got angry and had no trouble admitting it. In 1974, the year before UCLA won its last national championship under Coach Wooden, she said, "These should have been the best years of our lives, but they haven't been. Nine national championships in ten years is great. So are the winning streaks. But the fans are so greedy. They've reached the point where they are unhappy if John wins a championship game by only five points. If he even loses a game they're going to say that he's too old and he's lost his touch. You learn to prepare yourself for the worst, and then hope it doesn't happen."

In 1991, Wooden admitted to a reporter that he wasn't always as calm as he seemed. "After almost every game, I hardly slept at all," he admitted. "I'd play the game over and over in my mind, looking at all the things we did right or wrong. Even if you win by twenty points, you do a lot of things wrong."

Daily life was no happy romp at the beach, even for the most successful coach in college sports history. But through it all, he and Nell always strove to make sure their marriage was a much higher priority than wins and losses on a basketball court. And although Nell may have had her frustrations about the way she saw her husband being treated by the general public and the media, she was completely content with her marriage. You could tell by the twinkle in her eye.

Their granddaughter Christy Impelman says that John and Nell Wooden "fit so well together, they were almost like one person. They always did everything for each other." She adds, "Obviously, my grandparents had a very special relationship. That was just how I was brought up, and how things should be—to have a caring relationship and be supportive of each other. I didn't realize until I became almost an adult how rare it is to find that one right person with whom you want to share everything."

Coach used to laugh about what happened during one particular game when UCLA had a big lead and went into a four-corners offense to run out the clock. John heard a worried voice shouting from the stands, "Too soon! Too soon!"

"It was Nellie," Coach said, "and she was right. We almost lost the game."

Coach learned very early in their life together that it was a good idea to pay attention whenever Nellie spoke. Former UCLA player Bob Webb remembers an incident during a game on the road during his junior year when Coach was getting on the referees pretty good, "probably because Bill Walton was getting beat up on the post." Webb recalls that the refs warned Coach a couple of times to calm down, but he kept at them. "Mind you, I was just a reserve on this great team, but I was still as much a part of the team as any starter. During the timeout, I was standing, facing the seated players, as Coach gave instructions. I looked into the stands and Nellie was standing up gesturing to get my attention. 'Bobby!' she said, 'Get him quiet and away from the refs.'"

Webb wasn't about to tell Coach to "cool it," but Nellie was persistent. "After Coach finished talking to the team, he turned around and started yelling at the referees again—and Nellie once more gestured for me to quiet him down." Webb took a deep breath, put his hand on Coach's shoulder and tried to turn him away from the refs and back to the huddle. "When he turned around to see who was touching him, I almost had a heart attack," he says. "But I continued to turn his body completely toward the crowd and pointed at Nellie. As soon as he saw her, she yelled, 'John! Calm down before you get a technical!'"

To Webb's relief, Coach did exactly as his wife had requested. "Then Nellie smiled and gave me the okay sign and I took my seat on the bench. Before play started, Coach walked down to where I was on the bench and said, 'Well, Bobby, I guess you know who's the boss in our house.' We smiled at each other and I said, 'Yeah, Coach, and I think that's a good thing for me.'"

When Nell Wooden's heart stopped beating on March 21, 1985, Coach's life came to a standstill. He didn't want to go on without her. In his book, *My Personal Best*, he wrote, "If you dropped a small pebble into the deepest part of the ocean on the darkest night of the year—that was me without Nell. Her death brought grief down on me in a terrible way. I was desolate, unable to function day after day, week after week; I was alone, immobilized by what seemed unendurable."

He refused to attend the NCAA's Final Four tournament because it reminded him too much of Nell. He and his wife had attended thirty-six of those tournaments in a row. It took a tremendous amount of coaxing from his children before he was ready to get on with the daily business of life. Even now, he visits Nell's grave every Sunday, and he writes a letter to her once a week.

"Nellie and I were married for fifty-three years," he said. "We were sweethearts for sixty. When I lost her, it was difficult, and I didn't want to do much for two or three years. . . . I just sort of existed." He explained that he would never move from his condominium in Encino, California, because "I see her everywhere. I miss her as much now as I ever have. It never gets easier. There are friends who would like to see me find another woman for the companionship, but I wouldn't do it. It would never work."

He told a newspaper reporter that he looked forward to being reunited with Nell in heaven some day. Explaining that he has no fear of dying, Coach said, "It's my chance to be reunited with Nellie, and that's how I feel. The only important thing is the life you lead. You'll be judged, and it will be a fair judgment. I believe that." Even now, when he sends a gift to a family member for a special occasion, he sends it in his and Nell's names. "That pleases Nell," he says.

Hall-of-Fame broadcaster Dick Enberg says of Coach, "He lamented her loss for a long time and appeared to have lost his desire to live. His family and friends finally helped him recover."

A woman named Cheryl Forsatz told me about working at the McDonald's High School All-Star Basketball Game at Madison Square Garden in 2001. She admits she had never heard of John Wooden before, but she found herself deeply moved by what he had to say. "I will never forget his words on marriage," she said. "You could just see the love and passion he still had for his late wife. He told the players the ultimate success doesn't come on the basketball court but from the love you have for your family."

These days, Coach dotes on his children, his grandchildren and his great-grandchildren. When asked what he regrets most about the effects of his advancing age, he says it's the fact that he can't get down on the floor and play with the great-grandkids like he wants to. Granddaughter Caryn Bernstein says that Coach "absolutely loves kids, and not just those he's related to."

Children have always been of special importance to him. Former UCLA assistant coach Jay Carty, who has known him for years, says, "Children are more important to him than adults. If there is a child in the room, John is totally focused on him or her. He believes all of us need to start making decisions based on the welfare of children."

Bernstein says, "The kids love to hear him tell stories about when he was a kid. He tells them about when he was growing up and life on the farm." Referring to her own daughter, who was born shortly after Nell Wooden's death, Caryn says, "From the time she was nine months old, when my sitter couldn't watch her, he would. Picture this seventy-six-year-old man down on the floor with a baby, crawling around and playing with her; he just absolutely loved it. They developed a real special bond early on."

Another story about Coach's love for children came from Mike Kunstadt, a high school basketball coach from Irving, Texas, who often came to California during the summer to work at Coach's basketball camps. Kunstadt told me that when his daughters were little, Coach would bounce them on his knee and impersonate the characters from Sesame Street. "He'd teach them about being good girls, about having manners and so forth," Kunstadt said. "He was like the grandfather the girls never had, and he still fills that role to this day. He left a strong impression on our family."

John's niece Judy Sherbert remembers taking her young grandson, Ryan, to visit Coach. Ryan had just started karate lessons and was eager to show what he had learned. Coach watched, seemingly intrigued while Ryan demonstrated his best moves. Then, after telling the boy how impressed he was, he asked to see those great moves again.

Judy said, "Later, when Uncle John's friend Morgan Wootten arrived, he asked Ryan to repeat the routine for him!" How many adults do you know who would give that kind of gracious attention to a child?

Yet that behavior is not unique for Coach. On another occasion, Judy and her husband, Ron, went with "Uncle John" on a trip to a hotel in Colorado Springs. This time, another grandson, six-year-old Bay, went with them.

"They took Uncle John to his room on a golf cart, and he insisted that Bay ride with him. In the room was the largest hospitality basket I have ever seen. The two of them went through it all, item by item. After they were finished, Uncle John took a couple of small items for himself and told Bay he could keep everything else, including the basket!"

Ron Sherbert recalls visiting Coach's condo in Encino and being impressed by the dozens of trophies, plaques and other honors that filled his small study. When Sherbert asked his uncle which of those awards brought him the most pride, Coach knew immediately. He picked up a small trophy that was inscribed "California Father of the Year." That meant more than any of the ten national championships—and most likely more than all ten of them put together.

Former college coach Hal Wissel told me that when he was starting out in his career, he attended many basketball clinics where Coach was teaching. "After one of them, he asked about my family, and I showed him a photo of my infant son. Then he showed me a picture of his grandchildren." The two men spent thirty minutes or more talking about their families. It amazed Wissel that an icon like John Wooden would spend that much time with him—but that's Coach, and that illustrates the importance he has always attached to family.

Coach's love for his family is apparent to anyone who's spent more than a few minutes with him. He loves them dearly, and they love him right back. Lacey and Ashlyn Wooden, ten and eight years old, told me how they feel about their famous great-grandfather. "He's nice," Lacey said. "He's fun and he talks to me—and he listens, too." Ashlyn adds, "He's nice and he makes me feel safe."

* * *

My Papa is the coolest great-grandfather ever. He's a lot of fun because he has a special spirit about him. He's full of love.
—Coach's great-granddaughter Cori Nicholson

* * *

John and Nell Wooden always made their relationship with each other their top priority. In retrospect, it seems amazing that John Wooden was able to get so many top-ranked high school recruits to play basketball for him at UCLA because he didn't want to fly all over the country on recruiting trips. Oh, he did it, but not like some coaches who spend half their lives on airplanes. As far as he was concerned, the basketball season was more than enough travel. When the season was over, he wanted to stay home.

* * *

Papa is my role model because of everything he does for people. He's always telling me to try my hardest and never give up.
—Gailend Robbins, Coach's
eleven-year-old great-granddaughter

* * *

When son Jim was born in 1936, someone sent the Woodens a "congratulations" card with a poem inside that impressed John so much he committed it to memory:

> A careful man I must always be
> A little fellow follows me.
> I know I dare not go astray
> For fear he'll go the self-same way.
> I cannot once escape his eyes,
> What'er he sees me do he tries.
> Like me he says he's going to be,
> This little chap who follows me.
> He thinks that I am good and fine,
> Believes in every word of mine.
> The base in me he must not see,
> This little chap who follows me.
> I must be careful as I go
> Through summer's sun and winter's snow,
> For I am building for the years to be
> This little chap who follows me.

"I did like that," Coach says, "and I had it framed and hung where I
could see it almost every day."

Jim says he was never a particularly good student and knew that he was
not good enough in basketball to play the game in college. "It must have
been frustrating for my father that I wasn't a good student, but he never let
on that it was," Jim recalls. "He always backed me in everything I did."

In his book, *Be Quick—But Don't Hurry*, former Bruins player Andy Hill
says, "As much as Coach wanted to win, he never sacrificed family obligations for the sake of the basketball program." That was true of his own
family, and it was also true of his players' families. Hill tells of the time
when one of Wooden's players, Eddie Sheldrake, and his wife were awaiting the birth of a child. "Eddie's wife was expecting to deliver their first
child at a time when the Bruins were scheduled to play a crucial game out

of town. Eddie and Coach often did not see eye to eye—but in a surprising twist, it was Coach Wooden who insisted that Eddie miss the trip and be with his wife. Though there are some players today who might insist on being present for the birth of their children, it is hard to imagine any contemporary coach who would *insist* that a key player miss a game so he could be in attendance."

His example in this part of his life has been a great example to others. Brian Burmeister, who has known Coach since the early sixties, says that he and a brother were estranged for several years, until "I started listening to Coach talk about the importance of family and about being willing to forgive others." Burmeister says Coach made him realize that he had much to gain by reaching out to his brother. "Now, I have never mentioned this to Coach, but the fact is that my brother and I are very close now."

* * *

He's an awesome person who knows what he's talking about. He's nice to everyone, and he's funny. I want to be just like him.
          —Coach's great-grandson Eric Bernstein

* * *

Coach is evidence of a truth that has been proven time and again: A man who puts his family first generally does better in life than a man who makes his wife and children a lower priority than his career. It has been said that the best thing a man can do for his children is to love their mother. Actually, I think that cuts both ways. The best thing a man and a woman can do for their children is to love each other, respect each other, make their own relationship a higher priority than any other—except their relationship with God—and present a united front to their children.

That's exactly what John and Nell Wooden did.

Chapter Four

✥

If You Want to Be Like Coach: Love Other People

For success, either individually or for your team, there must be a level of friendship. It is a powerful force that comes from mutual esteem, respect and devotion.

—John Wooden

FRIENDSHIP IS THE THIRD of Coach Wooden's top three priorities.

Abraham Lincoln has always been one of his two heroes; Mother Teresa is the other. There are many obvious reasons that he admired these two great people, but another less obvious reason for his admiration of Lincoln has to do with Honest Abe's dedication to friendship.

Coach loves to tell the story about the time, near the end of the Civil War, when one of Lincoln's advisors thought he was being too conciliatory toward the Confederate states. "Mr. President," the man said, "you're supposed to destroy your enemies, not make friends of them." Lincoln smiled and replied, "Am I not destroying an enemy when I make a friend of him?"

Coach wrote, "Friendship takes time and understanding. Rarely will you find in working toward a common goal that others will be able to resist friendship if you offer it sincerely and openly. However, you may have to prime the pump first. Be brave enough to offer friendship." And, he warns, don't mistake kindness for friendship. "It isn't friendship when someone does something nice for you. He or she is simply being a nice person. Friendship is mutual, doing good things for each other. There's no real friendship when only one side is working at it. Both must give for there to be friendship."

Bill Wooden said of his brother John: "He never tried to put on airs or show off. He was more interested in other people than himself. He made them feel important."

John Vallely, who played for UCLA in the late 1960s, says that he was always impressed by the way Coach remembered people's names. "He has the ability to associate something that causes him to remember names. I found that really admirable for a man in a high-powered position."

When I spoke with Virginia Tech basketball coach Seth Greenberg, he told me an amazing story about Coach's ability to remember names. Seems Greenberg ran into Wooden at an airport and introduced him to his wife Karen and two-year-old daughter Paige. "About two years later, my wife was waiting to pick me up at an airport and, amazingly, saw Coach sitting alone on a bench. She went over and introduced herself, and he asked, 'How's Paige?'" Then, another three years after that, Seth and Karen attended a coaches retreat, where they encountered Coach again. Before Greenberg had a chance to "reintroduce" his wife, Coach greeted her warmly, "Karen, how are you? And how's Paige?" Greenberg says, "I thought, *How does he do that?* Then it hit me—he takes the time to listen and hear, which is a lost art. Coach talks with and to people, not at them."

Says Coach, "Friendship is so valuable and so powerful. We take it for granted, but we shouldn't."

Bill Oates, basketball coach at the Masters College in California, told me, "Everyone respects Coach's accomplishments, but people will never forget how he did it. He did it with integrity and humility and has never been enthralled with his accomplishments. Success never changed him. In 2003 he went to the White House to receive the congressional medal from President Bush. Afterwards, he told me, 'I couldn't believe I was there. I am just a simple farm boy.' He has remained untouched by all his success. John Wooden thinks of others first, and he is so humble. He is also a loyal friend. Every time I see him, he asks questions about how I'm feeling and what's going on in my life. He is genuinely interested in me."

Oates describes his old friend in these terms: "He is an educator and teacher. He reads books, writes poetry, listens to good music and—as a result—there is a tremendous depth to the man. He is fascinating to be with because he is so well read. He also has a true servant's attitude."

Every summer Oates takes Coach to lecture at an all-sports coaching clinic in Palm Springs. "There are about one thousand people there to hear him speak, and he always gets a ten-minute standing ovation. When Coach was ninety-two, he signed balls, books and photos for people for three hours after he spoke. Who else would do that? People had tears in their eyes when they approached him. Some were shaking. He touches people that way. People were awed that a legend had walked in the room. He has a love for people and makes himself accessible to all of them. When I drove him home he was exhausted and his hand was cramped. But he just wouldn't let anyone down."

Author/speaker John Maxwell told me about an appearance Coach made before a group of businessmen in Atlanta. "We did a Q-and-A session together, and I asked him what he wants to be known for when his life is over. He replied, 'Well, I know it is not the titles and trophies I won.' Then he paused—and the crowd was on the edge of their seats. After a moment he said, 'I want it said that I was considerate of others.' That's who John Wooden is, and that's why he is so special."

* * *

Papa has a genuine love of people. He's totally open to everyone and will give them as much time as he's able.
                    —Coach's granddaughter Cathleen Trapani

* * *

Here are some important things John Wooden can teach us all about friendship:

• OTHER PEOPLE ARE JUST FRIENDS WAITING TO BE MADE.

In my research for this book, I heard dozens of stories like this one from Mike Tschirret, a former high school coach, athletic director and principal in Florida. Tschirret told me that in 1974, he made a trip to the Final Four in Greensboro, North Carolina. He was eating breakfast with some other high school coaches on the Saturday of the semifinals, in which UCLA would be playing. All of a sudden, John Wooden walked over to their table and asked, "Do you mind if an old man joins you?"

Tschirret says, "We ended up talking with him for about ninety minutes, about basketball, life in general, religion, all sorts of things. At one point I asked, 'Coach, don't you have anything better to do than talk to a bunch of high school coaches—especially when you have to play such an important game today?' He just smiled and said, 'I can't think of anything I'd rather do.'"

That's Coach, making friends wherever he goes. Wherever John Wooden goes, people recognize him and want to talk to him—and he's always happy to oblige. Daughter Nan admits that she sometimes gets impatient with all the people wanting a piece of her father's time—but he never does.

Saul Rowen, who played for Coach in the 1950s, remembers, "When I first got to UCLA he was always asking me about my family." He was surprised that his coach took such a personal interest in him. But as Rowen quickly discovered, John Wooden truly cared about his players. "Coach had high standards and maintained them his entire life," Rowen says. "He wanted to bring out the good in people."

UCLA sports information director Bill Bennett was born on the same date as Coach, so they always call to wish each other a happy birthday. Bennett says, "Last year, I got to the office especially early because I wanted to be the first one to leave a Happy Birthday message. But when I got to my desk, I saw that I already had a message. Of course, it was from Coach Wooden, beating me to the punch. I saved that message and now every day, for almost a year, I start my morning by listening to Coach Wooden singing 'Happy Birthday' to me!"

How like Coach!

"He gets a tremendous amount of mail," Nan says of her father, "and it's from all over the world." She adds that many people write just to ask for her father's autograph. For years, he responded to every one of those letters, even when no return envelope was enclosed. But when "he became more limited in his ability to get to the post office," he stopped being able to answer those requests.

In his famous Pyramid of Success, Coach says that friendship "comes from mutual esteem, respect and devotion. Like marriage, it must not be taken for granted, but requires a joint effort."

* * *

He [Coach] draws people to him, young and old, because he's so sweet and has such a great sense of humor. People will go up to meet him at UCLA games, and I love to see their faces light up.
—Carleen Wooden, Coach's daughter-in-law

* * *

I love this quote from Samuel Johnson: "If a man does not make new acquaintances as he advances through life, he will soon find himself left alone. A man, sir, should keep his friendships in constant repair."

• YOU CANNOT PUT A PRICE TAG ON FRIENDSHIP.

As I mentioned earlier, Earl Warriner was John Wooden's basketball coach in elementary school in Martinsville, Indiana. His daughter, Francine Abbot, recalls a time, during the 1960s, when UCLA was coming to Indiana to play at Notre Dame. Her father sent a letter to Coach, asking if he could possibly get Warriner a few tickets for the game. Along with his letter, he enclosed a signed, dated check, leaving the "amount" line blank so Coach could fill it in.

By return mail, Warriner received the tickets he had requested, along with his check. On the line for "amount" Coach Wooden had written, *"Friendship far too valuable to be measured in dollars."* Warriner's daughter remembers, "My dad carried that check with him for a long time."

- **NO MATTER HOW GOOD A FRIEND IS, HE OR SHE IS GOING TO HURT YOU ONCE IN AWHILE—AND WHEN THAT HAPPENS, IT'S UP TO YOU TO FORGIVE THEM.**

John Wooden had some tough battles with players during his long tenure at UCLA. Not everyone who played for John Wooden loved him. Walt Hazzard threatened to quit the team after Coach benched him because of his flamboyant style of play. (Coach wanted him to quit "showing off" on the court, dribbling the basketball behind his back, between his legs and so on.) Coach had a well-known showdown with Bill Walton over a team rule about hair length. A patriotic man who fought in World War II, he was not at all thrilled when some of his teams in the early 1970s joined in protests against the Vietnam War.

Coach was also faced with the same tough decision that confronts every coach: Who would make the team, and who would be cut. After that, he had to decide who got a lot of playing time and who didn't. Because UCLA had so many supremely talented players in those days, many who might have been starters elsewhere wound up sitting on the bench in Westwood. Naturally, they didn't like it, and more than a few of them left UCLA with bitter feelings. But Coach was always ready to forgive and forget past troubles.

Andy Hill left UCLA with a decidedly unpleasant taste in his mouth. But thirty years after his graduation, Hill, now a successful executive in the entertainment world, decided to attempt to reconnect with his old coach. He didn't know what to expect. I think it would be best if I let him tell the story:

> *After a couple of rings, a machine started to play, "Hello, this is John Wooden. Please speak slowly and distinctly, and leave your name and number after the tone." Hey, this wasn't so hard. I would just leave word, try my best not to expect a call back so my feelings wouldn't be hurt, and move on. The message machine beeped, and I started to speak. "Hi Coach . . . this is Andy Hill." Wham, the phone was picked up, and that familiar voice was on the other end. "Andy, where are you, where have you been?" It was Coach, and his voice was unchanged. It was like being thrown back in time nearly three decades.*

But the forbidding Coach of yesteryear wasn't getting on me for a bad crosscourt pass, or annoyed at me for some ill-conceived idea I was asking him to support. He just wanted to know when I was coming to see him. In fact, he really wanted to see me.

Hill goes on to say:

Spending time reconnecting with John Wooden has been one of the most deeply satisfying and rewarding experiences of my life. I've had the opportunity to take my sense of bitter disappointment and resentment and replace it with a sense of accomplishment and gratitude—a wonderful trade-off. And writing this book with him has given me the perfect excuse to see him regularly and to know him in a way that I never thought possible. The mentor relationship is a very powerful one; so is the soul-satisfying completeness of reconnecting and getting to say a proper thank-you.

- **WHEN IT COMES TO FRIENDSHIPS, BE WILLING TO MOVE BEYOND YOUR OWN COMFORT ZONE.**

I mentioned earlier that Coach's best friend during his time at UCLA was Press Maravich, who coached the Tigers of LSU. These two men were pretty much complete opposites. Wooden was a dignified, refined, straight arrow. Maravich was an earthy fellow who couldn't seem to utter a sentence without at least one swear word in it. How did the two men become so close to each other? By moving beyond their own comfort zones and being willing to discover each other's good qualities.

- **BE FRIENDS WITH YOURSELF.**

Eleanor Roosevelt said, "Friendship with oneself is all-important because, without it, one cannot be friends with anyone else in the world."

Jesus said, "Love your neighbor as you love yourself." Implied in that statement is the understanding that it is right and proper—and even necessary—for us to love and respect ourselves. Coach has always believed this.

In his Pyramid, he says that one of the building blocks to personal success is "Loyalty to yourself and to all those dependent upon you. Keep your self-respect." If you would be like Coach when it comes to friendship, remember these words of wisdom:

Good relationships don't need working on; they need participating in.
Relationships grow; they don't just happen.
Relationships are a gift; you don't make them.
Self-centeredness destroys relationships.

Coach genuinely cares about others. I am reminded of a story told by Bill Marsden, UCLA's assistant manager from 1969 to 1971. Every year at UCLA's season-ending awards banquet, it was traditional for each of the seniors to give a farewell speech. Marsden recalls, "Bill Seifert, a reserve forward, ripped into Coach Wooden pretty good during his speech because he didn't feel he'd had a fair opportunity to prove himself. Athletic director J. D. Morgan then got up and said that Coach didn't have to respond to Seifert's charges. 'His record speaks for itself,' Morgan said. But when it was Coach's turn to talk, he thanked J. D. for his comments, but said that Bill's feelings were not invalidated by his teams' records, and that he hoped to be able to understand and redress the differences between Bill and him."

Marsden told me, "It would have been so easy for Coach Wooden to take the same approach as J. D. Morgan. But his own value system wouldn't let him do that. I'm sure you know that he and Bill did get together and worked out their differences."

Just before this book was due to go to press, I received the following message from Jaleesa Hazzard, wife of all-time UCLA great Walt Hazzard. Her poignant words made a deep impression on me, and I share them with you now:

When Walt came out to UCLA from Philadelphia, he was the product of a very solid home, with a father who had a PhD in theology since the 1950s. Walt's strong upbringing was supported by the example he found in Coach Wooden, who reinforced what

Walt had been taught about discipline and work ethic. Walt was a team player, and this was the foundation of Coach Wooden's philosophy. Coach Wooden appreciated that Walt would always hit the open man, had tremendous court vision and would make the smart play. He loved to play, didn't mind the tough practices and set a strong example as a team leader. Actually, Walt always loved the practices as much as the games, and when he became a coach he followed Coach Wooden's example of timing out the practice schedule and sticking to it. He worked on fundamentals and believed like Coach that what you did in practice made the games easy. Coach Wooden made sure they were well prepared, not on what the other teams were doing but on what they were doing—the press, the high-post offense, etc.

Every year on October fifteenth after Walt left UCLA he always called Coach Wooden on the first day of college practice. It was a routine that continued until Coach retired. When Walt had his stroke, Coach Wooden came to the hospital with Mike Warren and sat by his bed and talked to him, even though none of us were sure that Walt even knew what was going on. Coach encouraged Walt and spoke to him like he always had as his coach, about his toughness, his talent, his ability to overcome difficulty and succeed. I think all of us believed that Walt could feel Coach's presence, and he responded very positively. Even today when they see each other, Coach continues to push him on to continue to recover. He will always be Walt's Coach!

Four-time NBA all-star Willie Naulls referred me to the thirteenth chapter of first Corinthians and said, "The characteristics of love's actions in that chapter describe Coach Wooden." Then he added, "I have tried to walk the walk of love most of my adult life but have failed consistently. Where most of us miss the mark is through approaching love as an academic pursuit. No! Love is a state of being, of choice. Coach Wooden is God's walking and doing expression of love to all of us. That's what makes him special!"

After a trip from Indiana to Los Angeles to visit him, Roger Dickinson, the executive director of the Indiana Basketball Hall of Fame, recalled to me:

As I drove to the airport I thought to myself, *I had just met the most remarkable person ever in my life.* Here is an individual that is a legend in his own time, yet he is humble, wholesome, moral, respected, decent, and honorable and the type of person that anyone would be happy to call Coach, dad, grandpa, friend, counselor or servant of God. Coach Wooden continues to set a standard of excellence that is beyond most people's grasp. He demonstrates every day that by staying active and pushing one's self mentally that life can be good at any age.

To sum up what we've discussed so far, if you want to be like Coach, build your life on a solid foundation of godly character enhanced by a proper relationship with God, your family and other people.

Jesus talked about what happens to the man who builds on a proper foundation: ". . . the rain descended, the floods came, and the winds blew and beat on that house; and it did not fall, for it was founded on the rock" (Matthew 7:25). May we all strive to follow Coach's example in building a foundation that will never give way.

PART TWO

BUILD WITH KNOWLEDGE AND WISDOM

༺✦༻

All knowledge is of itself of some value.
There is nothing so minute or inconsiderable
that I would not rather know it than not.

—Samuel Johnson

Chapter Five

⌘

If You Want to Be Like Coach: Strive to Be a Teacher

I always considered myself a teacher rather than just a coach. Everyone, everyone is a teacher. Everyone is a teacher to someone; maybe it's your children, maybe it's a neighbor, maybe it's someone under your supervision in some other way, and in one way or another, you're teaching them by your actions.

—John Wooden

WHY IS IT THAT SOME coaches are winners everywhere they go?

The answer, says Coach, is simply that some coaches are better teachers than others are. "Among experienced coaches in sports, there is little difference in their technical knowledge of the game," he says. "All leaders basically evaluate the same information, draw from the same talent pool, and are constrained by similar financial considerations. Not always, but most of the time. The difference usually comes down to the ability of a leader to be an effective teacher of what it takes to 'move the ball' in the process of creating a winning organization."

* * *

Many years ago, when I had the great honor of leading others, I truly felt that if I had been a good teacher, I could sit in the stands during a game without witnessing any diminution in the quality of UCLA's performance—but only if I had done my job correctly, if I had taught competitive greatness to our team.

—John Wooden

* * *

I heard about an anthropologist who was studying the culture of a small tribe that lived on an island in the South Pacific. The people were primitive, superstitious, and had limited contact with the outside world. They were, in other words, a fascinating study. After some time on the island, the anthropologist was able to gain the confidence of one of the tribe's healers, and he asked the shaman if he could help him obtain an audience with "the most important man" on the island. The medicine man agreed, and the two men set out on a winding path through the jungle.

Naturally, the anthropologist assumed they were on their way to meet the tribe's king. Suddenly, the shaman stopped in his tracks and pointed. There, in a small clearing just ahead, stood an elderly, white-haired gentleman, surrounded by children.

"Is that your king?" asked the anthropologist.

"King?" The shaman seemed surprised. "You said you wanted to meet the most important person on the island. So I brought you to our teacher."

Obviously, that tribe was not nearly as primitive, nor as superstitious, as the anthropologist had first thought. They were advanced enough to know there is no one quite so important as a good teacher.

John Wooden was and is a good teacher. He always strove to do more than teach his players how to play basketball. He taught them how to succeed in the game of life: in their careers, in their relationships with others and, through his example, in their relationship with the Creator of the universe.

During Coach Wooden's final season at UCLA, his use of language during practices and games was monitored for research purposes. It was discovered that 75 percent of the time, when Coach opened his mouth, it was to give specific instructions—in other words, to teach.

Kareem Abdul-Jabbar says he first realized what a good teacher Coach was during a close game against Colorado State his sophomore year. "During timeouts, his instructions were clear and precise. I had never doubted him before, but when the game ended [and UCLA had won] it was obvious that he had been thinking three moves ahead of us, calm and cool as always."

Says Wooden, "A coach should remember that he's there to teach. He should remember that he's there to get a player to learn. . . . If he's recruiting just to have great players, he shouldn't be there. He should be a teacher."

Years after he retired from coaching, John Wooden was asked what he missed most about coaching. "The practices," was his surprising reply. "Not the rings or the titles. I'm a teacher, and I miss teaching the young men."

Former Bruins superstar Bill Walton agrees with Coach's description of himself as a teacher. "Above all, John Wooden was a teacher," Walton said. "He taught life, not basketball. The way he taught us how to learn changed my life."

When asked by a reporter what he liked most about coaching, Wooden answered, "Dealing with boys on an emotional, mental, psychological plane, as well as physical. When I taught English, I never reached my students in this many ways. I never got as close to them as I do to my players."

No wonder NBA scout Marty Blake called John Wooden "the first 'brain' coach." Said Blake, "John Wooden was a teacher as much as a coach. He was the first to organize his practices. He was very analytical in his coaching and tried to mold his offense and defense for each game. He'd treat each game as a separate entity."

From the time John and his three brothers were small children, their parents sought to instill in them a love of good books and a thirst for learning. It's no surprise then that, as adults, all four of them entered the teaching profession. Brother Daniel became assistant superintendent of schools in Alamogordo, New Mexico. Maurice, better known by his nickname of "Cat," served as principal of West Covina High School in California. And William taught in La Porte, Indiana.

Although John Wooden eventually came to be revered as a teacher, his career in the profession did not get off to a promising start. Shortly after he and Nellie were married, they moved to Dayton, Kentucky, where John was hired to coach football, baseball *and* basketball, plus teach English. (He was to do all of this for the princely salary of fifteen hundred dollars a year.)

Coach did alright in the classroom, but based on his first year as a coach, nobody would have predicted great things from him. On the football field, he was challenged by a player who snarled, "You're not man enough to make me," when Coach told him to practice harder. Even though the player was a 250-plus-pound lineman, Wooden proceeded to show the player that he *was* man enough.

Looking back on the incident in his book, *My Personal Best*, Coach said, "It was terrible behavior from someone trying to follow the examples of my coaching mentors. Even more, it went against my father's teaching." He added, "These days I'd be fired, rightfully, but on that hot, humid afternoon, we just moved on and continued practice."

Things didn't go a whole lot better on the basketball court. There were no physical altercations, but Coach was frustrated by his players' inability to understand what he was telling them. The Green Devils won only six games that year, while losing eleven, the only losing season that a John Wooden–coached team ever experienced.

Coach says he wasn't the type to scream or yell at his players, but he let his frustration and disappointment show, which caused his players to feel discouraged. "Since everything had come easily for me as a player, I didn't understand why these young men couldn't do the same. It was extremely upsetting to demonstrate something correctly only to watch them do it incorrectly—over and over. Patience is a most valuable asset for a leader. I lacked it, just as young coaches and teachers usually do."

It didn't take Coach very long to understand that he needed to show the same degree of patience on the basketball court that he exhibited in the classroom. He came to see that a pat on the back or an encouraging word helped a whole lot more than a harsh criticism. As he put it, "Young people need models, not critics."

Reflecting on his time at Dayton High, Coach said, "They didn't have people who were 'just coaches' back then. I was an English teacher. All the coaches I knew in my day taught class." He thought for a moment and said, "I think coaches today should all teach, too. I'm sure they'd do a better job of coaching because coaching is teaching, nothing more."

During his second season, the Green Devils won nine more games than they had the year before, finishing with a 15–3 record. John Wooden's reputation as a coach began to grow. Dayton High figured to be a contender for the Kentucky state championship the following year, but when Indiana's South Bend Central High came calling, Wooden accepted the job and returned to his home state. Central didn't have much of a team. But under Coach, they became a powerhouse, at one time winning thirty games in a row.

During those early years of his coaching career, Wooden also played professional basketball for teams based in Hammond, Indiana, and Indianapolis. (These were in the years prior to the founding of the National Basketball Association.) He made fifty dollars a game and led the National Basketball League in scoring. He set a league record by scoring sixty-seven points in one game for the Kautsky Grocers of Indianapolis, and he also hit 138 free throws in a row. But despite his heroics as a player, he quickly saw that his future lay in teaching the game.

Years later, looking back on his career, Wooden said, "Teaching is the most wonderful profession. The two most important professions in the world are parenting—that's the most important—and teaching."

Kareem Abdul-Jabbar, who revolutionized college basketball as a Bruin and starred for years in the National Basketball Association, said, "It's pretty clear that if Coach wasn't passionate about being a teacher—and loving the game of basketball at the same time—he wouldn't have had the effect on his players and students that he had."

Coach Wooden constantly stressed to his players the importance of an education. "You're here, first of all, to get an education," he told them. "The second reason is to play basketball." Every year he gave the members of his team a handout with the following information printed on it:

- You are in school for an education. Keep that first in your thoughts, but place basketball second.
- Do not cut classes and do be on time.
- Do not fall behind and do get your work in on time.
- Have regular study hours and keep them.
- Arrange with your professor in advance when you must be absent.
- Do not expect favors. Do your part.

- Arrange for tutoring at the first sign of trouble.
- Work for a high grade point average. Do not be satisfied by merely meeting the eligibility requirements.
- Do your assignments to the best of your ability, but never be too proud to seek help and advice.
- Earn the respect of everyone.

Michael Sondheimer, now associate athletic director at UCLA, never dreamed of playing basketball for the Bruins. As a freshman in Westwood in 1973, he stood five-foot-five, not exactly the size player Wooden was looking for. But long before he enrolled in classes at UCLA, Sondheimer dreamed of being UCLA's student manager. He interviewed for the position, felt that he made an excellent case for getting it, and was shocked when it went to someone else.

"I talked with assistant coach Frank Arnold, and he was surprised and suggested I talk to Coach Wooden about it." Sondheimer told me he was "scared to death" to talk to Coach about his disappointment, but decided to do it anyway. "I came into the athletic department and did what was probably the hardest thing I'd ever done, asking the secretary if I could see Coach Wooden." Within a matter of minutes, he was sitting in Coach's office.

Coach offered this bit of advice: "Michael, you came to UCLA first and foremost to get a great education. I know how disappointed you must feel right now, but you need to remember that in life things have a way of working out for the best. You may not believe that now, but that's how it will happen in the future."

Sondheimer said he left Wooden's office that day still disappointed and not really believing what Coach had said. But within a year, Sondheimer was covering UCLA basketball for the campus newspaper, *The Daily Bruin*, and he went on to fulfill his dream with a twenty-eight-year career in the school's athletic department. "I have been running the men's basketball recruiting from an administrative standpoint since 1985–86," he told me.

Today, Sondheimer describes Coach as "the greatest person I know, and the one I respect the most." He adds, "Yes, life worked out best for me. That talk with Coach Wooden lives with me every day of my life."

Another great story came from the late Steve Patterson, who was a high-post center at UCLA: "Coach was always getting on me about dropping the ball down too low where it could get stolen. One day at practice I couldn't take it anymore, so I stormed off the court and went to my locker. I was in tears and thinking of quitting. Coach left the floor and came to my locker and apologized to me. He told me he cared about me and just wanted me to be the best I could be. That meant so much to me. Coach realized he had gone too far and was humble enough to apologize, and that kept me going.

"That was 1971, and we went on to win another title that year, beating Villanova." Patterson had twenty-nine points in that title game, his career high. Patterson said, "Coach's desire to learn and communicate is the capstone of his life. He has continued to refine his craft into his nineties, and as a result he is the old master at the peak of his game."

Rich Levin—a longtime Major League Baseball publicity director who played for Coach in the sixties—told me that every fall at the start of practice, Coach Wooden would hand out reams of paper with outlines of practices and other information, including the Pyramid of Success. Rich said, "Many of us would make paper airplanes out of them, little realizing that what Coach was teaching us would impact us for the rest of our lives."

Another excellent illustration of Coach's skills as a teacher came from Rick Majerus, the legendary coach of the University of Utah. In 1973, Majerus was twenty-four years old and just starting out in coaching, as second assistant to Al McGuire at Marquette. He needed some information on coaching so he wrote a letter to Coach with nine specific questions. "Within a short period of time, Coach sent me the best letter I've ever received," Majerus told me. "He answered all my questions in a comprehensive, right-to-the-point manner. His answers were concise, but very informative, thorough, detailed and professional. I was just a twenty-four-year-old kid trying to make it as a coach, but John Wooden treated me like the top guy in the industry. How gracious of him!"

YES, YOU ARE A TEACHER!

In 1974, the Final Four was in Greensboro, North Carolina. A bunch of us went to the UCLA hotel to visit with Coach Wooden.

Bill Miller, the Elon College coach, had a beer in front of him. When Coach walked into the room, Bill hid the beer behind his chair. Can you imagine a grown man doing that? That's how Coach affected people.

—Danny Roberts, former Campbell College head coach

Now, you may be thinking, "What does all this have to do with me? I'm not a teacher." Oh, yes, you are. Whether you realize it or not, you are teaching others through the things you say and do. Everyone has a sphere of influence, and you have more impact on other people than you realize. John Wooden's students were America's best college basketball players. Unless you make your living as a coach or teacher, your students are probably your children, your neighbors, your coworkers and other people you come in contact with every day. You may not be aware that people are watching you, "taking notes" and learning from the things you say and do, but they are.

In an interview with Ronald Gallimore and Roland Tharp for *The Sports Psychologist* in 2004, Coach Wooden said, "I think everyone is a teacher. *Everyone!* Maybe it's your children, maybe it's a neighbor, maybe it's someone under your supervision in some other way. In one way or another, you're teaching them by your actions."

Craig Scalise was student manager of the UCLA basketball team in the late 1980s. Even though Coach had long since retired, his presence was felt very keenly during those years. Scalise told me, "I am grateful every day for Wooden's life lessons that reached me through UCLA basketball." He explains, "In 1987, when I was a sophomore engineering student at UCLA, my respect for Coach Wooden motivated me to become the basketball team's student manager. Coach's influence was powerful, and I learned some of my most important life lessons through the privilege of working with the players and coaches whom he had influenced."

Scalise went on to give a specific example.

"One day I found myself having received three Fs just about a week before my finals were to begin. Having endured a lot that quarter, I felt defeated and called my parents to say that if my best efforts were leading to failure, then I didn't know if there was any point in my sticking around for my finals. I should probably go home and start over with something easier—but first I would go to basketball practice.

"While at practice Reggie Miller noticed that I was downcast and sneaking looks into my physics book while running the shot clock. He asked me what was wrong, so I explained my classroom difficulties and told him I didn't know what to do.

"Reggie told me it was obvious what I needed to do, and that was study, so he would do my job for the rest of that day's practice.

"Obviously, the coaches would never allow such a thing," Scalise says, noting that Miller had just been selected as an All-American, and the NCAA tournament was just about to begin. But "Reggie's critically timed compassion and simple encouragement, rooted in Coach Wooden's teachings, gave me the boost that I needed to recommit myself to 'doing my best to become the best that I am capable of becoming.'"

Scalise not only passed his finals, he went on to earn a PhD from the University of Chicago, one of the toughest engineering schools in the country. Then he started his own business, which has helped the Ukrainian government modernize its economy, designed American Red Cross and Department of Homeland Security training programs, and works with sports leaders with "strategic advice that links ethical and moral values. These are contributions that I probably would not have been able to make if I had quit that day at UCLA."

As a teacher, John Wooden:

● **WAS DIRECT AND TO THE POINT.**

During his final season at UCLA, Gallimore and Tharp were invited to sit in on a number of Bruins practices. They noted, "His comments were short, punctuated and numerous. There were no lectures, no extended harangues."

They said Coach frequently made comments such as, "Don't walk!" "Hard driving, quick steps." "Do some dribbling between shots." Coach learned early in his career that short, quick comments, repeated often to drive home the point, worked much better than long speeches (which is something I'm sure most children wish their parents would learn—including mine).

• WAS HIGHLY ORGANIZED.

Coach met with his assistant coaches for two hours every morning to plan that afternoon's practice. In fact, planning sessions often lasted longer than the practices themselves. *The Sports Psychologist* says, "Practices were tightly organized and conducted with clock-like precision. There was constant activity, with players moving from drill to drill quickly and efficiently, so that the intensity level was kept at a remarkably high level."

Denny Crum, who went on to have an outstanding career as a college basketball coach, told me, "As a result of playing for John Wooden, and coaching under him, I learned many valuable lessons. For example, he helped me with my organizational skills and taught me the importance of being totally prepared. He did everything in basketball and in life based on being fundamentally sound." Crum added, "He's the best teacher I've ever seen because he recognizes that the principles of learning are the same whether it's English, math or basketball."

Bill Walton, who succeeded Kareem Abdul-Jabbar as big man on the UCLA campus, wrote that practices at UCLA were "nonstop, electric, supercharged, intense, demanding . . . with Coach pacing the sidelines like a caged tiger, barking instructions, positive reinforcements and maxims: 'Be quick, but don't hurry.' He constantly changed drills and scrimmages, exhorting us to 'move quickly, hurry up.'" Games, Walton said, seemed to happen at a "slower gear" than practices, because "everything we did in games happened faster at practice."

George Terzian, who was coach at Pasadena City College when Wooden was at UCLA, says that he sometimes took his assistants to see the Bruins practice. "Attending a UCLA practice was like going to a well-played symphony with John Wooden as the master conductor," he says. "Specific warm-up, fundamental execution with quickness, detail, encouragement and correction, sustaining of intensity and crescendo during five on five. We would leave practices exhilarated and charged up at the hope of going back to our own team and getting the same results." He adds that "Coaches throughout Southern California and even throughout the nation and world profited by watching such excellence in team preparation."

• TAUGHT BY EXAMPLE.

When Coach saw something happening on the basketball court that he didn't like, he'd stop the action and use a three-step process to show how the move should have been made. This involved:

1) Demonstrating the right way to do something.
2) Demonstrating what the player was doing wrong.
3) Again demonstrating the right way to make the move.

Gallimore and Tharp wrote, "His demonstrations are rarely longer than three seconds, but are of such clarity that they leave an image in memory, much like a text-book sketch." Texas Wesleyan University administrator William Ward was right on the mark when he said, "The mediocre teacher tells. The good teacher explains. The superior teacher demonstrates. The great teacher inspires."

• TAUGHT BY REPETITION.

In the *Pyramid of Success*, Coach wrote: "The four laws of learning are explanation, demonstration, imitation and repetition. The goal is to create a correct habit that can be produced instinctively under great pressure."

To drive his point home, Wooden said, "To make sure this goal was achieved, I created eight laws of learning: explanation, demonstration, demonstration, imitation, repetition, repetition, repetition and repetition."

As a coach and a teacher, John Wooden understood that old habits can be hard to break. If you've been doing something the wrong way for years and years, it's not likely that you're going to start doing it correctly overnight. After the kitchen in our building was remodeled, I can't tell you how many times I went to the water-cooler for a drink, only to find that the cooler was no longer there. Intellectually, I knew that things had been rearranged. But habit kept taking me back to the place where I used to get a cup of water. After a week or two, I finally broke that habit and started turning left instead of right when I walked through the kitchen door.

A good teacher understands the power of habit and the ability of repetition to overcome that power.

• PLANNED FOR THE INDIVIDUAL AS WELL AS THE TEAM.

Former UCLA center Swen Nater said of Coach, "He knew me better than I knew myself." He knew all of his players well, understood where and how they needed to improve, and was always ready to teach what was needed. As Coach said, "If you're going to build a team, you have to know the individuals on the team." In his book *Wooden*, he said, "I could track the practice routines of every single player for every single practice session he participated in while I was coaching him." I'd be willing to bet that none of his former players would ever dispute that statement.

• AVOIDED NEGATIVISM.

Coach says, "I've always believed in the positive approach."

Swen Nater recalls that he "committed many errors" in practice and often needed correction. But he also says that these "corrections" never became personal or degrading in any way. "Corrections in the form of information did not address, or attack, me as a person," Nater says. "New information was aimed at the act, rather than the actor." He remembers that Coach gave "information" that could be used to improve a specific situation—and not a deflating "evaluation."

Steve Fisher, who coached at the University of Michigan in the early 1990s, told me this story: "In 1993, we lost to North Carolina in the NCAA Finals, in the famous timeout game which haunts Chris Webber to this day. (Webber cost his team a technical when he called a timeout near the end of the game, apparently forgetting that Michigan had already used up all of its timeouts.) Chris was a finalist for the John Wooden Award and had agreed to go to Los Angeles for the ceremony. But after that final game, he knew he wouldn't win and didn't want to go. Finally his father and I convinced him to go, and he went reluctantly. The day before the dinner there was a little luncheon that Coach attended. He could see that Chris was really down, so he took him aside in a little private room and gave him a pep talk.

"Thirty minutes later, Chris came out beaming. Coach had talked to him, signed a *Pyramid of Success* for him and really lifted him up. All the way home, Chris thanked me and told me how much meeting John

Wooden had meant to him. Chris will never forget that act of kindness, and neither will I."

As Wooden biographer Steve Bisheff said: "John Wooden is America's teacher. If everyone could spend an hour with him at that little condo in Encino, the world would be a better place."

Chapter Six

✦

If You Want to Be Like Coach: Learn These "Rules of Good Teachers"

My children went to Coach Wooden's basketball camp. He sat with them—not only with my kids, but with all the kids—and talked to them as if they were his own children. He also took pictures with every kid in the camp.

—Willie Naulls, former Bruin and NBA star

IN THE PREVIOUS CHAPTER, we discussed some of the characteristics that made John Wooden such a wonderful coach and teacher. In this chapter we'll take a look at some of the other characteristics that go into the makeup of a good teacher:

The first thing good teachers do is:

Demonstrate patience.

Coach put it this way: "No two cases are identical, but the teacher must always have patience. And you have to listen to those under your supervision. I think anyone in a position of supervision, if they're not listening to those under them, they're not going to get good results."

I'm reminded of a story related by Bob Thau, who played for UCLA's freshman team in the 1950s and went on to become an attorney in Los Angeles. Thau told me that in the seventies, two of his sons went to a John Wooden summer camp. "Our youngest, Jordan, was seven at the time, and after the second day he called and asked if he could come home. He was whimpering and crying, and when I asked him what was wrong, he said, 'It's not good here. I'm not a good player, and the other boys aren't being nice to me.'"

Thau urged his son to give it one more day. "The next evening, Jordan called and said, 'I met Coach Wooden today, and he wants to meet my parents. I asked why, and Jordan replied, 'Coach told me that if you're homesick that means you have a very good home.'" Coach also told Jordan that he was "the bravest boy in camp" because he was sticking it out, even though he was homesick. "I'm very proud of you," Coach told him. Thau remembers, "Jordan came home thrilled because Coach Wooden was so interested in him. It still amazes me that with almost seven hundred kids at camp, Coach would spend time with Jordan and show so much interest. It proves what a remarkable teacher and coach he is. He took the negative of Jordan's struggle and turned it into a positive."

John Wooden demonstrated his kindness and patience in dozens of other ways. He never swore at his players. He rarely lost his temper. When he taught young players in basketball camps, if they had trouble "getting" something, he never blamed them or made them feel stupid. Instead, he patiently demonstrated the technique—over and over again until his young students got it right.

Coach actually said that he was occasionally bothered because one of his teams didn't make enough mistakes in practice. "I wanted my players to be active," he explains. "I wanted them doing things and initiating. I didn't want them worrying about mistakes." He went on to say, "Mistakes made while expanding boundaries are what I wanted. If we weren't making mistakes, we weren't far enough out on the edge. If we weren't pushing against the walls of our capabilities, we weren't practicing properly. The time to cut down on turnovers is during games, not during practice."

He knew that players who were afraid of failure might not try hard enough, and they might be so fearful that they'd "choke" when the game was on the line. Wooden said, "For example, in my next to last game, we were two points behind Louisville with only a few seconds to go. We set up a play for Richard Washington. Afterwards, a reporter asked, 'Why did you pick Washington?' I replied, 'Because he's not afraid of making a mistake.

He thinks he's a pretty good shooter, and if he misses, he'll think, *Well, you can't make them all.* Therefore, he's harnessed his fear. The others might be thinking, *I've got to make it.* If that's what they're thinking, they'll be fearful about missing. I didn't want that. I wanted Richard. And, as you know, we won.'"

Coach also showed patience by his willingness to teach any time he was asked. Former NBA assistant coach Brendan Malone told me: "Years ago, I was at a clinic at the Marriott Hotel in Newton, Massachusetts. I ended up alone in the lobby with John Wooden for thirty minutes. He went over his three keys to success: conditioning, fundamentals and teamwork. Then he explained his four laws of learning: explanation, demonstration, critique of the imitation of the demonstration and repetition. The one-on-one session soon became a lesson for seventy-five. Coaches just flooded in to hear him teach."

Former broadcaster Merle Harmon also saw Coach's kindness and patience. Harmon, who worked with Wooden after Coach retired from UCLA, told me, "He was like a father or grandfather that every young man should have. He set an example that all of us respected and admired. He never demanded special treatment from any of us and was a humble and caring person."

The second thing good teachers do is:

Break complex issues down into the simplest details.

Little things done well is probably the greatest secret to success. If you do enough small things right, big things can happen.

—John Wooden

Bill Walton says that Coach Wooden turned his Bruins teams into winners by breaking down every aspect of the game in practice. If you've ever looked over the shoulder of a coach while he diagrammed plays, you know that basketball is not a simple game. As all those Xs and Os and arrows and dotted lines testify, it can get pretty complicated. A basketball player has a lot to think about while on the court.

But Coach Wooden did what the best teachers do: he taught the game one simple step at a time. Then he put it all together like the pieces in a puzzle. Walton says, "Coach Wooden broke it down so the players could master the fundamentals and therefore could play up to their full potential. That's the thing I remember most about UCLA basketball. The practices were more important to me than the games. . . . I remember those simple fundamentals, about getting inside yourself, looking in the mirror and making sure that you did everything that you're supposed to do, and everything else would take care of itself."

Pete Blackman, who played basketball at UCLA from 1958 to 1962, says he has always remembered, and tried to live by, these few words of wisdom from Coach Wooden: "Do the basics right, and do as well as you can with what God gave you, and you will be surprised at how far you can get in life."

From time to time, other coaches or sportswriters would say that UCLA's basketball teams were much too predictable. They didn't do anything that shocked opponents or caught them by surprise. Everyone knew what they were going to try to do, but they did it so well that no one could stop them anyway! The Bruins were like a major league pitcher who throws a ninety-eight-mile-an-hour fastball. The batter knows what's coming, but still can't hit it!

When he was told that others called his offense "predictable," Coach simply said, "I am not a strategy coach. I'm a practice coach." Besides, as Wooden says in his book, *Practical Modern Basketball*, "There are no real secrets to the game, at least not for very long."

Now, if you were to take a poll of basketball players and ask them what they like most about the game, the most popular answer, by far, is sure to be "scoring." Nothing beats seeing the ball swish through the net and hearing the roar of the crowd.

Coach drilled the fundamentals into his players. He made sure that everyone on his teams understood the basics of the game from A to Z. He wanted well-rounded players, not one-dimensional guys who scored at will, but wouldn't, or couldn't, play defense. And as all those championship banners in Pauley Pavilion attest, it worked.

Coach didn't expect his players to learn too much too fast. He explained his teaching style this way: "The greatest holiday feast is eaten one bite at a time. Gulp it down all at once and you get indigestion. I discovered the same is true in teaching. To be effective, a leader must dispense information in bite-size digestible amounts."

Ex-UCLA basketball coach Jim Harrick said, "John Wooden has been described as one of the greatest teachers who ever lived. His subject was basketball and the court his classroom. He emphasized that basketball is a very simple game. Many times, coaches make it more complex than it really is. You learn to win games from 3:00 to 5:30 every day at practice, certainly not the night of the game."

Coach agrees: "What I taught was as simple as one, two, three. But, without being self-congratulatory, I believe I taught 'one, two, three' fairly well."

The third thing good teachers do is:

Strive to instill character.

Over the years, each good teacher redirects hundreds of lives.
—Tracy Kidder, author

Sometimes reading the sports page is a lot like reading a police blotter. This athlete was picked up on an assault charge. That one is accused of robbery. Still another has been charged with sexual assault. Too many college coaches look the other way and pretend that nothing is wrong. All they care about is winning, and if you can win with thugs and criminals, then they're going to recruit thugs and criminals. But John Wooden was never that way. He demanded that his players act like gentlemen on and off the basketball court. He insisted on a quality of character that went right down to the clothes they wore and the way they cut their hair. He felt that if his players looked like gentlemen, they would act like gentlemen.

Bill Walton said that Coach "rarely talks about basketball, but generally about life. He never talks about strategy, statistics or plays, but rather about people and character. And he never tires of telling us that once you become a good person, then you have a chance of becoming a good basketball player or whatever else you may want to do."

Coach is right. A good character is the foundation upon which a successful life can be built. An excellent teacher does more than impart practical knowledge—how to solve a math problem, how to write an essay and so forth. He enables his students to understand the difference between right and wrong, and helps them choose the right.

John Wooden exerted a positive influence that has changed hundreds, and perhaps even thousands, of young minds. That reminds me of Henry Adams's statement that, "A teacher affects eternity. He can never tell where his influence stops." Coach believed, "You won't know what kind of teacher you were until twenty years after the fact."

When Coach was at UCLA, before he'd even consider recruiting a young man to play basketball for him, he wanted to know what kind of character he had. "While I can't prove that a person of good character has more potential as a team player . . . that's the person I want to coach. A scientist might find otherwise," he admits, "but scientists don't make their living teaching young men and women how to play basketball."

Before the team hit the floor for the first practice of the season, Coach handed them this list of twenty "suggestions" and said, "Our chance of having a successful team may be in direct proportion to the ability of each player to live up to the following":

- Be a gentleman at all times.
- Be a team player always.
- Be on time whenever time is involved.
- Be a good student in all subjects—not just in basketball.
- Be enthusiastic, industrious, loyal and cooperative.
- Be in the best possible condition—physically, mentally and morally.
- Earn the right to be proud and confident.
- Keep emotions under control without losing fight or aggressiveness.
- Work constantly—improve without becoming satisfied.
- Acquire peace of mind by becoming the best you are capable of becoming.
- Never criticize, nag or razz a teammate.
- Never miss or be late for any class or appointment.
- Never be selfish, jealous, envious or egotistical.
- Never expect favors.
- Never waste time.
- Never alibi or make excuses.

- Never require repeated criticism for the same mistake.
- Never lose faith or patience.
- Never grandstand, loaf, sulk or boast.
- Never have reason to be sorry afterward.

In other words, do your best to demonstrate good character at all times. As he presented his list to the players, Coach reminded them that, "The player who gives his best is sure of success, while the player who gives less than his best is a failure. Everyone knows your reputation," he said, "but only you know your character—and that is what really counts."

Kareem Abdul-Jabbar says, "John Wooden was a constant teacher and role model. I really appreciate what he was able to impart about how to live your life, how to enjoy success and not let fame destroy you. I got that first-hand. Success destroys a lot of people."

Coach was furious whenever any of his players engaged in showboating or tried to show up their opponents in any way. Lucius Allen remembers, "I used to like to throw the ball behind my back, because I had the ability to do it, but that was not the proper way to make the pass. . . . I'd make my behind-the-back pass and the crowd would go crazy and we'd score the lay-up. I'd be feeling great about the play I'd made. But when the horn sounded and we came off the floor, I'd get an angry look from Coach—and he'd tell me to sit down.

"The first half would go by and the second half would be halfway through. And finally, Coach would say, 'You ready to play basketball now, Lucius?'

"'Yeah, Coach, I'm ready to play.' So that's the way I learned not to throw the behind-the-back pass. He was a master of psychology. He knew what buttons to push to get us to do what he wanted us to do, and he knew when to push them."

Roy Williams, who is now head basketball coach at the University of North Carolina, told me about a game at Pauley Pavilion when he was coaching the Kansas Jayhawks. Early in the first half, Jayhawks center Raef LaFrentz dunked on a UCLA player and then danced in celebration. Williams says, "Raef is the best kid in the world, but I took him right out because I didn't believe in anything like that. After the game, I ran into Mike

Warren, one of Coach Wooden's great players, and he asked me why I took Raef out of the game. I explained my actions and he said, 'Coach Wooden would've done the same thing.' I took that as the ultimate compliment."

The fourth thing good teachers do is:

Show their students that they really care.

You cannot live a perfect day without doing something for someone who will never be able to repay you.

—John Wooden

When Wilt Chamberlain was traded to the Los Angeles Lakers in the mid-1960s, he said something that Coach never forgot. "One of the writers at the press conference announcing the trade asked him, 'Do you think Bill Van Breda Koff can handle you?'" Chamberlain responded, "No one handles me. I'm a person, not a thing. You handle things—you work with people."

Coach adds, "Shortly before that, my book had a chapter titled *Handling Your Players*. I came home and crossed it out and put *Working with Your Players*. Then I called the publisher and told them I wanted to change it for the next edition. Because when you stop and think about it, that's what you do—you work with people."

Coach recalls that when he started out in coaching, he thought, "Everything was either black or white. But I've come to see that there are gray areas, and I made two mistakes that I regret very much because I didn't see the gray area."

The first regret: "I had a rule in high school that smoking was cause for automatic dismissal from the team. And my finest player, my only center, I caught him smoking and I dismissed him. Well, he never finished high school, and he could have gone on to college. I think I should have handled it in a different way."

The second regret: "I had another player in high school who didn't qualify for his letter. He was a fine person who worked very hard, but just didn't qualify. Anyway, his dad came in one day and asked me if his son was going to get his letter." When Coach replied that he hadn't decided yet, the father said, "If he doesn't, I'm going to have your job."

Coach sighs, "I didn't like that, and I ended up not giving the boy his letter, and I feel, deep down in my heart, that I would have given him the letter if not for his dad—and that's wrong."

Over the years, Coach Wooden came to believe that his number-one priority was the personal well-being and development of his players.

Broadcaster Al Michaels remembers traveling with the UCLA basketball team to a game in Pullman, Washington, on a bitterly cold winter weekend. The team had a couple of hours to practice, then they showered, dressed and prepared to walk a couple of blocks back to the hotel. But before letting his players walk out into the frosty weather, he went around the room and felt every player's head to see if his hair was dry. He wanted to make sure that none of his boys caught a cold. Michaels says, "It tickled me so much. I thought, here's John Wooden, so loved, so admired, so respected by his players, and clearly a man who's a father figure. And he's not only a father figure, but he's going to be their mother, too."

No wonder former Bruin Larry Ruben said, "John Wooden was an educator who cared very much about all of his students." Ruben added that Wooden's desire was always to make a lasting, positive impact on his players. Most often, he succeeded.

Ed Powell played high school basketball for Wooden in Indiana during the 1930s, served as an assistant coach at both Indiana State and UCLA, and has maintained a lifelong friendship with his old coach. From the beginning of his career, Powell says, Coach was willing to do anything he could to help his students. "He was highly regarded," Powell says. "He was one you would seek out for advice. Sometimes when I think of John, I think of a father figure. Sometimes I think of a brother. A coach, but always a friend. He'd go out of his way to assist you. He would work with you on schoolwork if it needed to be done. . . . That's the way he was."

Ed Ehlers also played for Wooden in South Bend, before going on to play professional baseball and football. He recalls, "I kept getting my nose broken all the time and couldn't breathe. Then one day a doctor came to the house and said he wanted me to come to the hospital because he was going to operate on me. He straightened my nose out, and I never paid a cent." Officially, Ehlers never found out who arranged or paid for the surgery. Unofficially, he has always known Coach Wooden was involved. "He's always helping somebody."

Ehlers says, "Coach was different, in that he wanted you to be a success in any endeavor you chose."

Like all good coaches, John Wooden expected his players to do their best, but he did not browbeat them when their best wasn't good enough. He let them know that he believed in them, that he knew they had enough talent and strength to win. But even if they didn't win, he was happy with a solid effort. "A coach is a teacher," he said, "and one of the most important lessons to be taught is that players are successful when they do their best, even if the final score goes against them."

Former NBA player Tommy Hawkins says that Coach Wooden taught his players all the skills they needed to succeed in life, even if they didn't realize it at the time. He was what news anchor Dan Rather calls "a teacher who believes in you, who tugs and pushes and leads you on to the next plateau—sometimes poking you with a sharp stick called truth."

The fifth thing good teachers do is:

Love learning as much as teaching.

Who dares to teach, must never cease to learn.

—Motto of Kean College,
written by John Cotton Dana

Wooden once said, "I prefer to call myself a teacher rather than a coach. I am also a learner. In fact, I like to think that during my last year of coaching, I was a better teacher than I was the year before. I tried to improve each year," he said, adding, "If I am ever through learning, I am through. You either have to go forward or you'll go backward. You rarely move rapidly upward, but you can go downward very fast."

Coach continues, "If I've learned anything in my ninety-plus years, I have come to understand that it's what you learn after you know it all that really matters." In *The Sports Psychologist*, he is quoted as saying, "I hope I was learning the very last year [I coached]. I don't think I learned as much the last year as I did my first year, but I hope I learned a little bit each and every year." He continued, "I think I learned more my first year of teaching than I ever did any other year. The second year I think I learned more than the year after that, and so on."

Former British Prime Minister Benjamin Disraeli put it this way: "As a rule, he who has the most information will have the greatest success in life."

The sixth thing good teachers do is:

Help their students put into practice what they've learned in the classroom.

The purpose of the teacher is to "draw out"—not to "cram in." We must create an interest in the heart and mind that will make the learner reach out and take hold upon the things that he is taught.

—Henrietta Mears, teacher/author

Former UCLA star Gail Goodrich recalls the "pep talk" Coach Wooden gave to the 1964 Bruins before they went out and won the national championship.

"Who finished second last year?" he asked.

Coach searched the faces of the young athletes gathered around him. Nobody knew.

"See?" he said. "Nobody remembers who finished second. Now go out and play the way we prepared."

"And that," Goodrich remembers, "was his pep talk."

Coach didn't say, "Go out and win this thing."

He knew that if his players just remembered to play the way he had taught them—if they utilized a pressing defense and a fast-break offense—there was a very good chance they'd be cutting down the nets after forty minutes of play.

Goodrich remembers that practices during his years at UCLA were tightly controlled. Coach Wooden had a certain number of minutes allocated for each drill, and he stuck to it. "He was certainly prepared. Boom, boom, boom. There certainly wasn't any free time, but it was fun because it was so organized. And it was a learning experience."

He adds, "Life is preparation. If you've been in or anticipate a situation, it's no pressure."

The seventh key to being a good teacher is:

Communicate, communicate, communicate.

The greatest aspect of John Wooden's coaching was his ability to communicate with his players.

—Gail Goodrich

Gail Goodrich's father was an outstanding college basketball player, and captain of the team, at the University of Southern California, UCLA's crosstown arch rival. Why, then, did Gail decide to play ball for the hated Bruins? Two words: John Wooden.

Goodrich, who played on UCLA's 30–0 national championship team in 1964, said, "Coach had the ability to communicate with his players and motivate them. He took players from different environments and motivated them to work together as a team, to understand their roles within the team, and ultimately to be successful."

Goodrich said that he knew he wanted to be a Bruin after he saw his first UCLA practice while still in high school. "I had never seen anything so organized and precise in my life," he said.

Coach always took the time to communicate with his players. He often oversaw Bruins practices from a high vantage point in the stands, while his assistant coaches put the team through its paces. Every so often, he would call a player to come up and sit next to him. They would talk for a few moments, with Coach carefully and thoroughly explaining how the player had been out of position on a certain play, how he had reacted improperly to an opponent's move, and so on. Then, the player would return to the court.

Coach has always believed in open, honest, direct communication, and he continues to be a great communicator today. Wherever he goes, he's recognized by dozens of people who want a few words, and he's always more than happy to oblige them.

Steve Kelly, a writer from Seattle, remembers that when he was a twenty-four-year-old writer, just starting out, he ended up in the locker room with John Wooden, and was "one-on-one with him for thirty minutes. He talked basketball with me for the whole time . . . and I could see he loved it because he's a teacher. It wasn't an interview, but a teaching session. I couldn't believe he did that."

Claude Terry, a former NBA player, tells a similar story. "When I was coaching at Seattle Pacific University, I would go visit Coach at the start of season to get my batteries charged. He was always so gracious to me. We would go to his favorite coffee shop for breakfast where everyone knew him. Then we went back to his condo for a day of Xs and Os."

The eighth and final key to being a good teacher is:

Practice what you teach.

I admire Coach Wooden. He didn't tell us to do anything that he didn't do himself. He set a good example for us to follow. And what an example!

—John Green, former UCLA player

As Coach said, "Being a role model is the most powerful form of educating. Youngsters need good models more than they need critics. It's one of life's greatest responsibilities and opportunities."

Willie Naulls, who went on from UCLA to a stellar career with the Knicks and Celtics (the Celtics won three NBA championships in a row when Naulls was in Boston), relates, "John Wooden is a great family man, an honorable man, a particular man, a teacher. He loves all of us. We were his boys." Naulls adds, "I have observed Coach Wooden's interaction with thousands of people during our more than fifty years of unbroken association, and what makes Coach Wooden special is that he treats everyone he meets with the same attitude—just as he did me all those years ago when we first met. My mom told me when I was very young that 'you can judge a man's heart by what he does.' She said, 'A godly man will demonstrate love in his life's encounters.' My love/hate relationship with Coach Wooden over the many years of our association has always been stabilized by God's love through Coach to me."

In his *Practical Modern Basketball*, Coach wrote that, "The coach must never forget that he is a leader, not just a person with authority. The youngsters under his supervision must be able to receive proper guidance from him in all respects, and not merely in regard to the proper playing of the game of basketball."

He also wrote, "The coach must be extremely careful in his judgment and consider all matters in the clear light of common sense. He must have a sense of discretion and tact comparable to that of Solomon. A sense of values in regard to men, games, techniques and training is a must for him."

"I'd rather be remembered as a good man than a good coach," he said. "Sometimes it's hard for us to keep things in proper perspective."

Pete Blackman, former UCLA player, told me,

> Coach drove everybody, but with a conception that always had value: Make yourself as good as you can be: Always. There was very little emphasis on the opposition . . . very little attempt to understand what they were going to do on the theory that if you do the best you can, you're going to statistically come out well. These are lessons of a profound nature. Focus on yourself, your own values, doing things correctly.

One morning when Coach was having his usual breakfast (eggs, dry toast and brittle bacon) at VIPs, the restaurant near his house, a man came up and asked him, "Coach, by the way, what year did you retire from coaching?" "I retired from teaching," Coach said, emphasizing the word, "in 1975." John Wooden has always considered himself to be first and foremost a teacher, a molder of young lives.

In his book *My Personal Best*, he says, "Common sense, an ability to read human nature, and good judgment are among the most valuable assets a teacher and coach can possess—much more important than just ABCs or Xs and Os. . . . We need to couple firm discipline with fairness and reason, understanding and compassion." Wise words from a wise teacher.

Chapter Seven

❧

If You Want to Be Like Coach: Drink Deeply of Good Books

There are ten thousand books in my library, and it will keep growing until I die. This has exasperated my daughters, amused my friends and baffled my accountant. If I had not picked up this habit in the library years ago I would have more money in the bank today. But I would not be richer.

—Newspaper columnist Pete Hamill

WHERE DID WE EVER get the idea that "real men don't read books"?

We talk about someone being "bookish," and the picture we get is of a timid Casper Milquetoast type with thick, horn-rimmed glasses, a pale complexion and a soft voice. A scaredy-cat Barney Fife type of character who doesn't have any real adventures in life, so he lives vicariously through adventures on paper.

What a lie!

John Wooden learned early in life the importance of reading good books. He realized that reading is essential to the development of a well-rounded character. He loved poetry, philosophy and the Bible. He has always felt, as I do, that it would be a tragedy not to read the world's greatest books—because those books contain the collected wisdom and knowledge of the ages. I have been to his condo in Encino and seen the shelves of books, especially books about Abraham Lincoln, his favorite American.

Coach understands that good books provide us with the opportunity to learn the thoughts of the greatest men and women of history. Books give us the wisdom and strength we need to overcome our troubles—and they can teach us how to do just about anything that is "doable." The reading of books allows us to "stand on the shoulders of giants," and thereby see further into the future.

The experiences that John Wooden had while growing up in rural Indiana supplied the foundation for his future success. Living on a farm during tough economic times taught him the importance of virtues like hard work, teamwork, sharing, thriftiness and dependence on God. He also learned a great deal from the poems, stories and books his father would read to him and his brothers at night beneath the flickering glow cast by a small oil lamp.

Andy Hill, author of *Be Quick—But Don't Hurry*, which I've mentioned several times already, believes these early lessons from his father were instrumental in shaping Coach Wooden into the man he is— "an American icon who reminds us all that the pursuit of success does not require that you compromise your morals and values."

Because of his strong moral foundation, Coach was never seduced by the glitter and glamour of Hollywood. Hill remembers, "The culture of Los Angeles in the 1960s was so self-consciously hip that John Wooden's provincial Indiana roots made him appear to be from another planet. Unlike the style-conscious L.A. glitterati, he was very secure in who he was and where he came from. In a city where everyone wanted to be cool, this man clearly had no interest in imitating the world of movie deals, cutting-edge fashion, rock music and air kisses."

He continues, "If Pat Riley was the quintessence of L.A. style as coach of the Lakers in the 1980s, Coach Wooden was its antithesis, bringing to the limelight the solid Midwestern values of substance over showtime. Even as a young boy I could sense that there was something special about a man like this. . . ." Here is yet another testimony to the learning and wisdom contained in books.

BOOKS: IMPORTANT SINCE THE BEGINNING

One year at Christmas we took a road trip to Michigan State and Bradley. A couple of us had to take an English lit exam at the hotel, and Coach Wooden served as the proctor. I'll never forget how he talked with us about poetry and his love for the written and spoken word. He could have taught the course.

—Bill Johnson, former UCLA player

Coach has always understood that good books nurture the human spirit, just as good food nurtures the body. The philosopher Erasmus said it like this: "When I get a little money, I buy books; and if any is left I buy food and clothes."

I suppose I'm an Erasmus type of guy. When I was just a boy, my mother taught me through her example to appreciate good books. I love to read, and a week rarely goes by that I don't read at least seven or eight books. Right now, I have over two hundred books on the shelves in my office, arranged by topic, which I intend to read over the next several months. John Wooden has always been a voracious reader as well.

Brett Vroman, who played for Wooden at UCLA, told me, "I was one of the few players Coach Wooden ever came to personally recruit. We lived in Provo, Utah, and my mother was an English teacher. They really hit it off talking English, reciting poetry." By the time Coach flew out of Salt Lake City International Airport, on his way back to Westwood, he had a commitment from Vroman. His parents couldn't imagine their son playing for anyone else!

Andy Hill says, "I've heard Coach speak, and out of nowhere he'll start reciting a poem I've never heard before. His daughter Nan will tell me she has no idea where he came up with it, something he learned years ago that just came out. I've also heard him speak and he'll be in the middle of a poem and fumble over a line briefly. He's not really fumbling. It's just his way to get the audience's attention and shake 'em up a little bit."

In today's world, it seems that many people feel they don't have time to read. And so we lurch along from one slogan to the next. We are captivated by the sound bite and the catchphrase. Advertising agencies spend millions of dollars trying to come up with a "tagline" the public will remember and hang on to, such as "You deserve a break today" or "A mind is a terrible thing to waste."

Such slogans aren't bad in and of themselves. But what is bad, in my opinion, is that those who don't read are going to find themselves following a path of style over substance. For no matter what Madison Avenue may say, image is not everything.

Reading good books helps us understand the world. It requires discipline and initiative, traits that help make an effective leader. Beth Moore, who played her college basketball at UCLA in the late seventies, told me, "When you enter Coach's condo, the first thing that hits you are the books you see. He has an abiding love for poetry and the written and spoken word." Fred Slaughter, who played on Wooden's first NCAA championship team in 1964, said, "Coach is an intellectual. He has a wealth of knowledge on a number of topics, including basketball. He knows what he's doing."

How important is reading? Author Brian Tracy cites research that shows the highest-paid Americans read for an average of two to three hours every day. The lowest-paid Americans do not read at all. He says, "The key to expanding your knowledge is reading. Perhaps not all readers are leaders, but all leaders are readers."

My long career in professional sports has given me the opportunity to meet many extremely successful men and women from all arenas—sports, entertainment, politics, literature, medicine, religion, business, you name it—and one thing almost all of them have had in common is a love for good books. Again:

If you want to be like coach, you must acquire a love of reading.

I am certain John Wooden would agree with these words from the philosopher Cicero:

Books nourish youth, delight old age, adorn prosperity, afford a refuge and solace in adversity; forming our delights at home; anything but hindrances abroad; they are our nightly associations; our indoor and out-of-door companions.

Chapter Eight

༺❧༻

If You Want to Be Like Coach: Seek Wisdom

If any of you lacks wisdom, he should ask God, who gives gener-ously to all without finding fault, and it will be given to him.

—James 1:5

WHEN DENNY CRUM ARRIVED at UCLA as an assistant coach in 1968, the Bruins were defending national champions. In fact, they had won three of the previous four NCAA tournaments, falling short only in 1965 when Texas Western's Miners shocked the world of college basketball.

Obviously, John Wooden knew how to coach. By that point in his career, he might have been tempted to think he knew all there was to know about the game. Because of that, Crum says that when he first came to UCLA, he wasn't sure that any suggestions he made would be accepted or seriously considered. But the new coach quickly discovered that John Wooden was not the least bit close-minded or arrogant: "He was very open to suggestion and change. I think that's what impressed me about him more than any-thing else—and I think it was unusual, given the success he had already had to that point."

Crum remembers that, "I'd say, 'I think if we tried this it might work a little bit better,' and he'd say, 'Well, show it to me.' Then I'd diagram it on the blackboard and we'd talk about it." Coach didn't agree to anything right away. He wanted time to think about it and see if he really thought it would work. But neither did he reject anything just because it wasn't his idea. Whereas Coach's foundation stayed the same, he changed and grew with the times—as the sport of basketball changed.

During his years as head coach at UCLA, John Wooden had this sign on the wall in his office: "It's amazing what you can accomplish when you don't care who gets the credit." Because he's always tried to live up to that ideal, he has been open to ideas and suggestions from others. As he once told NBC sports announcer Jim Gray, "When everybody thinks alike, nobody thinks."

Coach understands that an open mind is one of the basic requirements for anyone who wants to be wise. You can't believe everything you hear, but neither can you reject everything you hear. A wise person seeks to be open-minded without being gullible, discerning without being cynical. That's a difficult line to walk, but John Wooden has managed pretty well.

When I asked University of Alabama basketball coach Mark Gottfried to give me his impression of Coach, his eyes lit up and a grin spread across his face. "When you're with John Wooden, you'd better be wearing a catcher's mitt to catch all the pearls of wisdom," he said. "You can be sure that you're getting good counsel."

Coach has always been a seeker of wisdom—in all areas of life. Former UCLA head coach Jim Harrick calls John Wooden "the wisest man I ever met. We can talk about politics, or world affairs, or the budget. It seems to me that he could solve all of the world's problems. He could bring countries together and get leaders with huge differences in thought to sit down with each other and end up working their troubles out. He is a true humanitarian, a true gentleman."

Harrick told me, "Wooden's wisdom makes him special. Sometimes I'll hear him say something particularly wise and wonder, 'Why didn't I think of that?' He's a master at life lessons, and that's why his ex-players come back to see him all the time. When they were playing at UCLA, they may have rejected some of his teachings, but now that they're older and deeper into life, they realize how right he was."

Harrick added that whenever he spends time with Coach, he asks him all sorts of technical questions about basketball. "I ask him about an out-of-bounds play when he is one point down. Or about going to a full-court pressure defense when he's behind. He folds his arms and says, 'Jim, I never expected to be in those situations.' Then he'll laugh. Coach loves to tease you if he knows you well."

A similar viewpoint is expressed by Lorenzo Romar, head coach at the University of Washington. "When a problem or tough situation arises, my first reaction is to see what Coach has to say about it," Romar told me. "He has so much wisdom about life. There is not a subject where he doesn't have experience."

The world is full of wisdom, but it's up to us to seek after it. It's not going to come floating into our minds for no good reason at all. As Coach said, "There are no secrets. Study and learn all you can."

Where can you find wisdom? In the Bible, first of all. Wisdom can also be obtained from watching the right television shows, reading the right books, attending thought-provoking plays and movies. Wisdom can be found in the writings of the great thinkers. It can be found at museums, art galleries and lectures. Wisdom comes through spending time with wise people. And, in my opinion, it comes most of all from a daily relationship with God.

John Wooden clearly understands the difference between wisdom and knowledge, and he seeks after both. Knowledge consists of data: facts, figures, dates, mathematical formulas, mechanical information and so forth. Wisdom is knowing how to put all that knowledge together and use it. For this reason, wisdom transcends knowledge. For instance, knowledge is required to build a nuclear weapon, but wisdom teaches you to never use it. It takes knowledge to know that your friend is wrong about something he or she insists is true, but it takes wisdom to keep quiet and avoid hurting his feelings. Knowledge is being completely familiar with every play in a playbook hundreds of pages thick. Wisdom is knowing which of those plays is going to work in a pressure situation with the game on the line.

Wisdom is taking the time to reflect on the things you've learned and letting them sink down into your soul so you can see clearly how they apply to you.

At the beginning of this chapter, I quoted from the biblical book of James. I love what James has to say about the importance of following through on what you know:

Do not merely listen to the word, and so deceive yourselves. Do what it says. Anyone who listens to the word but does not do what it says is like a man who looks at his face in a mirror and, after looking at himself, goes away and immediately forgets what he looks like. But the man who looks intently into the perfect law that gives freedom, and continues to do this, not forgetting what he has heard, but doing it—he will be blessed in what he does.

—James 1:22–25

I recently came across these "Tips for Living" in a newsletter from a mental health clinic. As I read them over, I realized how clearly each of them has been demonstrated in the life of John Wooden:

- **Concentrate on your good qualities.** Whatever it is about you that's best—a generous nature, a deep, sympathetic ear, an infectious smile, a deep sense of loyalty—remember to always keep that in the forefront of your own image of yourself. Coach not only concentrated on his own good qualities, but on everyone else's good qualities as well. Paul Saunders, president of Saunders Systems, played for Coach in the late forties, and later served as a scout for the Bruins. He told me about a time when a newspaper columnist came to Wooden's office and told him that a young man who had played briefly at UCLA had just been sentenced to five to ten years in prison. Saunders said everyone associated with him knew this young man had been in trouble with the law just about all his life, and several of them started talking about all the bad things he had done. "Coach Wooden didn't join the discussion, so the columnist turned to him and asked him for his comments on the situation. Coach smiled and replied, 'I understand he was a good father,'" said Saunders. "Coach Wooden found something very positive to say even in a very negative situation."
- **Face your problems honestly**. If you can, get help from a friend. Learn what's going wrong and what you can do to improve things. UCLA trainer Tony Spino told me, "John Wooden's thought process is amazing. He will evaluate a situation for you and then give a simple,

calm answer because he cares about other people. His common sense is beyond anything I have ever seen." Then he added, "That's why everyone comes to John Wooden for everything: advice, wisdom and reassurance."

- **Make sure others get something positive from their association with you.** Kelvin Sampson, head basketball coach at the University of Oklahoma, told me, "John Wooden keeps us all grounded." When I asked him to elaborate, he said, "He has done things as a coach the rest of us can only dream about—yet he is this gentle, humble soul with a warm, sweet spirit. In the 2002 finals we lost to Indiana—but as I listened to Coach Wooden speak at a luncheon after that game, his words of wisdom reminded me why I got into this profession in the first place. It's not about the fame and fortune the game brings you, but about giving back to others." Willie Naulls told me, "The Bible says that God loves the man who gives cheerfully. Coach's life mission has been that of a sower of God's seed of generosity, which has grown into a harvest of good deeds done. His giving proves the reality of his faith!"

- **Be kind to people—avoid hurting them.** Look for good qualities, not faults, in yourself and others. Don't go around criticizing people or expecting them to let you down. College coach Dustin Kearns told me, "John Wooden's philosophy of life is very basic: Treat others well, respect their views, be considerate of them."

- **Be tolerant—accept people as they are.** Try to bring out in them the behavior that is best for both of you. Above all, bear with them. Remember that this world hasn't seen a perfect person in more than two thousand years now, so it's highly unlikely that anyone you know falls into that category. Sonny Smith told me that when he was a young man, he desperately wanted to be a college basketball coach; however, because he was always "playing the comedian" and trying to make people laugh, some potential employers wouldn't take him seriously. Then he had an opportunity to work with Coach in a basketball camp one year, and Coach told him, "My advice to you is, don't ever change. You have to coach to your own personality." Smith says, "Coach really impacted me with that comment." Armed with renewed self-confidence, Smith went on to a successful career as a college coach.

- **Look upon your failures as lessons to be learned.** And examine them carefully so you can avoid repeating them. But after you've examined them for a time, put them away and don't allow yourself to bring them up again. As Coach's old friend, Dutch Fehring, told me, "If you want to be like John Wooden, just look at his Pyramid of Success. His philosophy is very direct: Always strive to be the best you can be. He always lived and coached that way. Then, win or lose, he could always look in the mirror and say, 'I did the best I could.' That's all any person can do." Some people get so distracted by the failures they've experienced that they take their eyes off the big picture of their lives. For most of us, the path toward success zigs and zags rather than moving in a straight line. We take two or three steps forward, fall back a step or two, and then take a couple more steps forward. It's only when you step back and look at the overall picture that you can see the steady progress you're making.

- **Remember that everyone is occasionally worried or discouraged, including you.** Accept this fact of life and keep on moving toward your goals. Despite all those amazing winning streaks, undefeated seasons and national championships, Coach also knows what it's like to walk off the court a loser. And he admits that when his teams lost a game, he sometimes felt discouraged and depressed—especially if he felt his team had failed to play up to its full potential. "I wanted to win as much as anybody else," he says. "I'm fiercely competitive. However, the best competition I have is against myself, to become better. I did this with my teams, too. I wanted us to always be the best we could be."

- **Promise, readily, to do things for others.** But only promise the thing you fully intend to do and are able to do. In other words, don't make promises you can't keep. In 1964 the Bruins won their first national championship under John Wooden, trouncing Duke in the title game to cap off an undefeated season. Immediately, Coach was in demand for appearances at banquets and television shows all over the country. And yet, on an April evening within one week of that title game, Coach was the featured speaker at a church league awards banquet in

Inglewood, California. Jim McFerson, who was a walk-on for the Bruins in 1957, told me the story:

My brother was the director of our local church basketball league in Inglewood, and he wanted to end the season with an awards banquet with a special program. He asked me if I could get Coach Wooden to be our speaker, and I said I would try. I was still attending UCLA as a graduate student, so I visited Coach at school one day, and he agreed to come to our awards program, which, at the time, was still several weeks away. In the meantime, the UCLA basketball team was on its way to an undefeated season. But in order to keep a commitment to one of his obscure former players, one week after winning his first national championship and being much in demand as the toast of the Los Angeles sports scene, Coach Wooden appeared at our humble awards night to discuss his Pyramid of Success. I don't think anybody ever did figure out how my brother and I pulled that one off, but it was because of Coach Wooden's integrity and loyalty to a former player.

- **Never forget that people are more important than things.** Jeff Dunlap, who played basketball at UCLA during the 1985–86 season, told me, "John Wooden welcomes you into his world and there is no prerequisite required. He's so pure and genuine and grounded in love. I've never seen it in anyone else. Coach is always good to others and teaches us all to love one another." Then he added what so many others have said about Coach, "He lives what he preaches and is a living example for all of us."

You never know where you'll find the nuggets of wisdom that can change your life. I found these words, unattributed, in a bulletin from a Baptist church:

- I've learned that it takes years to build up trust and only seconds to destroy it.

- I've learned that it's not what you have in your life, but who you have in your life that counts.
- I've learned that you can get by on your charm for about fifteen seconds. After that, you better know something.
- I've learned that you shouldn't compare yourself to the best others can do.
- I've learned that you can do something in an instant that will give you heartache for the rest of your life.
- I've learned that you can keep going after you can't.
- I've learned that you are responsible for what you do, no matter how you feel.
- I've learned that either you control your attitude or it controls you.
- I've learned that heroes are the people who do what has to be done . . . when it needs to be done, regardless of the consequences.
- I've learned that I sometimes have a right to be angry, but that doesn't give me the right to be cruel.

One final piece of advice about wisdom: Sometimes, the wisest thing you can do is just admit that you don't have all the answers. Sometimes, things happen in life that are unfathomable to even the wisest among us. For Coach, one of those events was the long illness and death of his beloved Nell. Coach admits that Nell's passing knocked the props out from under him. For a time, he withdrew from all of his normal activities, withdrawing into the safety of his condominium. His belief system was shaken, and for a brief period, he struggled to hold on to his faith. But eventually, the love of his family and friends, and the birth of his great-granddaughter Cori, brought him back from the edge of despair.

In his book *My Personal Best*, Coach says: "Certainly, the old must make way for the new, however painful that may be. Nell was taken, but my life was renewed when I recognized and accepted the love of Cori and her little brothers, sisters and cousins. Everywhere I look, then and now, I see Nell. Everywhere I look, I see the Good Lord's plan.

"The deep sense of loss I feel without my sweetheart has never gone away, not for one single day. But the spirit of love I've regained is stronger than ever, and it gets stronger every day."

But what about the long days Coach spent sitting in Nell's hospital room as she lay in a deep coma? What can we say about those days, except to admit that the Lord's purposes are often beyond our comprehension and our wisdom? As Chuck Swindoll writes, "When you follow God's will and find yourself in a situation that you cannot explain, don't even try. If you do, you'll use human wisdom and you'll just mess things up. Call it like it is. It's another of his mysterious surprises. Practice using words like 'I don't know,' 'I don't understand,' 'This is beyond me,' and 'It doesn't make sense to me, but that's okay. God knows.'"

I'd like to close this chapter with some of my favorite quotes on wisdom from John Wooden:

- **A man makes mistakes**, but he isn't a failure until he starts blaming someone else.
- **An athlete** who says that something cannot be done should never interrupt the one who is doing it.
- **Consider the rights of others** before your own feelings and the feelings of others before your own rights.
- **Don't let what you cannot do** interfere with what you can do.
- **Failure is not fatal**, but failure to change may be.
- **It's the little details** that are vital. Little things make big things happen.
- **Never fear failure**. It is something to learn from. You have conquered fear when you have initiative.
- **Never try for a laugh at another's expense**. Try to laugh with others and never at them.
- **People are usually as happy** as they make up their minds to be.
- **There are many things** that are essential to arriving at true peace of mind, and one of the most important is faith, which cannot be acquired without prayer.
- **There are no secrets**. Study and learn all you can from those with whom you come into contact.
- **Things usually turn out best** for people who make the best of the way things turn out.

PART THREE

BUILDING A WINNING TEAM

꧁❖꧂

There is one star that counts, and that's the team.
Any organization whose leader seeks stardom
at the expense of the team is one
I would not want to join, regardless
of the paycheck.

—John Wooden

Chapter Nine

꧁꧂

If You Want to Be Like Coach: Be Part of the Team

Each of us must make the effort to contribute to the best of our ability according to our individual talents. And then we put all the individual talents together for the highest good of the group. . . . Understanding that the good of the group comes first is fundamental to being a highly productive member of a team.

—John Wooden

JOHN WOODEN SAYS he learned the importance of teamwork from Piggy Lambert, his basketball coach at Purdue University. Lambert stressed that everyone on his team was equal. No one was to be treated as if he were more important than anyone else—and that included a flashy young All-American by the name of Johnny Wooden.

When Wooden became a coach, he carried Lambert's philosophy with him. He says he always told his players that, together, they were like the components of a powerful car.

Maybe a Bill Walton or Kareem Abdul-Jabbar or Michael Jordan is the big engine, but if one wheel is flat, we're going no place. And if we have brand-new tires but the lug nuts are missing, the wheels come off. What good is the powerful engine

99

now? It's no good at all. A lug nut may seem like a little thing, but it's not. There's a role each and every one of us must play. We may aspire to what we consider to be a larger role, or a more important role, but we cannot achieve that until we show that we are able to fulfill the role we are assigned. It's these little things that make the big things happen.

The Apostle Paul says something very similar in the twelfth chapter of First Corinthians:

The body is a unit, though it is made up of many parts; and though all its parts are many, they form one body.

It's no secret that John Wooden's UCLA basketball teams featured some great players:

Kareem Abdul-Jabbar
Bill Walton
Walt Hazzard
Henry Bibby
Keith Wilkes
Sidney Wicks
Lucius Allen
Gail Goodrich
Keith Erickson

The list could go on for pages. But it wasn't the talent that won basketball games so much as it was John Wooden's ability to meld that talent into a unified group of players who were willing to put the team ahead of their own personal success. Sometimes, he admits, his players didn't like each other personally, but that didn't stop them from playing together as a team.

"One of the great misconceptions," Coach told a magazine reporter, "is to feel you have to have great camaraderie to have a fine team. For instance, Tinker, Evers and Chance were probably the greatest double-play combination there ever was in baseball. That may be hard to authenticate, but a poem was written about them—they had to be good. But the truth was, they hated each other. . . . I've had players—a couple of forwards—who detested each other, yet we had a fine team that year. I also had two guards who didn't like each other."

Despite such personality conflicts, Coach insisted that his teams play together as a unit, and that included relying on each other and trusting each other in pressure situations.

With conviction in his voice, Coach says that any player who is more concerned with his own statistics than the welfare of the team is someone "I welcome on the opponent's side of the court. The presence of such an individual weakens the team and makes it vulnerable during competition to a disciplined group filled with team spirit.

"Team spirit is one of the most tangible 'intangibles' I have ever encountered. It's difficult to see; you feel it. And it's a powerful feeling for an organization to have."

In an interview with *New Man* magazine, published in the July/August 2005 issue, Wooden is quoted, "The athletes today and their athleticism are just remarkable. But as it has improved, in my opinion, I don't think teamwork has progressed at all. . . . I don't like to see a fellow score a basket and point at himself and strut around."

Bob King, former Purdue head basketball coach, says of Coach, "I think his biggest ability was that he stressed the team concept. There were great stars, but it was still UCLA, it was not Alcindor. It was not any other particular player, it was UCLA."

All of the players mentioned above were superstars in their own right. But each also demonstrated an important quality Coach calls *team spirit.* If you have team spirit, he says, you will be willing to sacrifice personal consideration for the welfare of all.

For an individual with team spirit, "The team is the star, never an individual player." As Coach said, "Ten strong horses could not pull an empty baby carriage if they worked independently of each other."

Part of team spirit is believing in the team, expecting every member to do their part and to function at an optimum level. Ron Ekker, former assistant coach for the Orlando Magic, told me an interesting story about a conversation he had with Coach when Ekker was head basketball coach at West Texas State University in Canyon, Texas.

Wooden had come to town to give a speech at the university, and afterwards, Ekker drove him back to the airport in Amarillo. "It was a windy, dreary night, and as we got in the car, Wooden said, 'It's got to be a tough job recruiting here.' I said, 'Well, it is isolated and there's no social life, but that allows the players to concentrate on basketball.'

"Then he said something very interesting: 'In coaching, you've got to find a way to win. When I went to UCLA in 1948, I was convinced we couldn't win big. It was a football conference. Our facility was poor. Then, at the start of the 1963–64 season, for some reason, I felt good about the team. Of course, we won it all that year, and that started our run. When I reflect back, it wasn't the players who were losing—it was me. I had to believe we could win before the players could. My staff kept saying, 'We can't recruit. We can't do this or that.' You've got to get rid of that attitude before you can succeed.'"

Toby Bailey, who was a freshman at UCLA during the 1994–95 season, remembers that he felt bad because he believed he wasn't getting enough playing time. Consequently, when he did get a chance to play, "I did a lot of individual stuff, thinking that it would impress the coaches." One of Wooden's former players, Mike Warren, decided that Bailey needed to hear some wisdom about the importance of teamwork, so he arranged for the three of them to have lunch together. Bailey said, "Coach told me the team must always come first, and after that, the individual accolades will come. He told me to be patient and work hard and my time would come. That lunch turned my season around, and in many ways, it turned my life around. I'll never forget it."

I've already mentioned how Coach left Jack Kent Cooke fuming when he refused Cooke's offer to coach the Lakers. One of the primary reasons that John Wooden was never much interested in the pros is because he saw a lack of teamwork at that level. "The pros don't interest me generally because of all the fancy stuff and the reduced role of real teamwork," he said. "I believe basketball is a team sport and should remain so."

"The team was everything to Coach." That's the view of Tommy Curtis, who played for UCLA during the Walton era. "You had to buy into the team plan Coach presented, and not your personal plan," Curtis said. "When I was at UCLA he had fifteen first-team, high school All-Americans on the squad. He had to be the best psychologist in Southern California to deal with all those guys."

Jonathan Chapman was a very rare creature during Coach's tenure at UCLA—a walk-on. As you can imagine, he didn't get a whole lot of playing time on a team filled with the top high school recruits from all over the country. Chapman sat on the bench, watched, listened and learned. After graduation, he went to Europe to play pro ball. His coach there, Elwin Heiny, who later coached the University of Oregon women's team, asked him to interpret the basketball style played at UCLA so their team could copy it. Chapman told me, "It was unusual for me to be asked to supply so much input into how a team I was on was going to play. It caused me to think critically about what was really key to UCLA's success."

He came up with these hallmarks of Bruin basketball:

1) It was a system that allowed for hard work to result in key stats. We had a player, Rich Betchley, who attended a Rick Barry camp. He often quoted Rick's mantra, "If you hustle, you get twenty." While Coach would probably be surprised to be lumped with Rick Barry, he did recognize that players would be more content to play in a high-scoring system.

2) Practices were supremely efficient. Coach used to tell us every year about his survey of West Coast programs. "We practice for fewer minutes than any team in the West," he told us. The implied message: "Practice hard, and it will stay that way." We were in movement every minute except those short breaks to shoot free throws. We would seldom get stuck in any drill for more than seven to ten minutes. There was always enough variation in practice sequence and content to keep things interesting. Every year, when we went to the NCAA tournament, we got to see other schools practice. Without exception, we would observe jaw-dropping misuse of practice time.

3) As an English teacher, Coach had a keen command of the language. At no time was anybody even slightly confused about what they were supposed to do in practice or in a game. Clarity reigned supreme.

4) Coach motivated in positive ways. He rarely, if ever, was overly critical. During my career as a teacher/coach and administrator, I've

often recalled Coach's clear distinction between punishment and discipline.

Finally, Chapman says of Coach, "It was clear he walked the talk, which made anything he said that much more credible."

John Wooden might be described as a "basketball purist." He never liked the slam dunk because he thought it emphasized the individual over the team, and he said he preferred watching "the rhythm of the game—the beauty of a play as it unfolds and leads to a basket."

Coach Wooden's definition of teamwork is:

A cooperative effort on the part of a group of persons acting together as a team or in the interests of a common cause.

Similarly, he says that a team is:

A group of individuals who are committed to a common purpose.

He has always taught that the key concepts of teamwork are best expressed in these six statements:

- **Happiness begins where selfishness ends.** Coach Wooden insisted that his players always acknowledge the help and support they received from other members of the team. For example, a player who scored a basket after receiving a pass from a teammate was expected to acknowledge the assist as he headed back up the court to play defense—usually by pointing, smiling, winking or nodding at the man who had helped create the scoring opportunity.

Some players asked, "But Coach, what if he [the teammate who gave the assist] isn't looking?" "Believe me," Wooden replied, "he'll be looking!"

Coach also suggested that three points should be awarded when a team "runs a screen and roll, give and go, then cuts in and makes a nice basket. That requires skill from several players at the same time, so make it worth three points." (He later said he wasn't really serious about the three-point play but "was merely emphasizing the importance I put on teamwork.")

So anyone who wants to be like Coach must learn how to put aside his or her own selfish interests for the good of the team. I know that's not so easy to do, but as all those championship banners in Pauley Pavilion attest, it is well worth the effort involved.

- **Politeness is a small price to pay for the goodwill and affection of others.** Coach has always been pleased by letters he received from the custodial staffs of schools where the Bruins had played, thanking him for leaving their locker rooms in a neat, clean condition. He said, "The locker rooms were clean when we departed because I asked the players to pick up after themselves. I believe this is just common courtesy. In basketball we often have orange slices or gum at the half. I see no reason that you should throw those orange peels or gum wrappers on the floor. There are receptacles for those."

Wooden said he also believed that being neat and courteous helps make a person feel better about himself. "I believe this encourages teamwork and team unity. It establishes a spirit of togetherness that helps mold the team into a unit. I really believe that. In fact, perhaps I should say I know it. I've seen it work."

- **The best way to improve the team is to improve ourselves.** Every team needs highly skilled players. According to Coach Wooden, "Skill means being able to execute all of your job, not just part of it. This is true whether you're an athlete, an attorney, a surgeon, a sales rep or anything else. You'd better be able to execute properly and quickly."

During my forty-four years in professional sports, I have known many "superstar" athletes. One thing most of them had in common is that they all worked very hard to improve their skills. They were determined to get better, and therefore make their teams better, no matter how much they had already accomplished.

Always remember, your team is counting on you!

- **Forget favors given, but remember those received.** John Wooden has always been a giver. During my interviews in preparation for writing this book, I heard dozens of stories from players, coaches and ordinary citizens who told me how John Wooden spent quality, one-on-one time with them, sharing his knowledge about basketball.

Dick Versace, who went on to become general manager of the Memphis Grizzlies, was a high school basketball coach during Wooden's championship run at UCLA. He told me, "In those days, I would go to hoops clinics all over the country. To go to a John Wooden clinic was the ultimate experience for any aspiring young coach at any level. After a clinic, you could walk right up to him, ask a question, and he would dig in with you and go over it all one-on-one. He would spend as much time as you wanted. Not many big-time coaches would ever do that."

Homer Drew, coach at Valparaiso University, remembers a basketball clinic he attended when he was a coach in St. Louis. "I sat down with my box lunch. Pretty soon, a man joined me, and it was John Wooden. I started shaking. He said to me, 'What is your favorite out-of-bounds play?' Can you imagine?" Drew shakes his head in wonder at the memory of that moment. "We ended up talking basketball, and he just opened up and shared his knowledge with me. He was very kind. He's always been willing to talk with people and share his wisdom. He always has time for you, and he listens."

A young man from Baltimore, Brett Greenberg, told me: "I wasn't good enough to play for my high school team but I love basketball and wanted to be a coach. When I was seventeen I wrote a letter to John Wooden and told him about the goals in my life. Within a week, he wrote back, gave me his phone number and said to come visit him when I was in Los Angeles. My dad and I agreed we should take advantage of the invitation, so in August 2003, we flew to California to see Coach. We spent three-and-a-half hours with him, and we talked mostly about life, not Xs and Os. Coach spent an hour reading us poetry, most of it written by Swen Nater. He even played us a song Swen had written and recorded. As the afternoon unfolded, I tried to remember every word because as Coach was speaking I felt it was a prophetic vision from the wisest man in the world."

Brett went on to say, "Two themes came through to me: faith and patience. He told me, 'Things work out best for those who make the best of how things work out.' He also told me, 'If you work hard and love what you do, what could be better?' That sure makes sense to me."

Perhaps one reason John Wooden has always been quick to give favors is that he follows his own advice and remembers favors given. For example, when his UCLA teams were struggling on defense, Coach called one of his archrivals, Pete Newell, who was then at the University of California, and asked for help. Wooden wound up sending two of his assistants to Berkeley, and Newell worked with them for an entire day.

Can you imagine a rival coach spending an entire day helping the UCLA Bruins become even better? That's exactly what Pete Newell did. And who knows? Perhaps he did it because he remembered when someone else did a similar favor for him. Just think what a wonderful world this would be if everyone was determined to pass along the favors other people have done for them. That's what would happen if we were all like Coach.

- **The main ingredient of stardom is the rest of the team**. When I asked former UCLA star Greg Lee what he remembers most about John Wooden's coaching style, he replied, "What set Coach apart from other coaches was his consistency. He did the same things with his stars that he did with his scrubs. He was always focused on the details and never wavered from the first day of practice to the last day of the season." Lee also said something that I've heard from dozens of other former players: "He was a teacher who happened to be a basketball coach. All he wanted to do was help people become the very best they could be."

In *The John R. Wooden Course*, developed by Coach for American Agencies, he has this to say about teamwork:

> *It's amazing what can be accomplished when no one is concerned with who gets the credit. This simple concept involves cooperation and team spirit. When we cooperate, we believe that what is right is more important than who is right. When we have team spirit, we have consideration for others and an eagerness to help the team achieve its goals.*

Wooden says that when he was a coach, he expected his players to be as enthusiastic about the success of others on the team as they were about their own success. I'm sure this wasn't always easy, especially for some of the players who spent most of their careers sitting on the bench. Most of us find it difficult to remain in the shadows while others we know always seem to be in the spotlight. But we need to remember that those "background roles" can be just as important.

Every football team needs a good blocker who can open a hole for the star running back.

Every baseball team needs a middle-reliever who can set the table for the superstar closer.

Every basketball team needs good sixth and seventh men who can keep their team in the game while the superstars catch their breath on the bench.

And so on. As Coach said:

The individuals who aren't playing much have a very important role in the development of those who are going to play more. They are needed, and you must let them know it. Everyone on the team . . . has a role to fulfill. That role is valuable if the team is to come close to reaching its potential. The leader must understand this.

Coach didn't like it if he saw one of his players becoming arrogant and self-important. When that happened, "I would say to some of the other players in a stern voice loud enough for the star to overhear, 'You fellows are as important to the success of this team as anybody. Everyone has to fulfill their role for this team to reach its potential. Nobody is bigger than the team. Nobody! Remember that.'"

Former Bruins player Chris Hibler says, "Coach insisted that there be chemistry among his players. His players respected, feared and loved him. He treated the twelfth man almost like he treated his stars."

And there's this from Shaquille O'Neal, who told me: "John Wooden sat me down in college a long time ago and said, 'Being great ain't all about scoring and making fantastic plays. It's about how everybody else plays around you.' I've always been that type of player. Guys depend on me, but I also depend on them."

It's so important to trust the other members of your team. And yes, anyone who trusts will occasionally be disappointed. But as Coach says, "You'll live in torment if you do not trust enough. Trusting is part of our higher nature. Doubting is a lower instinct. The latter is easy to do, the former more difficult, but so much more rewarding."

- **True happiness, freedom and peace cannot be attained without giving them to someone else.** Bobby Pounds was the first black player John Wooden recruited at UCLA, joining the team in 1950. Pounds remembers, "I grew up in Fresno, California, farm country. In the summer of 1949, I was out picking grapes all day. The next year I was at UCLA. Coach took me out of the grape fields and into the big time." Pounds says that Coach wanted to win, but more than that, "he wanted to make you a great person. You wanted to please him by trying to be as good a person as you could be. I love the guy." Pounds later went into coaching "because I wanted to help kids just like John Wooden helped me."

So far in this chapter, we've seen that teamwork is an important key to achieving success. But how do you develop a cohesive team? *The John R. Wooden Course* lists these steps:

STEP ONE: Set the team goal. All team members work together by fulfilling their roles and helping each other to succeed.

As strange as it may seem, Coach's goal was never, simply, to win games. At the first practice of the year, he told his players that they wouldn't hear him talk much about winning during the season. His goal was to see his players become the best they could possibly be, as individuals and as a unit. "If you do your best on the court, and your best isn't good enough to win, I'll still be satisfied," he told them.

One of his former players, Larry Gower, told me that Coach meant what he said. After a loss to Ohio State—with Jerry Lucas and John Havlicek—during the 1961–62 season, Gower says some of the Bruins were sitting in front of their lockers with their heads down. "Coach Wooden walked in and asked, 'Why are your heads down?' Someone said, 'Because we lost.' Coach said, 'You lost to a team that was a little better tonight, but you played the best you were capable of playing, and that's all I can ask of you. Be proud and walk out of here with your heads up high.'"

Gower went on to say, "That message has stayed with me my whole life.

Coach always talked about that concept, but that night he showed us about living it after a tough defeat."

Then again, he had some talented players. He had to know that if they did their best they were just about always going to win—and they did.

For Coach, winning was always secondary. It was much more important that everyone on the team try as hard as they possibly could. When they didn't give their all, he was disappointed, even if they won by thirty points. On the other hand, if they gave it everything they had, but still lost, he was satisfied. Coach once said, "We just do our best on every possession and assume we will win, but sometimes we simply run out of time."

Craig Scalise—who, as I mentioned earlier, was student manager of the Bruins basketball team during his undergraduate days at UCLA—has been working with former Bruins coach Steve Lavin to put together the John Wooden Institute. One of the key components of the Institute is a general education course that presents Coach's teachings as a comprehensive philosophy. Scalise told me that he and Lavin want to ensure that John Wooden's teachings are "explicitly preserved, reflected upon and transmitted to future generations."

In a paper titled "Coach Wooden's Philosophical Fundamentals," Scalise writes:

> *Perhaps the best test of how you truly define success is how you react to pressure. If success depends on outcomes, then the demand to succeed—pressure—increases with the rewards provided by a challenge's outcomes. This pressure generates stress because achieving success through outcomes is beyond your control, and this stress can greatly interfere with performance when challenges' outcomes offer more to gain or lose, intensifying the demand for success.*
>
> *However, this stressful pressure is an illusion to those who accept Coach Wooden's definition of success. Within Coach Wooden's definition of success, the demand to succeed never changes. Rather, all tasks—whether big or small, in the spotlight or seen by none—provide the same opportunity to succeed by*

"knowing that you did your best to become the best that you are capable of becoming." This is free from stress because achieving it is always fully under your control. Those who truly accept this should be able to maintain a high level of performance, unaffected by the intensifying pressure of greater challenges.

Coach always appreciated and congratulated those who did their best, whether they were playing for or against him. Adrian Dantley starred for the Notre Dame team that stopped UCLA's eighty-eight-game winning streak in January 1974. For Dantley, the upset victory over UCLA was even sweeter because he had been a fan of Bruins basketball as far back as he could remember. "As a kid growing up in Washington, D.C., I'd stay up late to watch the UCLA games on tape delay," he says.

Dantley says that during the Fighting Irish's historic one-point upset of the Bruins, "I'd look over at Coach and see him twisting that game program. He'd give me a little nod. I think it was a nod of respect for the way I played, and I've always appreciated that."

Of course, that loss was a difficult one for the UCLA basketball team to endure. But what made it even worse for Coach was that he felt his players had not played up to their potential. They had not achieved their goal. It was a precursor of things to come, including an 80–77 double-overtime loss to North Carolina State in the NCAA tournament. Prior to that, the Bruins barely eked out a triple-overtime win over Dayton in the tournament, a team that Coach felt should have been no match for UCLA.

After the loss to Notre Dame, a heartbroken Sidney Wicks told Coach, "I just can't believe we lost!" Coach replied: "Then I suggest not to do it again."

In his book *My Personal Best*, Coach looks back and says, "The mark of a champion, I believe, is consistency of performance at your highest level under pressure. That's the apex, the highest block, of the Pyramid of Success.

"The Bruins exhibited competitive greatness for two full seasons and portions of two others—an extraordinary time during which every single team we faced wanted to be the one who stopped UCLA."

Coach says it is because he prizes effort over result that "I have such pride in our loss to Cincinnati in the 1962 NCAA Final Four. The Bruins' extraordinary effort during that season was nearly 100 percent and culminated in a wonderful, but losing, performance against Cincinnati. Conversely, I have no pride in UCLA's triple-overtime victory against Dayton in the 1974 NCAA tournament. The difference was in the quality of the effort of those under my supervision."

As you build your team, you have to know what your goal is and how you're going to get there. And everyone on your team needs to know what your goals are and how they are expected to help you reach those goals. Whether your goals are simple, or complicated, it's important to spell them out so the entire team can work together to meet them.

STEP TWO: Determine the roles that are necessary for the team to succeed. Emphasize that all roles are of equal importance.

Most of the young men who were recruited to play basketball for UCLA were superstars in high school. They were used to scoring lots of points and being the best players on their teams (if not in their entire conferences). But when they arrived at UCLA, for the first time in their lives, some of them weren't good enough to start. They sat on the bench—and had a tough time doing it. Coach did his best to let them know they were an important part of the UCLA team, even if they didn't get much playing time. He said, "Every member of your team needs to feel wanted and appreciated. If they are on the team, they deserve to be valued and to feel valued."

Gail Goodrich remembers that when he came to UCLA, he was used to having control of the ball for most of the game. "At the high school level, I was the best player on the team, and I was always a good scorer. But when I came to UCLA, Walt Hazzard was playing the other guard. He was the passer, the play-maker, the ball belonged in his hands." Coach stressed to Goodrich the importance of playing well without the ball, of getting in position to get the pass from Hazzard. For the benefit of the team, he had to learn how to change the way he had always played the game—and he did.

"Coach always chose players to fill roles that were necessary to meet certain goals," Goodrich explains.

In other words, you can't have a basketball team made up entirely of point guards, nor a football team made up of quarterbacks and receivers. Nor can you have a company where everyone is a "big idea" person. If there's nobody around to take care of the details, then those big ideas will never become reality. You can't have a team where everyone leads and nobody follows. Nor can you have a team where nobody leads and everybody follows. To a great degree, success comes from having the right people in the right roles.

STEP THREE: Carefully evaluate and place the right team members in the right roles. Explain what that role is and why it is important to the team.

Coach once remarked that anyone who wants to develop a winning team "should always make sure you have better players than your opponent." Of course, that's not always an easy thing to do. But it often comes as the result of working with the members of your team, developing them into the best they can possibly be, and then making certain they are filling the right roles. Consider Dodgers closer Eric Gagne. Gagne was a bust as a starting pitcher, bouncing back and forth between the major leagues and AAA. But when Gagne was moved into the closer's role, he became one of the biggest stars in all of baseball.

STEP FOUR: Allow each team member to develop within that role. They must be given freedom to create new and better ways to do the job.

According to Kareem Abdul-Jabbar, Coach Wooden "was always working on improving himself and maintaining whatever improvements he'd already made."

During his first twelve seasons at UCLA, Wooden changed the UCLA Bruins from an also-ran to a college power. But he wasn't satisfied. He felt that the Bruins could be even better. He already had his sights on an NCAA championship. He spent hours looking at films, reviewing extensive notes, talking with assistants and replaying games in his mind, trying to figure out what he was doing wrong. He finally came to believe that he was working his players too hard in practice. He felt they were worn out by the end of the regular season, and they ran out of gas at tournament time.

Wooden responded by implementing a rotation system at practice that allowed his five starters to get more rest. The system also improved teamwork by giving reserves more time on the court. He also introduced a full-court press, which created numerous scoring opportunities by forcing turnovers. The innovations paid off, and in 1964 the Bruins won their first national championship. It may surprise you to know that UCLA's tallest starter that year was six feet, five inches.

A couple of years later, when Kareem Abdul-Jabbar (then known as Lew Alcindor) joined the team, Coach Wooden changed his game plan again. This time, he went from the high-post, which he had used for thirty years, to a low-post offense to take advantage of Jabbar's seven-foot, one-inch height. The offense allowed Jabbar to perfect his "sky hook," and turned Westwood into the undisputed center of the college basketball universe.

When asked about his years at UCLA, Jabbar remembers that Coach cared about more than basketball, and he did what he could to help his players succeed in other areas of life. Jabbar told me, "I started out as an English major, and I'd ask him questions about my classwork. He always knew the answers. It wasn't just about going to the gym. There was more to your life than that, and he expected you to see that and apply yourself to getting your education." For that reason, Jabbar says, "I would put his graduation rate for the guys who played for him against any program you could name."

STEP FIVE: Evaluate, evaluate, evaluate.

When David Greenwood was about to graduate from high school, he was pursued by basketball coaches from colleges throughout the country. Most of them told him how great he was. As Greenwood put it, "They told me I was the greatest thing since sliced bread."

Wooden was different. He told Greenwood there were a few areas of his game that needed refining. Greenwood remembers, "I'm going, 'Wait a minute. Everybody else is treating me like I'm a god—and you're criticizing me.' But it made me respect the guy, and that was one of the reasons I chose to play at UCLA."

Even when his teams were going through entire seasons undefeated, John Wooden never stopped analyzing and evaluating. In his book *Wooden*, he said that his teams won championships because he was able to analyze players, get them to fill their roles as part of the team, and pay attention to details and fundamentals.

He also said, "The statement has often been made that we learn from adversity. However, you can learn as much through winning, in my opinion, as you can from losing."

STEP SIX: Hold regular meetings to:

- Ensure that everyone understands the team goal.
- Remind everyone that the performance of the team is what matters most, and not individual success.
- Remind every team member that he or she has an important role in determining the overall success of the team.
- Remind team members that the best thing they can do for the team is to continue improving themselves.
- Encourage team members and remind them that they are appreciated for their contributions to the team.
- Look for ways to recognize good work that has propelled the team toward its goal, and to acknowledge the good progress that has been made.

Former Bruin Eddie Sheldrake remembers that, "Coach had a meeting with his assistant coaches every morning at ten. And that meeting was going to go on no matter what. He wasn't going to change that meeting time for anyone—even the president of the United States. All of his coaches knew he was going to have that meeting, and they knew that they'd better be there."

Coach agrees with that assessment. He said that in his latter years at UCLA, he spent at least two hours every morning with his assistants, getting ready for that afternoon's practice. "I have a record of every practice session in a loose-leaf notebook," he says.

Every one of Wooden's assistant coaches and managers carried three-by-five cards to practice everyday so they knew exactly what was going to happen and when. They knew the precise moment when two basketballs were going to be needed at one end of the court for a drill, when the team was to switch from practicing rebounding and passing to dribbling and pivoting, and so on. Name a date—any date—from any season when Coach was at UCLA, and he can tell you what the team did at practice that day. His practices were that organized and his records are that thorough.

ROOT, ROOT, ROOT FOR THE HOME TEAM!

"Every family and every business requiring two or more individuals is a team," says Coach Wooden. "Selfishness, envy, egotism and criticism of each other can crush team spirit and ruin the potential of any mutual endeavor."

A marriage won't work—can't work—unless the husband and wife see themselves as a team, working together for the mutual benefit of each partner. John and Nell Wooden had a great partnership that lasted over sixty years. As former DePaul coach Ray Meyer told me, "John did everything with his beloved Nell. He never went anywhere without her. They had a true partnership."

Before Nell died in 1985, John spent over fifty nights in a row with her in the hospital. Today, he still writes her notes, and says, "I'm not afraid of death, because when I die, I'll get to see Nellie again."

Paul Westhead, who coached the Los Angeles Lakers to the NBA championship in 1980, told me about the time he dropped by the Woodens' condo to talk basketball. "We set up a date and I arrived at his apartment at 10 A.M. We talked basketball until 11:45, at which point Coach said, 'We need to end now because Nell and I go out for lunch every day. Would you like to go?'" Westhead went with them to a nearby Denny's, where John and Nell ordered the same thing they ordered every day—chicken noodle soup and grilled cheese sandwiches. "After lunch, we returned to the apartment and Wooden said, 'My wife is not well, and I spend thirty minutes with her now. You're welcome to stay and we'll continue our discussion.' I waited and we talked some more." Westhead says, "I've forgotten most of the basketball talk, but I'll never forget seeing the devotion of a man to his wife. I learned more from that than all the basketball stuff."

Former college coach Sharm Scheuerman said, "Coach Wooden had a unique marriage. They had a real partnership. He included Nell in his life and career, and they went everywhere together. That made an impression on me." Coach has always made his family a high priority. He credits his great-grandchildren, in fact, for helping him recover from grief over the loss of his beloved Nell.

Coach said, "Although I didn't recognize it at the time, that same year—1985—the one that brought me such sorrow, also brought my survival, the birth of Nell's and my first great-grandchild, Cori. Initially, I hardly took notice of the blessing because I was too deep in grief. But she is the reason I began recovering. The Good Lord first took Nell, but then sent the love of Cori and great-grandchild after great-grandchild, until their love and the love of all of all our grandchildren was everywhere around me like a field full of flowers. . . . Slowly, I began getting back my old self as I saw their smiles, laughter and love."

Chapter Ten

✤

If You Want to Be Like Coach: Work Hard to Achieve Your Goals

I've learned that winning games, titles and championships isn't all it's cracked up to be, and that getting there—the journey—is a lot more than it's cracked up to be.

—John Wooden

RAY ALBA WAS ONE of the basketball players John Wooden inherited at UCLA when he came from Indiana to Southern California in 1948. Before Coach's arrival, the Bruins football team made all the headlines. The basketball team won a few, then lost a few more, and nobody seemed to care all that much.

Alba remembers that all the players thought the previous coach, Wilbur Johns, was "a good guy." They were losing, but they were happy. Then, with Coach Wooden's arrival, the relaxed atmosphere suddenly disappeared. "The workouts were very difficult," Alba recalls. "At first I was angry and said, 'What the heck is this guy doing?'"

Alba didn't like the difficult workouts, nor did he care for the new rules. He says: "Wooden inaugurated a bed check when we were on the road. He'd have Ducky Drake, the trainer, come in at 9:00 or 9:30 and check each room to make sure all the boys were there." Alba says he would get in bed with all his clothes on, and "the minute the bed check was over, I'd jump up and meet one or two of my friends and we'd go out on the town."

That ended when Drake caught Alba and a couple of his friends in a bar in San Francisco one night.

"There was a big debate about whether they were going to send us back home and take us off the team or not," Alba says. "He [Coach] finally decided to give me another chance, and from then on I made all my bed checks."

As the season wore on, Alba discovered that his playing had improved. In fact, the entire team was better. Everyone seemed to be performing better than ever. UCLA, which had been picked to finish last in the Pacific Coast Conference, surprised everyone by winning the championship. They finished the league schedule with back-to-back wins over archrival USC.

Alba says that he finally came to realize that John Wooden is "a master teacher and a marvelous person." He smiles, "I learned from John Wooden that it takes hard work and perseverance to get what you're going after. If you and somebody else are going after something, you have to have more training or perseverance. Success is a lot of hard work. It isn't something magical that comes along, or a lucky break. It's you working for the break and working very hard."

Alba chuckles when he remembers encountering Coach on the UCLA campus long after his playing days. "Here I hadn't seen the coach say in, I don't know, twenty years, and I said, 'Hello, Coach.' And right away, he answers, 'Hello, Ray.'" Alba says he was astounded that Coach Wooden knew him after all those years. "But I'm sure he remembers most of the people's names."

How does he do that?

Simple. He works at it! Just like he works at everything.

What Alba didn't know, during Coach's first season at UCLA in 1948–49, was just how hard his coach was working. Being a college coach was Wooden's *afternoon* job. Every morning, from 6 A.M. until noon, was spent working at a local dairy "because I needed the money. I was a dispatcher of trucks in the San Fernando Valley and was a troubleshooter. After all the trucks made their deliveries and came back, I would call in the next day's orders, sweep out the place and head over the hill to UCLA."

And what was the first thing he did when he got there? He and his assistant Ed Powell mopped the gymnasium floor to get it ready for the afternoon's practice.

We talked earlier about the fact that John Wooden learned the importance of hard work from his parents at a very early age. He was also a humble man who, when he saw something that needed to be done, did it himself instead of waiting for someone else to do it for him. Even if what needed to be done was a good cleaning of the gymnasium floor.

When Coach was a boy, he and his brothers got up well before school to help milk cows and take care of other chores around the farm. When they got back home in the afternoons, there was plenty more to do, plus homework and basketball practice.

Coach recalls that when he was a child, he was certain that his father was the best man he had ever known. Today, at ninety-five years of age, long after the distorted views of childhood have faded away, he still feels that way about his father.

"He was the one who set the course that guided me through life—what I believe, what I do and how I do it." He says that his father taught his sons "in word and deed that the simplest values and virtues are the most important ones."

One of Joshua Wooden's favorite sayings was, "Don't try to be better than somebody else, but never cease trying to be the best you can be." He also told his sons, "Boys, always try to learn from others, because you'll never know a thing that you don't learn from somebody else—even if it's what not to do."

Today, Coach says, "You lose, you feel bad—sometimes very, very bad. But a much worse feeling is knowing that you haven't done everything you possibly could have done to prepare and compete."

Coach also saw hard work modeled in the life of his mother, Roxie Anna Wooden. Mrs. Wooden made almost all of her children's clothes, and John says he doesn't ever remember her buying a new dress for herself. "Only on rare occasions did she purchase new shoes. When she did, they had to last her for a long time."

When she wasn't sewing, baking or tending to the other needs of her large and active family, Roxie Wooden could generally be found in her garden. There, she grew peas, carrots, tomatoes, beans, celery, radishes and more. Most of what she grew went straight from the garden to the family dinner table. What wasn't eaten immediately was canned and stored in the fruit cellar, like money in the bank for a rainy day. Thinking about it now, Coach says that he knows his parents had a very rough life when he was a boy. "But for my brothers and me, growing up on that little farm was almost perfect."

In reality, life was far from perfect for John's mother. Her only two daughters died while they were still children. The first, Cordelia, died from diphtheria before reaching her third birthday. The second died soon after birth, not even living long enough to be given a name.

Coach says, "I doubt if Mother ever really recovered from the deaths of her two little girls. Perhaps she survived because farm life offered no time for self-pity. Maybe she survived because of her strength and her religion. Like my father, my mother placed her faith in the Good Lord, and they taught us to do the same."

While I was writing this book, I went back and spent two days in Martinsville, Indiana, to help me really capture the flavor of Coach's early life. We gathered about fifty-five people from his past at Poe's Cafeteria for a six-hour session to talk about John Wooden. I collected all their stories and their reflections, and it was a marvelous experience! So many wonderful stories were told.

Then I took the John Wooden tour. First, we went to the gym at the high school, which is the same gym he played in, then out to his boyhood home, which still stands. His elementary school is no longer there, but you can see where it was—and the farm he worked on is still a farm. The day I was there the corn was growing high, and I'm sure the fields looked very much as they did in the 1920s.

After that, we went over to the little cemetery where Coach's mother and father were buried. As we were walking among the grave markers, we heard a commotion over by a wire fence. When we went to see what was going on, we discovered that a potbellied pig was giving birth to a brood of piglets. And I thought to myself, *This is the home turf! Nothing much has changed since Coach grew up here over ninety years ago. This is the soil in which his values were born, nurtured and cultivated.*

During his teen years, Coach Wooden worked a variety of jobs. He worked as a garbage collector, in a cannery, in an ice cream factory, as a bagger in a grocery store, and he helped the phone company erect telephone poles. It seems that John Wooden was almost never without a paying job—and this was in addition to all the chores he was responsible for at home, as well as the hours he spent practicing and playing basketball, baseball and track. (His senior year of high school, Coach finished in sixth place in the state finals for the one-hundred-yard dash.)

During the summer of 1927, before his senior year in high school, Coach and a high school teammate hitchhiked to Kansas to work in the wheat fields there. The Martinsville High School team had won the Indiana state championship that year, so the boys wore their state championship letterman jackets on the road in order to increase their chances of getting a ride.

When they reached Lawrence, the boys discovered, to their dismay, that the wheat crop was not yet ready for harvest. So, instead, they got a job pouring concrete for the University of Kansas' new football stadium, Memorial Stadium. At night, they slept on the floor of the campus gymnasium. Memorial Stadium is still in use today, and Wooden chuckles, "I think I did an excellent job."

When John graduated from high school and went off to play basketball at Purdue, he carried with him the strong work ethic he had learned from his parents. A few years ago, Curt Conrad, then ninety-two, reminisced about the season he spent as manager of the Purdue team in 1931–32: "I saw every practice Purdue had that year," he told me. "John Wooden played hard in practice and never got tired.

"Our coach, Piggy Lambert, would say, 'John, go get some rest.' John would say, 'I want to stay out here. I need the experience. I'm not tired.'"

Conrad continued, "John had a heart bigger than anyone, and he had more endurance than anyone. After every practice John would go shoot twenty-five free throws. He wouldn't leave until he'd done it." It was during that season that a sportswriter dubbed him "The Indiana Rubber Man." Dutch Fehring remembers that the nickname was given because Wooden would "drive to the hoop, score and get knocked into the seats. But he'd bounce right back up and beat everyone down the floor."

Former college coach Alex Omalev said, "When I was a kid in Detroit,

I got to see Purdue play at Michigan. John Wooden was a great player, and tough, too. Michigan had some football players on their team, and they'd knock John around. He'd bounce up and come back like a bulldog."

John Wooden was a three-time All-American at Purdue, and the Boilermakers were national champions during his sophomore and senior years. But that didn't mean he was treated like a star, nor that he sailed through college on a full scholarship. The basketball court wasn't the only place where John Wooden demonstrated his willingness to work hard. During those days, Purdue's biggest football game of the season was played at Soldier Field in Chicago, against a University of Chicago team coached by the legendary Amos Alonzo Stagg. Hundreds of Boilermaker fans traveled to Chicago by train to cheer for their team each year, and John was there, too—walking up and down the aisles, selling sandwiches and soft drinks.

He says, "One of my biggest moneymakers was something I manufactured myself. I'd go to local department stores that donated gold and black ribbons (Purdue's colors). They'd throw in a big box of safety pins, and I'd spend several hours cutting and crossing ribbons to create little lapel pennants." Coach smiles. "They cost me nothing, and I sold them for ten cents a piece. And I sold plenty."

During the basketball season, Coach also published and sold the official Purdue program. He wrote the copy, sold the ads and turned the crank on the mimeograph machine. Then he hired local high school students to sell them for a dime apiece. After the game, he and his "sales crew" split the profits. John also made money by working as a "taper" during the football season—wrapping ankles, arms and legs—and he helped to paint the football stadium, earning thirty-five cents an hour for that difficult job. Then he had to find time to study! He was up to the challenge, finishing nineteenth from the top in his class.

THE EFFORT'S THE THING

During Coach's senior year in high school, the Martinsville team lost the final game in the state play-offs by one point. Coach still remembers how disappointed he felt—but, unlike the other players, he did not cry when the final buzzer sounded. He knew that he'd worked hard and done his best, and that helped to ease the sting, even though the outcome wasn't what he had hoped for.

When he was at UCLA, Coach said, "For me it is never simply a case of win or lose, because I do not demand victory. What I demand—and that's exactly the word—is that each player expend every available ounce of energy to achieve his personal best, to attain competitive greatness as I define it." He continued, "Victory may be the by-product, but the significance of the score is secondary to the importance of finding out how good you can be. This is only possible with ceaseless, not selective, effort toward that goal."

Former Bruin Jack Arnold remembers that John Wooden expected, and got, very hard work from his teams. "Every minute was really well organized. Coach ran us to death. We'd finish a practice and then he would run us so hard we thought we would die. I would be so tired I couldn't even walk downstairs to the locker area. We won a lot of games in the second half just because we were in better shape."

Another ex-UCLA player, Pete Blackman, agreed with that assessment. Blackman told me, "At the end of practice we would run laps and then go to the free throw line. Coach would hand us a ball and if we hit the free throw we'd go downstairs to shower. If we missed it, we'd run more laps and then come back and have to hit two free throws in a row. We were getting practical application of being dog tired but ready to hit two free throws with a few seconds left against USC."

Coach Wooden says he considers hard work to be so important that he made it one of the two cornerstones of his Pyramid of Success. (The other cornerstone is enthusiasm.) He said he called it "industriousness" instead of "work" because "it involves more than merely showing up and going through the motions. Many people who tell you they worked all day weren't really working very hard at all, certainly not to the fullest extent of their abilities." He goes on to say, "You can work without being industrious, but you cannot be industrious without work."

When asked if hard work is always so important, he says, "I challenge you to show me one single solitary individual who achieved his or her success without lots of hard work. . . . Hard work is essential, and only you really know if you're giving it everything you've got. People who always try to cut corners will never come close to realizing their full potential."

He cites Grantland Rice's famous poem, "How to Be a Champion":

> You wonder how they do it,
> You look to see the knack,
> You watch the foot in action,
> Or the shoulder or the back.
> But when you spot the answer
> Where the higher glamours lurk,
> You'll find in moving higher
> Up the laurel-covered spire,
> That most of it is practice
> And the rest of it is work.

Andy Hill says that after his book with Coach was published, the two of them attended a promotional event, where they had to autograph nearly one thousand books. Hill says, "That's a big task for anyone, let alone an eighty-eight-year-old man." Hill noticed that Wooden always signed "Best Wishes, John Wooden," and said to him, "Coach, it will be a lot easier if you just sign your name."

Hill recounts that Coach "gave me that look like I was nineteen again and said, 'I thought you wanted this done right.'"

John Wooden has never been willing to cut corners to avoid hard work, which is one of the many reasons for his tremendous success. Coach would agree wholeheartedly with Dallas Cowboys Hall-of-Fame quarterback Roger Staubach, who said, "Nothing good comes, in life or athletics, unless a lot of hard work has preceded the effort. Only temporary success is achieved by taking shortcuts."

As someone once said, "The harder I work and the better I plan, the luckier I get."

Here are a few specific principles about the importance of hard work that have guided Coach Wooden during his life:

1) WORK TO DEVELOP YOUR GOD-GIVEN GIFTS

Nobody ever worked harder than me. Sure I had talent, but the key to my success, like all the great ones, is hard work.

—Joe DiMaggio

John Wooden had a succession of highly talented players at UCLA. They were already excellent basketball players when they showed up for their first practice. But Coach wasn't content to let them stay at that level. He always made them work hard to develop and improve their skills. Gail Goodrich, who went on to a long, successful professional career with the Los Angeles Lakers and Phoenix Suns, said, "John Wooden enjoyed coaching and teaching in practice more than the games. He used to say, 'Failure to prepare is preparing to fail.' Coach was so into detail on everything. Everyone we knew played our offense, but it was always a matter of execution. That's where he excelled."

Coach explains why he worked his teams so hard: "Next to condition is the knowledge of and ability to execute the fundamentals. That's the coach's job. You have to teach them the fundamentals, but there's more to it than that. They must be able to execute them properly at the right time—and quickly. Quickness is the most important asset in athletics in my opinion. If you can't do it quickly it doesn't do any good. If you can't get a shot, it doesn't do you any good to be a good shot. You have to be able to do both. The same thing is true in playing defense or rebounding or whatever it might be."

2) WORK WHEN YOU'RE SUPPOSED TO BE WORKING

Successful people have learned to make themselves do the thing that has to be done, when it has to be done, whether they like it or not.

—Aldous Huxley

Author Brian Tracy says that one of the most important habits anyone can develop is that of working all the time you are at work. He writes,

"According to Robert Half International, the average employee works only 50 percent of the time. The other 50 percent of working time is largely wasted. It is spent in idle chitchat and conversation with coworkers, late arrivals, extended coffee breaks and lunches, and early departures. It is dribbled away making private phone calls, reading the newspaper, taking care of personal business and surfing the Internet."

If that's true, and I have no reason to doubt it, just imagine how much people could accomplish if they worked all the time they were supposed to be working!

3) HARD WORK PUTS YOU IN A POSITION TO WIN

Doing the best at this moment puts you in the best place for the next moment.

—Oprah Winfrey

Coach has always believed that hard work puts a person in the position he or she needs to succeed in life. And even when his teams were winning championships year after year after year, Coach never cut back on the hard work or the preparation. He warned, "How you respond to past success can be damaging if you let it diminish your preparation for the future."

Coach wrote: "You must be conditioned for whatever you're doing if you're going to do it to the best of your ability. There are different types of conditioning for different professions. A deep-sea diver has different conditioning requirements from a salesperson. A surgeon has different physical conditioning requirements from a construction worker. A CEO has different conditioning requirements from a food server."

Coach goes on to explain that when he talks about conditioning, he means getting yourself ready physically, mentally and emotionally. "Some believed my teams were simply in better physical condition than the competition," he says. "That may have been, but they also had tremendous mental and emotional conditioning. . . . It is impossible to attain and maintain desirable physical condition without first achieving mental and moral condition."

Wooden quotes his hero, Abraham Lincoln, who said, "I shall prepare myself and my opportunity must come."

4) HARD WORK WILL CHANGE YOUR LIFE—AND YOUR WORLD

The difference between what we do and what we are capable of doing would solve most of the world's problems.

—Mohandas Gandhi

John Wooden changed the world through hard work, and by getting others to work hard as well. In 2002, when he was asked what had been most rewarding about his coaching career, he replied, "The fact that almost all of the players that I had in my twenty-eight years at UCLA graduated, got their degrees, most of them in four years. And practically all have done well in their chosen professions. I think there are over thirty attorneys. There are eight ministers. There are ten or eleven dentists, ten or eleven doctors, and lots of teachers and people who are successful in the world of business. And that makes me feel good."

Coach always demanded that his players give their best, both on and off the basketball court. He did that because he knew it would change their lives for the better.

He said there is no shame in finding out that someone is better than you at something. But, on the other hand, he wrote that "Shame is an appropriate response" when someone is better than you only because you haven't done your best to develop your innate potential; in other words, because you haven't worked hard enough to become the best you can possibly be.

Coach didn't believe in trying to get players "up" for big games. He expected them to be motivated and ready to give their very best at all times, against all opponents. He said, "There should never be a need for me to give a pep talk to instill motivation. The motivation must come from the players' belief—deeply entrenched—that ultimate success lies in giving their personal best. More than anything, I wanted players to love the process of doing that. Unlike a pep talk that might generate temporary enthusiasm, loving the process of working to be your best isn't temporary."

Coach demands maximum effort in every area of life—from himself and from others. UCLA alumnus Mitchell Gold told me about attending a John Wooden basketball camp when he was fifty-two. "We were divided into teams and instructed in fundamentals, and then we practiced and played games against other teams. During one of those games I was on defense and actively trying to guard my man. Coach Wooden was the ref at the time. He yelled at me, 'Mitch. Stop reaching. Come up. Come up!' Now, you have to understand that this was not really a significant game, and, at fifty-two years old, I didn't have much of a future as a guard no matter how well I defended the ball. But that was Coach. Always the teacher. Always the perfectionist. Forever trying to ensure that the game was played the way it was supposed to be played no matter who was on the floor."

Coach has always worked as hard as possible to be the best he can possibly be in every endeavor of life. For that reason, he is justifiably proud of the honors he earned as a college basketball coach. But he is even more proud of honors like these:

- California Father of the Year, 1964
- The Whitney Young Urban League Memorial Award for Humanitarian Service, 1973
- The Christian Church Humanitarian Award for Service to Mankind, 1973
- The Layman's Leadership Institute Velvet-Covered Brick Award for Christian Leadership, 1974
- California Grandfather of the Year, 1974
- California Sports Father of the Year, 1975
- Lexington Seminary's Humanitarian of the Year Award, 1995
- The Reagan Distinguished American Award, 1995

I could go on, but you get the picture. Coach has won dozens of similar honors, all of them testimony to the impact his hard work has had on those around him. He truly has changed the world for the better!

5) HARD WORK WILL HELP YOU FIND FULFILLMENT IN LIFE

To love what you do and feel that it matters—how could anything be more fun?

—Katharine Graham

I am quite certain that John Wooden would have been a tremendous success in any profession he chose. But I can't imagine him doing anything other than the thing he really loved—coaching basketball and shaping young lives in the process. Coach discovered, when he was still in grade school, what he really loved to do—and then he spent the rest of his life doing it.

Similarly, I believe that only when you discover something that you love to do, and then do it with all your might, will you find true success in life. Some people complain and grumble because they have to work so hard. But you know what? Those people just aren't doing what they ought to be doing. If they were, they'd know that work is one of the greatest blessings God has given us. Coach says: "Tomorrow is, in large part, determined by what you do today. So make today a masterpiece. . . . Apply yourself each day to become a little better. By applying yourself to the task of becoming a little better each and every day over a period of time, you will become a lot better. Only then will you be able to approach being the best you can be."

Chapter Eleven

❧

If You Want to Be Like Coach: Be a Leader

Great leaders are always out in front with a banner, rather than behind with a whip.

—John Wooden

DO YOU CONSIDER YOURSELF to be a leader?

Or are you one of those people who says, "I'm a great follower, but I don't want to be in charge. Some people just aren't cut out to be leaders?"

Well, either way, the truth is that there are significant areas of your life where you are called to be a leader, whether you want the job or not! Whoever you are, whatever you do, there are people who look up to you, learn from you and follow your example: children, your siblings, your neighbors or coworkers—it would probably surprise you to know how many people are "following" you in some way.

Because we all have leadership responsibilities, it's important that we all do what we can to develop and improve our leadership skills. I know of few better examples of leadership than John Wooden. And I believe that anyone who pays attention to his words and his example will become a much stronger and better leader as a result.

WHAT IS A LEADER?

What comes to mind when someone says the word "leader"? Chances are, you think of someone who is driven and demanding—especially if your idea of a leader is a sports coach—someone who is always shouting orders and pushing his followers to their limit, like an army drill instructor on an obstacle course.

John Wooden has never been like that. He never was the type to motivate his teams by berating them or instilling fear. He rarely raised his voice. He never swore. And yet he had such an impact on his players that many of them still stay in touch with him on a regular basis, thirty or forty years after putting on the UCLA uniform for the last time.

Former University of Delaware coach Irv Wisniewski, who has been running his Varsity Day Camp basketball camp for fifty-six years, tells about sitting with Coach at the Final Four in 1966. When a TV reporter asked Coach how he managed to recruit such great talent year after year, he replied, "I don't recruit. My former players do it for me." Certainly, Coach has no bigger fans and supporters than the men who played for him. After all, they're the ones who know him best and, therefore, love him most!

Sportswriter Jim O'Connell told about attending a business breakfast where Coach Wooden was the featured speaker. "I was amazed at what took place," he said. "These big, powerful corporate types didn't move as Coach spoke—and all around the room, the busboys and waiters stopped what they were doing to listen to him as well. They were all totally focused on him." Of course they were. They knew they were in the presence of greatness, even if he didn't shout and carry on like a politician running for office.

Coach describes his leadership style this way: "There are coaches out there who have won championships with a dictator approach, among them Vince Lombardi and Bobby Knight. I had a different philosophy. I didn't want to be a dictator to my players or assistant coaches or managers. For me, concern, compassion and consideration were always priorities of the highest order."

He also said, "I believe effective leaders are, first and foremost, good teachers. We are in the educational business. Whether in class or on the court, my job was the same: to effectively teach those under my supervision how they could perform to the best of their ability in ways that best served the goals of the team. I believe the same is true for productive leaders in any organization. We must get our players to believe that the best way to improve the team is to improve themselves, and, in doing so, we must not lose sight of the fact that the same principle holds true in regard to the coach."

Coach believes leaders should always strive to influence their followers in a positive way. "They must be interested in finding the best way rather than having their own way. Most important, leaders must always generate enthusiasm if they wish to bring out the best in themselves and those under their supervision."

He also says, "Regardless of whether you're leading as a teacher, coach, parent or businessperson, you must have enthusiasm. Without it, you cannot be industrious to the full level of your ability. With it, you stimulate others to higher and higher levels of achievement."

Bill Walton told me, "Coach Wooden was truly happy when others succeeded. His greatest joy in life came from seeing the accomplishment of others. His life was dedicated to making others' lives better. Coach teaches you how to feel better about yourself. He's so positive, so upbeat. There's never any negativity with Coach."

Positive enthusiasm is the first quality of an excellent leader. Here are eleven other important characteristics of a good leader from the John R. Wooden course on "Coaching for Life":

1) **The leader is a servant.** As the master of men expressed it, "And whosoever would be chief among you, let him be your servant."
2) **The leader sees** through the eyes of his or her followers.
3) **The leader says,** "Let's go!" and leads the way, rather than saying, "Get going!"
4) **The leader assumes** followers are working *with* him or her, not *for* him or her. The leader sees that they share in the rewards and glorifies the team spirit.
5) **The leader is a people builder.** The more people he or she can build, the stronger the organization will be, including himself or herself.
6) **The leader has faith in people.** The leader believes in them, trusts them and thus draws out the best in them.
7) **The leader uses the heart** as well as the head. The leader is a friend.

8) **The leader plans** and sets things in motion. The leader is a man or woman of action as well as of thought.

9) **The leader has a sense of humor.** He or she is not a stuffed shirt but has a humble spirit and can laugh at himself or herself.

10) **The leader can be led.** The leader is not interested in having his or her own way, but in finding the best way. The leader has an open mind.

11) **The leader keeps** his or her eyes on high goals. The leader strives to make the efforts of the followers contribute to the enrichment of personality, the achievement of more abundant living for all and the improvement of all.

Let's take a closer look.

1) The Leader Is a Servant.

When someone asked John Wooden to describe a good leader, he replied, "Someone who doesn't try to be a leader." He went on to explain what he meant:

> *Someone who is not lost in himself, not consumed with himself. A good leader is one who makes every effort to let those under his supervision know that they are working with him to accomplish something.*

Myron Finkbeiner is founder of the Humanitarian Hall of Fame. He said, "John Wooden has a down-home personality with no pretension at all. Anyone can approach him, and he will make you feel comfortable. Despite his success and fame, Coach doesn't intimidate people—he makes them feel special. His priority is always serving others first." Finkbeiner was coaching at Pasadena Nazarene College (now Point Loma) during Coach's early days at UCLA. "Sometimes I would get down and discouraged as a coach, so I would go down to watch a UCLA practice. It was an inspiration to watch Wooden teach and see how his players responded to him. I would go back to my team all revved up and energized to be a success."

2) THE LEADER SEES THROUGH THE EYES OF HIS FOLLOWERS.

In other words, if you want to be someone people respect and want to follow, you'd better be close enough to them to know what they're thinking. Think about how it is in politics. We want to vote for men and women who understand what we're going through—who know what it's like to pinch pennies and stretch a paycheck—who feel with us when we worry about crime in our neighborhoods or who share our concerns about the condition of the schools in our neighborhoods. Nobody votes for someone because he or she is a professional politician who's completely out of touch with the folks back home. That would be crazy!

Some coaches at John Wooden's level have very little direct interaction with their team. They communicate with assistant coaches, who in turn communicate with the players. The coach's orders trickle down from on high, like an edict from Caesar. That's not the way John Wooden did it. He made sure that he stayed in close contact with his players. Obviously, that paid off beautifully!

Longtime NBA player and coach Paul Silas told me about the time he wound up sitting next to John Wooden on an airplane flight. He said, "I was amazed that he was reading a couple of psychology books." When Silas asked about his choice of reading material, Coach replied, "All the time I was at UCLA I took psychology courses. It's the key to coaching—understanding the human mind and how players think."

"That impressed me," Silas says. "I was coaching the Clippers at the time [then one of the worst teams in the NBA], so I thought I'd better get some psychology books of my own."

3) THE LEADER SAYS "LET'S GO" AND LEADS THE WAY.

The effective leader won't ask his followers to do anything he's not willing and ready to do himself. For example, if a situation comes up that requires a lot of overtime, he or she is willing to work long hours right alongside everyone else on the team. Whether the job is a glamorous one that brings attention and glory, or a menial task that no one will notice, if he or she expects others to do it, the good leader will be willing to lead the way.

Franklin Adler was a student manager for the UCLA basketball team from 1964 to 1968. He spent his first year with the freshman team, but for the next three seasons he served as manager for the Bruins varsity and says, "I saw and worked with Coach Wooden every practice and game day during that time." He told me, "One of Coach Wooden's frequently repeated orders on road games was that we were to leave the locker room cleaner than when we first entered, as that would reflect upon our school." Adler told me that he was usually the last one out of the locker room. "I'd rush around picking up scraps of tape, orange peels, papers and other assorted trash and depositing them where they belonged."

After one game in Pullman, Washington, Adler remembers, "I was scurrying around between banks of lockers when I heard the sound of footsteps and the thud of objects landing in a receptacle. Thankful for any help, I assumed that a Washington State janitorial employee was making his rounds after the game. Imagine my surprise when I came around a corner and saw that my ally in cleaning up the room was Coach Wooden!"

Adler shakes his head in wonder at the memory. "Here was a man who had already won three national championships, a man who was already enshrined in the Hall of Fame as a player, a man who had created and was in the middle of a dynasty—bending down and picking up scraps from a locker room floor." Adler says that as he watched Coach picking up trash and straightening up, he wondered, "Did Knute Rockne, Bear Bryant, Vince Lombardi, Red Auerbach or Casey Stengel ever deign to do menial work after they became household names? Coach Wooden did—with me as the only witness."

Adler adds, "In a time and age when coaching only one team to a national championship leads to public adoration and deification, my story is a personal salute to a humble man who has managed to keep his personal values, dignity and integrity intact, even in the face of unmatched accomplishments."

4) The Leader Assumes His Followers Are Working with Him Rather Than for Him.

Coach says, "There is no area of basketball in which I am a genius. None. Tactically and strategically, I'm just average, and this is not offering false modesty." Then he goes on to say, "We won national championships while I was coaching at UCLA because I was above average in analyzing players, getting them to fill roles as part of a team, paying attention to fundamentals and details, and working with others.

"There is nothing fancy about these qualities," he continues. "They have wide application and equal effectiveness in any team endeavor anywhere. If there is any mystery as to why UCLA won ten national championships while I was the coach, that may clear it up."

Michael Marienthal was an assistant football coach at UCLA from 1946 to 1948. He also held the job of official scorer for the Bruins basketball team. When Wooden arrived in Los Angeles in the spring of 1948, he asked Marienthal to continue keeping score.

From the very beginning, Marienthal remembers, "He made me feel that I was an integral part of the basketball family." Marienthal kept score for all of the twenty-seven years Wooden was UCLA's head coach, and then he continued to serve as official scorer for another twenty-one years until 1996. During all of his years with John Wooden, Marienthal says, "I was included in the locker room before and after games. Being a good listener, I learned a great deal about being a successful and caring leader. His advice to basketball players could be applied to any business situation. In fact, I used many 'Woodenisms' in my career as a secondary school principal for more than twenty-five years—and they made my job much more successful."

Marienthal told me, "Our friendship and mutual respect continues to this day. Many times he publicly complimented me on my loyalty, demeanor and efficiency. He makes everyone feel good and always recognizes those who assist him. He is one of a kind."

Says Coach, "The most essential thing for a leader to have is the respect of those under his or her supervision. It starts with giving them respect. You must make it clear that you are working together. Those under your supervision are not working for you, but with you, and you all have a common goal." Coach adds that if you respect those under your supervision, "then they will do what you ask and more. . . . There is no clock-watching when a leader has respect."

5) The Leader Is a People Builder.

Coming out of high school in the early 1970s, six-feet, six-inch Gavin Smith seemed destined for stardom as a collegiate basketball player. By the time he was a sophomore at UCLA, during the 1974–75 season, he was the sixth man on a Bruin team that was on its way to another national championship. Yet, by Smith's admission, he was a free spirit who didn't care for all the rules Coach imposed on his players. He says, "Coach was trying to whip me into shape, to get me to be part of the team."

Then one day in practice, Smith went up and swatted away a shot by teammate Jim Spillane. To this day, Smith believes he got nothing but basketball. Coach didn't see it that way. Smith remembers, "I was pumped up and started celebrating, but Coach said, 'Gavin, you fouled Jimmy.'" When Smith got upset and started to argue, Coach said, "You also goal-tended."

Smith says, "That's when I lost it. I stormed down the court, cussing to myself. I even spit on the court." Then he turned around and saw, to his horror, that Coach had been behind him every step of the way. "He'd heard everything I said."

Coach didn't say a word. "He stared at me with those steely eyes, wiped up the spit with the sole of his shoe, and just walked away."

Smith quickly became the fourteenth man on a team with fourteen members. The rest of the season, he didn't get into a game until the outcome was no longer in doubt.

At the end of the season, with another NCAA banner in hand, John Wooden resigned. Smith played one more year at UCLA for new coach Gene Bartow, and then he transferred to the University of Hawaii. He never said another word to Coach—or anyone else—about the spitting incident, but it gnawed at him for thirty years. Then, recently, he went to Coach's condo to get a basketball signed for a charity donation.

In the course of their conversation, Smith brought up "the incident."

"Gavin," Coach said, "when that happened, I didn't know I was going to retire at the end of the season." Wooden went on to explain that he wasn't trying to destroy his young player, but rather to rein him in and help him become the player he was capable of being. "I knew that if I could get through to you, during your junior and senior years, I'd have a player of real value." Smith told me that tears rolled down his face as they talked about the incident, and he realized that Coach's only desire, all along, was that he become the man God had meant him to be.

Smith said, "What a painful lesson I had to learn. It's been part of me for my entire adult life." He went on to tell me, "Coach believes in certain things very strongly. If you didn't live up to his expectations, you wouldn't play for him. He had rules, and you must abide by them. You weren't going to curse and rant and rave and still play on his team. I've seen him stop practice if a player did something that violated his principles. He'd stop practice one hundred times if it was necessary. He just had this 'I know what's best' attitude. The next year, after he'd retired, we all looked at each other in practice one day and said, 'Oh, my. He really did know best.'"

Another former player, Kenneth Washington, says, "Coach Wooden is a great human being who utilizes his immense influence to teach others how to be successful and obtain peace of mind." He also told me, "Coach believes excellence is achievable with integrity, and he practices what he preaches. He is humble and well grounded, is passionate about what he believes, but not myopic or dogmatic in believing that he knows all he needs to know. He realizes life is a journey of continuous growth." What a wonderful description of this man who has spent his life building up those around him.

Coach has always been a constructive leader. Whereas some seem to think that you have to tear down first in order to build up later, John Wooden has never believed that. "I never wanted to teach through fear, punishment or intimidation," he says. "Pride is a better motivator than fear."

Coach says that pride is a natural outcome of respect and asks rhetorically, "Who would I prefer to work with, an individual who has great personal pride or one who is fearful of punishment? That's an easy choice for me. Fear may work in the short term to get people to do something, but over the long run I believe personal pride is a much greater motivator. It produces far better results that last for a much longer time."

He adds, "A leader must analyze carefully all of the people under his or her supervision, specifically recognizing the fact that no two people are identical. Two people may be alike in many respects," he says, "but what motivates one won't necessarily motivate another. There are no set formulas that will work with everyone. The goal is to bring out the best in each person."

If the leader is good enough, respected enough, he can even build people up just by his presence. Keith Owens, who played for UCLA from 1987 to 1991, recalls that his senior year "we had an underachieving team that did a lot of popping off and didn't show a lot of respect." Then one day, when the team gathered for practice, they were surprised to see an older gentleman sitting in the stands. John Wooden had come to watch the team practice, for the first time in over four years.

"He just sat there without saying a word," Owens told me, "but it was the best practice we had all year. Every player maxed out their effort just because of his presence, and the respect he had earned. We went on and won a few games after that, too."

Andy Hill says that Coach built people up by going out of his way to give credit and praise to players who were not starters or All-Americans. "Those players get plenty of praise," Coach said, "but the players on the bench need your encouragement."

6) The Leader Has Faith in People.

Bill Walton had an amazing collegiate career at UCLA, but that didn't mean he was the apple of his coach's eye. Walton and Wooden didn't see eye to eye on a number of things. And those disagreements often caused friction between them. Walton was an outspoken critic of the Vietnam War. Coach was a quiet conservative who wanted his players to stick to basketball, rather than making news because of political activities. Walton wanted to wear his hair long. Coach expected everyone on the team to keep their hair neatly trimmed. Walton thought he had a right to grow a beard and mustache. Coach said, "Of course you have the right. Go ahead. But we'll miss you on the team."

It's not as if they clashed all the time. Much of the "bickering" that went on between them was good-natured, and they both grew to respect each other during their four-year relationship as player and coach. But there were also some fairly stormy seas during those amazing years in the early 1970s.

Yet, looking back on those days, Walton told me, "Coach Wooden's leadership by example was so powerful. You never wanted to let him down." He added, "Coach Wooden taught us we were responsible for our lives . . . no griping or whining about things. We always had the ability to take control and not be victims."

Walton's eyes light up when he talks about his relationship with Coach since his playing days. "You just cannot say enough great things about him. I like everything about him. He's got such a marvelous sense of humor. He's so quick."

When Walton's children were growing up, he sent them to Coach's basketball camps and also took them to visit with Coach at his condo. He says he wanted his children to know Coach because "he taught us everything you need to know about the game of basketball and about life. The latter is what he really talked about. He rarely talked about basketball. Basketball was the vehicle, but it was really about life. To him, that was more important."

Walton adds, "Coach Wooden is an incredibly fiery competitor, but his goal was always about UCLA's success. It was always about the team. It was never about him."

7) The Leader Sees with the Heart as Well as the Head.

John Wooden loved his players. They may not have known it at the time because he was a tough disciplinarian and he worked them hard. But as the years have gone by, many—perhaps even most—of his former players have come to understand that Coach always saw them as much more than cogs and gears in his basketball machine. That's demonstrated by the fact that so many of them have stayed in touch with him over the years.

Longtime college basketball coach Stan Morrison told me about the closeness he has witnessed between Coach and former player Bill Walton. "I have been with Bill Walton and Coach Wooden at events and marvelled at how protective Bill is with his Coach. With over thirty surgeries on his legs, Walton is not the most physically capable of human beings. But with Coach Wooden hanging on to his arm, he is like King Kong. His affection for Coach Wooden is unabashed. Bill Walton is one of the most gracious and giving men, and I have no doubt where he learned to be that way."

"A leader who tries to lead without love will turn around one day and find there is nobody following," Coach says. "The family will have disappeared. Love is essential—for the competitive struggle itself, for the people on your team, and for the journey you and they are taking."

When Claude Terry went to Modesto, California, to serve on the staff of First Baptist Church, he discovered that another member of the staff was an avid fan of John Wooden. He called Coach, who invited the two men to drive down to Los Angeles to spend some time with him. Terry told me, "We drove down for what turned out to be a very special day. While we were there, Coach got a telephone call from one former player, and then the mail brought a recording of a song that Swen Nater had written for him. He played it for us, and we all cried. John Wooden impacted all of his former players' lives, and it was wonderful to see the way they still looked up to him, long after their playing days were over."

8) THE LEADER PLANS AND SETS THINGS IN MOTION.

Says Coach: "Leadership is about more than just forcing people to do what you say. A prison guard does that. A good leader creates belief—in the leader's philosophy, in the organization, in the mission. Creating belief is difficult to do where a vacuum of values exists, where the only thing that matters is the end result, whether it's beating the competition on the court or increasing the profit margins in the books."

Attorney Gary Stern said, "I have practiced law in Los Angeles for twenty-three years. I have the Pyramid of Success on my office wall and refer to it almost every day. It has been a real guide to me." He smiled and added, "Coach Wooden gets it. He gets what life is all about, and very few do. He has his priorities in order, and people sense that and gravitate to him. He has lived his life the right way . . . with utter class."

9) THE LEADER HAS A SENSE OF HUMOR

Another way to say this is that the good leader has the ability to look on the bright side. Business guru Peter Drucker noted, "There's an art to rallying the troops, and it begins with directing their attention to the opportunities ahead of them, not the problems around them." Drucker said, "Strong leaders don't open meetings by shouting 'Woe is us!' and then listing everything that's going wrong. They talk about what's right, then focus on shoring up weak areas."

Nothing diffuses tension like the ability to see the humor in things.

There's an old proverb that says, "Laugh and the world laughs with you, cry and you cry alone." I don't know about the "crying alone" part, but I do know that laughter is contagious—and that it's good for your body and soul. That's why the Bible says, "A cheerful heart is good medicine . . ." (Proverbs 17:22).

Numerous studies have shown that this is true. Dr. Bernie Siegel is an oncologist and the author of books like *Love, Medicine & Miracles*. He discovered that cancer patients who are able to maintain a positive, joyful view of life in spite of their disease generally live longer and respond better to treatment.

Other studies have shown that a good belly laugh is good for the heart and lungs, as beneficial as if you spent that time on a treadmill or riding an exercise bike.

Coach has always had a quick sense of humor, and at age ninety-five, he's still sharp as ever. Carroll Adams, who played for Wooden in the 1950s, told me that he saw Coach at a UCLA basketball game a couple of years ago. "I had just remarried so I said, 'Coach, I'd like you to meet my new wife.' He winked at her and said, 'Did you have your eyes examined before you got married?'"

Adams also recalled another time, over fifty years ago, when he experienced Coach's sense of humor and his fairness. Adams had broken his right hand—and he was right-handed—in a fight with an opponent. (Carroll had jumped off the bench and slugged the player because he thought the guy was trying to hurt one of his black teammates. "It was a very rough game, with the players on the other team's bench razzing our three black players the whole time," he remembers.)

Shortly after Christmas that year, the Bruins were scheduled to play in the Holiday Festival tournament at Madison Square Garden. Adams desperately wanted to make the trip and play in that prestigious venue, but Coach said no. He didn't think Adams could help the team because of his injury. Carroll was persistent, though, so Coach finally said, "I'll tell you what. If you can make forty out of fifty free throws left-handed, you can go."

Adams remembers, "At the last practice before the trip, Coach gathered the team and told me to start shooting. I think I made about forty-two out of fifty, and he said, 'Start packing. You're going to New York.'"

Kim Puckett, Coach's nephew, told me this story:

In 1999, my oldest daughter, Kelley, was a senior on the basketball team at Hart High School [in California]. For three years in a row, they had almost made it to the CIF [California Interscholastic Federation] championship. Twice they had lost in the semifinal game, and once in the quarterfinals. That year, their coach, Oliver Germond, asked if I could arrange for the team to visit Coach at his condo. Coach said he would be happy to have them come, but he felt that none of them would really know who he was. As usual, he was pretty much correct. What they knew of him came from their parents and grandparents.

On the day we got together, I introduced Coach to them, and then he said that rather than talk to them he'd be happy to answer any questions. After a moment or two, a young lady raised her hand and said, "Coach, I get real nervous before games. I was wondering if as a coach and a player you also got nervous—and if so what would you do?"

Without hesitation, and with that wonderful grin, he answered, "Oh yes. I would get nervous all the time and when that happened—why, I would just go to the bathroom." All the girls laughed, and it was obvious that this simple, honest answer had made a connection. Hands went up throughout the room, and Coach answered question after question for the next two hours. This coach who had retired twenty-four years before had just connected with a new team, with players who weren't even born when he won his last national title. And Hart went on to win the school's first CIF championship one week later.

Craig Impelman, who married Coach's granddaughter, Christy, says, "He has an incredible sense of humor, a very sharp wit. He's always reciting funny limericks."

Former UCLA standout Lucius Allen says, "John Wooden is a great speaker. He's very funny, and he generally makes fun of himself, so there's a dichotomy there. Everybody's looking at this great, great man who's telling them he's not so great." Allen also smiles as he recalls that Coach seemed more concerned about how he was doing as a human being than his performance as a basketball player. Adding that he was "pretty rebellious" during his college days, Allen says, "His focus was to make an All-American person out of me first. And if I happened to be an All-American basketball player, well, that'd be real nice, too."

How like Coach to put first things first!

10) THE LEADER CAN BE LED.

Coach says, "In my opinion, being an effective leader, one who can build a winning organization, requires being an effective listener. The most productive leaders are usually those who are consistently willing to listen and learn. Perhaps it stems from their understanding that success is more often attained by asking 'how?' than by saying 'no.'"

When he was coaching, John Wooden was always willing to listen to his assistant coaches and his players. That didn't mean he always did as they suggested. But he never had the attitude of "I don't have to listen to you. I'm the coach!"

Instead, he always strove to live up to his own advice: "Listen to those under your supervision. Really listen. Don't act as though you're listening and let it go in one ear and out the other. Faking it is worse than not doing it at all. A good motto is, 'Others, too, have brains.'"

With typical Wooden humor, he adds another important piece of information: "It's difficult to listen when you're talking." He is also quick to point out that the words "silent" and "listen" consist of the very same letters. The only difference is the way those letters are arranged.

11) THE LEADER KEEPS HIS EYES ON HIGHER GOALS.

What do you suppose Coach Wooden's top goal was each year? To win an NCAA championship?

No, you're not shooting high enough.

Coach's goal was always to help the young men on his team polish and refine their skills until they were as good as they could possibly be. And I'm not talking only about being good basketball players, but about being good people. It may sound trite. It may sound corny. But it's true. John Wooden's goal was to help the boys who came to UCLA to play for him develop into men who would experience true success in life.

Jim Steffen, who played basketball and football at UCLA from 1956 to 1958, told me, "One night, we were playing USC and it was a tough, physical game. I was sitting on the bench next to Rafer Johnson when a fight broke out, and I threw a punch at a USC player. After the game, Coach Wooden made me go to the USC dressing room to apologize. That was a hard thing for me to do." Steffen's story shows that Coach wanted his players to develop character that extended far beyond the lines of a basketball court.

Coach has always been extremely proud of UCLA graduates like Kareem Abdul-Jabbar, Bill Walton, Walt Hazzard and Gail Goodrich, who went on to outstanding careers in the NBA. But he's just as proud, perhaps even prouder in some ways, of those who never played a minute in the pros but found their niche as businessmen, lawyers, doctors, ministers, teachers and members of other professions. Some of them played only during mop-up time when they were Bruins. They didn't have the size and strength of Walton or Jabbar, or the speed or shooting eye of Hazzard, Goodrich or Sidney Wicks. But they worked hard to be as good as possible; they put their all into every minute they were on the court. And they left Westwood armed with skills that would carry them far into life.

Coach has always said that he considered his job as a coach to be "a sacred trust: helping to mold character, instill productive principles and values, and provide a positive example to those under my supervision."

He warns that we should not get distracted by matters that are beyond our control. "You can't do anything about yesterday," he says. "The door to the past has been shut and the key thrown away. You can do nothing about tomorrow. It is yet to come; however, tomorrow is, in the large part, determined by what you do today.

"So make today a masterpiece. Apply yourself, each day, to become a little better than you were yesterday. Over a period of time you will become a lot better! Only then will you be able to approach being the best you can be."

Joe Brown, the longtime general manager of the Pittsburgh Pirates and a UCLA guy, told me an amazing story. He once offered Coach Wooden the job of being manager for the Pittsburgh Pirates. Even though baseball was always Coach's favorite sport, he had no experience in professional baseball. Coach said no, but Joe kept offering him the job.

Coach said, "Joe, if I do this, we'll both be fired. These players know I have no baseball background. They're not going to respect me."

Still, Brown kept pushing. He knew a leader when he saw one and figured that Coach would be a success in any endeavor he attempted. "I did everything I could. I didn't have a doubt in the world that he was going to be successful," Brown told me.

That would have been one whale of a story if Coach had taken the job. One can only imagine how many championships the Pirates might have won with Coach at the helm!

Before we move on, take a few moments to think about these **"Nuggets of Wisdom for Leaders,"** from the mind of John Wooden:

- **Keep your emotions under control.** For every contrived peak you create, there is a subsequent valley. I do not like valleys. Self-control provides emotional stability and fewer valleys.
- **Use discipline** to help, improve, correct and prevent, not to punish, humiliate or retaliate.
- **To do better in the future**, you have to work on the "right now."
- **Dwelling in the past** prevents doing something in the present.
- **Quiet confidence** gets the best results.
- **If you lead a team** as coach, parent or businessperson, you must have enthusiasm or you cannot be industrious. With enthusiam you stimulate others to increasingly higher levels of achievement.
- **The goal** is not to satisfy everyone else's expectations, but rather to satisfy your own expectations.
- **If you're too busy** making a living, you're not going to make much of a life.
- **Everything revolves** around your faith, your family and your friends.

- **"Love" is the most important word** in the English language, followed by "balance."
- **Achieving love and balance** isn't hard if that's where you put your priorities.

"Remember, you can have respect for a person without necessarily liking that individual. Coach Amos Alonzo Stagg said, 'I *loved* all my players. I didn't necessarily like them all, but I did *love* them all.' What does that mean?

"You *love* your children, but you may not like some of the things they do."

"Profound responsibilities come with *teaching* and *coaching*. You can do so much good—or harm. It's why I believe that next to parenting, *teaching* and *coaching* are the two most important professions in the world."

"Winning a championship is what everyone is aiming for to begin with. But you don't think of it just as that. You think of it game by game. You'd like to get to that point, but if you start looking ahead too much you're not going to get there. You gotta take things day by day."

Chapter Twelve

❧

If You Want to Be Like
Coach: Practice Discipline

*John Wooden was a very difficult coach to play for in some ways.
He was very demanding and had strict principles.*

—Lynn Shackleford,
former UCLA player

JOHN GREEN WAS AN All-American at UCLA in the early 1960s, before the days of big men like Kareem Abdul-Jabbar, Bill Walton and Swen Nater. His eyes sparkle as he remembers playing for UCLA at the very beginning of the Bruins dynasty.

"Coach used the same plays year after year," Green says. "Everybody knew what we were going to do, but very few could stop us. That's because Coach had us do things over and over again until we did them right."

In other words, UCLA had practiced its plays so many times in practice that they worked to perfection in a game situation. "We knew where to go, where to be and that we'd better be there," Green says.

Green smiles, "Coach didn't let you waste your talent. He got the best out of every player. He was in the right profession."

When asked what made John Wooden such an outstanding coach, Green answers quickly: "Discipline, first of all. He was the boss. There was no messing around, no matter who you were. You did what he said. He demanded your respect, and he got it."

Along with dozens of others who played basketball at UCLA, Green remembers that Coach's practices were jam packed and on schedule from start to finish. "If there was a drill we just couldn't get right, he didn't dwell on it. We'd spend ten minutes on it and then go on to the next drill. But the following day, Coach would probably have us scheduled to work fifty minutes on that drill, until we were able to run it to perfection."

Disciplined practices were always a hallmark of John Wooden's coaching style. Ralph Bauer, who played for Wooden during Coach's first season at Westwood in 1948, says, "There were two things different about the way we played basketball. The first was that there was a tremendous amount of discipline. I don't mean discipline in the military sense, but we were very focused on what we needed to do. We were prepared, and the games were easy compared to practice."

The second? "We were unbelievably well conditioned. We were always in substantially better condition than the opposition."

Green agrees with that assessment. "He was tough. He didn't mess around in practice. He got us in shape. He once said that we might not be the best team, but we'd always be the best-conditioned team . . . and he wasn't kidding."

Coach agrees that he was a tough disciplinarian, but he always tried to make it clear that discipline is not the same as punishment. "The purpose of discipline is to help, prevent, correct and improve," he says. "Punishment, on the other hand, antagonizes."

"The more disciplined the team," he says, "the closer they will play to their potential in big games."

Former broadcaster Eddie Doucette told me, "John Wooden reeks with discipline and class. When he says something you know it's important. He had a plan for everything and the discipline to carry it out. When you talked basketball with him, it was like talking poetry with Robert Frost."

What does it mean to be disciplined?

Discipline is burning the midnight oil when you'd rather be sleeping.

Discipline is finding the strength to take one more step, and then another and another, until you reach your destination.

Discipline is being willing to go the extra mile when even one mile seems too far.

Discipline is the strength to resist temptation, in all of its various forms.

Discipline is the ability to delay gratification, or to endure momentary pain or discomfort, in order to earn greater rewards in the future.

As John Wooden proved year after year, discipline is also the soul of a basketball team. It was discipline that molded players of various temperaments, skills and backgrounds into a cohesive team. Red Auerbach, the incredibly successful coach of the Boston Celtics, described John Wooden's success this way: "A lot of coaches take great talent and screw it up. Wooden took good players and made them very good, very good ones and made them great, and great ones and made them greater. That's coaching."

Auerbach is absolutely right. And discipline was one of the important qualities John Wooden used to sharpen and improve the skills of the young men who played for him at UCLA. Coach has always understood and used these five important principles of discipline:

- **Every worthwhile achievement** comes as a result of discipline.
- **The very best way** to get what you want in life is to work for it.
- **Discipline is just as important** as talent—and perhaps even more important.
- **No one can achieve** truly great things in life without self-discipline.
- **The discipline you exercise** in the "quieter" moments of life will pay off when the game is on the line.

Let's take a closer look:

Principle Number One: Every worthwhile achievement comes as a result of discipline.

Or, as theologian and best-selling author Gordon MacDonald says, "Nothing of value is ever acquired without discipline." The UCLA Bruins didn't win all of those national championships because they were lucky. They were a disciplined, extremely well-coached team. Myron Finkbeiner recalls watching the Bruins practice during the Final Four in 1975. "It was amazing to watch them, because Coach put them through the same drills he had used on the first day of practice at the beginning of the season," he remembers. "They ran through simple little passing drills, pivoting moves, blocking-out routines. John Wooden was redoing the fundamentals all over again."

Carroll Adams agrees with Finkbeiner's assessment. "His practices were very arduous and repetitive," he said. "That's what made him so great. He just drilled you on the strict fundamentals, and when that situation came up in a ball game you handled it because it had become second nature to you."

Adams adds that Bruin players were working hard every moment of practice. "I see kids nowadays just throwing the ball up, or they're going up for layups and doing all kinds of dipsy-dos. You never missed a layup with him. If you did, you'd be running laps after practice." He believes it was the Bruins' disciplined approach to the game that "won the close games" for UCLA.

Former LSU coach Dale Brown remembers a time in the early seventies when he was standing courtside with Coach, watching UCLA practice prior to a game at Washington State. "He was talking with me in that very gentle manner when he saw Swen Nater doing some fancy dunks. Coach barked at him, 'Swen, get over here. Stop messing around or you will be on a bus back to Los Angeles—not a plane.' He never cursed or lost control, and then he continued talking with me in his soft, gentle voice."

In a 1986 interview with the *Christian Science Monitor*, Coach decried the lack of discipline in American society. "Having worked with young people all my life, I can tell you for a fact that today's kids are crying out for discipline, and most of the time they aren't getting it," he said. "Until we give them the proper standards to live by, we will continue to be a nation whose young people will be in and out of trouble."

Principle Number Two: The best way to get what you want is to work for it.

When John Wooden was a boy, there was no such thing as a credit card. It wasn't until 1950 that Diner's Club issued the first one, and that card was good only for meals at a limited number of restaurants. Eight years later, in

1958, American Express and BankAmericard (now Visa) came upon the scene. These days, most of us have wallets or purses filled with plastic.

But in 1920 Indiana, most of his neighbors had only a small amount of credit they could use at the local general store. This reflected the cyclical nature of a farmer's income. Credit was extended so families could have food and other essentials during the months of the year when they were struggling to get by. Otherwise, the closest thing to credit was layaway.

No one wants to return to the days when credit was unavailable, and I don't want to get into a discussion about the pros and cons of credit cards. But something was lost when it became too easy for people to obtain things they hadn't worked for first. We have more than our grandparents ever dreamed of having, but I don't think we appreciate it as much as our grandparents did. And, as a general rule, I don't think we have previous generations' understanding of the importance of self-discipline, self-sacrifice and hard work.

In *They Call Me Coach*, John Wooden wrote, "I tried to convince my players that they could never be truly successful or attain peace of mind unless they had the self-satisfaction of knowing they had done their best." He added that although he always wanted his players to win, "I tried to convince them they had always won when they had done their best."

When John Wooden first arrived at UCLA, he felt that he'd made a big mistake. He wanted to turn right around and run for Indiana and home.

"Immediately after accepting the position, I agreed to take a week off from Indiana State and go to Los Angeles to conduct spring basketball practice, which was then permitted. On my previous visit I had been all over the campus, visited various administrators and officials, but had not met one of the basketball players. When I went up on the floor for the first time in the spring of 1948 and put them through that first practice, I was very disappointed. I felt that my Indiana State team could have named the score against them. I was shattered. Had I known how to abort the agreement in an honorable manner, I would have done so and gone to Minnesota, or if that was impossible, stayed on at Indiana State."

The previous season's UCLA squad had finished with twelve wins and thirteen losses—and three of the starters from that team were gone. All of the experts had picked the Bruins to finish last in the Pacific Coast

Conference. Still, Coach has never believed in quitting. "I resolved to work hard, try to develop the talent on hand and recruit like mad for next year."

Coach's eyes twinkle as he remembers his disheartening first assessment of that club. "It was like starting from scratch," he laughs. From day one, he stressed fundamentals, conditioning and running plays to perfection. By the time the season started, that group of "misfits" had become a disciplined machine. The Bruins went on to win twenty-two games that year, the most ever for a UCLA basketball team. The final two games of the season were at archrival USC, and the Bruins won both of them, 51–50 and 68–65, to finish at 10–2 and capture the conference's southern division title.

Wooden still lists those two games against USC among the "most memorable" games he ever coached. He will never forget how the players on that team worked so hard to become better than anyone ever thought they'd be.

Principle Number Three: Discipline is just as important as talent— and perhaps even more important.

"One man can be a crucial ingredient on a team, but one man cannot make a team."

The above quote takes on greater significance when you discover that it comes from Kareem Abdul-Jabbar, the man who was the center of the UCLA dynasty for four years and who dominated college basketball like no other player in the sport's history. Coach has always said, "The team with the best talent usually wins," but he will also tell you that talent doesn't mean a whole lot if it's not channeled and focused. As Hall-of-Fame broadcaster Curt Gowdy told me, "UCLA won those titles with different types of teams. Some with great big men, others with smaller, faster teams."

One of Coach's many strengths was the ability to take the talent he had, fit it all together into a high-functioning unit, and make the individual parts even better.

In the world of sports, we've all seen teams with tremendous talent that didn't win because the superstars didn't play well together as a team. The 2003–2004 Lakers come to mind. It's unlikely that there has ever been an NBA team with such a strong roster—and yet, in the league's championship series, the Lakers were no match for the hustling, cohesive Detroit Pistons.

Kenny Heitz went from UCLA to Harvard Law School and then enjoyed a hugely successful career as an attorney. He played on those Bruins championship teams of the late 1960s and says that Wooden had "an exceptionally good set of values that translated to me." In what might be regarded as an understatement, Heitz says, "We had wonderful players." He smiles and adds, "But you could take players from different UCLA teams, from entirely different eras—players who have never played together before—and in fifteen minutes they'd be a functioning team." Heitz recalls that Wooden stressed stability, uniformity and unselfishness. "It was a sure way to get benched if somebody passed you the ball for a basket and you didn't acknowledge the pass."

"Coach Wooden may not be what you'd call a colorful character," Heitz says. "But he's a very solid, disciplined person."

Dave Meyers, who played on the last two Bruins national championship teams, adds, "Coach had a system, and you played within that system. He coached a lot of years. There were a lot of personalities that came through that school." He says, "It was amazing, the tremendous talent that went through there, but they had to play within the system to be successful. Coach was not into flash. He was not into the glide, the finesse. He was into hardworking cooperation from a team, so that we blended like an orchestra or a symphony."

Gary Colson is a longtime college basketball coach who had successful teams at Pepperdine, Fresno State and New Mexico. He told me that when he was at Pepperdine, he would go as often as possible to watch the Bruins practice. "Coach had the best players at UCLA, but he knew how to coach them, too," Colson said. "And that's not easy." Colson added, "John Wooden is a true gentleman, a word we've forgotten in our society—and over the years he hasn't changed a lick. All our sports legends are gone except Coach. We're looking to a ninety-five-year-old man to inspire us."

Another former college coach, Bill Berry, echoes Colson's assessment: "John Wooden had great talent at UCLA, but he knew how to put it all together, and then he coached the heck out of them. He was well organized, and his teams were well organized."

Coach himself will tell you that two of his favorite Bruin squads were the 1964 and 1975 teams. Both of those teams won NCAA championships, but neither was expected to be a national power. The 1964 group didn't have a player taller than six feet, five inches, but put opponents away with a hustling, sharp-shooting offense and a tenacious, pressing defense. The 1975 team wasn't expected to make it to the finals because the Bruins were without a dominating big man for the first time in many years. The previous season, UCLA had lost in overtime to North Carolina State in the NCAA semifinals, and this year they were playing without Bill Walton and Keith Wilkes, so expectations were not that high. Surprise! The Bruins breezed through the season and into the Final Four.

On Sunday, March 30, of that year, as Coach prepared to put his team through practice in preparation for the following night's national championship, he wrote:

> *Practice the day before the NCAA championship game vs. Kentucky and the day after a great overtime victory against Denny Crum's fine Louisville squad in a semifinal game. When you consider the play of each team, I felt this was the finest NCAA tournament game in which I've ever had a team involved.*

The Bruins went on to defeat Kentucky 92–85 in the final to give Coach his tenth and last national title.

Principle Number Four: No one can achieve truly great things in life without self-discipline.

Coach says that in order to achieve success in life, you've got to avoid becoming complacent, resist temptation and understand that past success doesn't guarantee success in the future. "It's so easy to relax, to cut corners, to let down," he told me. "You can't afford to fall into the trap of thinking you can just 'turn it on' automatically, without proper preparation. Once you reach the top, you have to keep working hard, or even harder, to stay there."

I doubt if it's ever been said better than by the late preacher Harry Emerson Fosdick: "No horse gets anywhere until he is harnessed. No steam or gas ever drives anything until it is confined. No Niagara is ever turned into light and power until it is tunneled. No life ever grows great until it is focused, dedicated, disciplined."

As a basketball coach, John Wooden always expected his players to exercise self-control, and he prided himself on his own ability to maintain his cool under pressure. He said, "I try to be very firm. You may have to raise your voice a little, but yelling is a definite weakness. It's like the use of profanity. It's a weakness if you have to swear to get your point across."

Coach may have learned much of his leadership style from something that happened when he was a small boy, living on a farm in Indiana. A neighbor was having a terrible time trying to get a couple of plow horses to cooperate. It was a hot summer's day, the horses were tired, and they didn't want to do another lick of work. The neighbor was yelling and swatting them with a whip, but they just stood there, ignoring him as he grew angrier and angrier.

John and his dad watched silently for a couple of minutes, and then Joshua Wooden said quietly, "Let's see if we can help." Together, they walked to the neighbor's field and asked if they could be of assistance.

"When they get stubborn, it's generally useless," the neighbor answered.

Coach says, "My dad then stood between the two beautiful animals, patting them on the head and talking to them in a gentle voice. They calmed down in just a few minutes. He then jumped on the plow, grabbed the reins, and off they went. My neighbor was surprised, ran to catch up, and switched positions with my dad. I'll never forget that."

In his "Essays on Repentance," Montaigne wrote, "It is a rare life that remains well ordered in private. Any man can play his part in the side show and represent a worthy man on the boards; but to be disciplined within, in his own bosom, where all is permissible, where all is concealed—that's the point."

That is the kind of man John Wooden saw modeled in the life of his father, Joshua, and it is the kind of man he himself became—a man who is disciplined and ordered within.

Coach says that self-discipline helps us achieve what he calls "balance."

Balance is important in many aspects of basketball. Besides physical, emotional and mental balance, we need squad balance,

rebounding balance, offensive balance, defensive balance, size
balance. Balance. Balance. Balance. The same thing is true in
life. We must have physical, emotional and mental balance,
balance between making a living and making a home. We must
keep things in perspective, both the good and the bad.

He adds, "Life is complicated, and it's easy to get things totally out of balance. That's when you have a problem."

Coach rarely let things get out of balance. He was always the epitome of self-control, sitting on the Bruins bench with his rolled-up program. Bob King, executive director of a basketball coaches association in Indiana, said, "John's philosophy was that if a coach can't control himself, how can he expect his players to exercise much control?"

Coach has written, "Sometimes we get so concerned with the things we don't have, the things over which we have no control, that the things over which we do have control become adversely affected."

Principle Number Five: The discipline you practice in the "quieter moments of life" will pay off when the game is on the line.

Over and over again, as I collected interviews for this book, I heard statements such as, "John Wooden's basketball practices at UCLA were amazing." I've heard them described as "precise," "fast-paced," "seamless" and dozens of similar adjectives. Matt Guokas, who was playing for the Chicago Bulls in 1970–71, told me, "UCLA came to town and practiced at DePaul after we finished. I stayed to watch, and it was an amazing sight. Coach Wooden sat in a chair at midcourt, blew his whistle and the first drill began. Ten minutes later, the whistle blew again and they moved immediately to the next drill. Coach never said a word. It was like a professor monitoring his classroom. His teams always prepared to play just the way they practiced."

Coach has often said that when game day came around, his job was pretty much over. When the ref blew his whistle to start the game, the Bruins were either prepared to play or they weren't. If they had practiced the way he expected them to, they were prepared.

Ralph Bauer, who I mentioned at the beginning of this chapter, says,

"John Wooden was a great teacher, and the key was the discipline he imparted. You saw the results of his teaching, and that encouraged you to pay even closer attention. I learned that discipline in athletics carried over to intellectual discipline in my life."

Bill Sweek, who played for UCLA in the late 1960s, told me, "John Wooden's uniqueness was his attention to detail in his teaching. We'd have entire practices that were focused on proper balance and footing, being in the right position, well-executed footwork. Coach would be the demonstrator, and it was amazing to watch." Thirty-five years later, Sweek says, "All the things he taught us made sense, and they last forever."

Sweek admits that he and his coach didn't always see eye to eye. At the Final Four in 1969, UCLA played Drake in the first game. Sweek says he wasn't playing as much as he thought he should play, so he wasn't very happy. Late in that game, which was closer than anyone expected, Coach told him to go into the contest. Sweek remembers, "I sauntered up to scorer's table in a funk, and Coach said, 'If you don't want to play, sit down!'"

Sweek stormed off the court, into the locker room and began taking a shower. UCLA beat Drake by just three points, and Sweek says, "As soon as the game was over, Coach came right in after me. He was very angry and just tore into me. But before the final game with Purdue, he forgave me and took me back on the team. That was an important moment for me. It impacted my entire life." Sweek was three for three from the field in the championship game, a twenty-point victory for the Bruins.

Lynn Shackleford says that he saw Coach's patient, disciplined approach pay off in terms of both the basketball season and a player's career. He didn't give up on players he believed in, but continued to work with them to help them improve. "He saw the long run of the season or the long run of the player's career," Shackleford said. He says that many times, the player who was "making turnovers or missing shots" in December had become a star by tournament time, because of Coach's patience and hard work with him.

This morning's mail brought a letter from Donald Johnson, a longtime college basketball coach who won All-American honors at UCLA in 1952. Johnson writes, "In my coaching career, which has now spanned some forty-seven years, I've found it difficult to keep up with all my former players, their activities, and to meet my obligations to them. When one considers the many young men who have competed for Coach Wooden, and the extraordinary demands made on his schedule, and his age, it is truly mind-boggling to understand that this man does NOT let people down."

He continues, "When I was inducted into my high school Hall of Fame, guess who was there? It was a surreal feeling sitting alongside John Wooden, both of us signing balls, programs and the like. Then again, at my surprise retirement party, guess who was present? John Wooden blended in with my former players, staff, friends and family, alongside my great junior college coach, Alex Omalev."

And then he tells of a memory that has been etched into his mind for over fifty years. One Sunday during the year he spent in the graduate program at UCLA, he became terribly ill. "I was convinced that my appendix was about to burst." His wife, Colette, knew there was only one person to call: John Wooden. Less than half an hour later, Coach was knocking on the door of their apartment, a doctor in tow. The illness turned out not to be as bad or dangerous as Johnson had feared, but as usual, Coach had been prepared to drop everything else and come to the aid of someone who needed him. "These are the kinds of things John Wooden does on a daily basis," Johnson writes.

He concludes by saying that he has been asked to introduce Coach at a number of banquets and other occasions and "I'm always flattered to do the honors, but also very frustrated—because I've never felt that I've been able to properly capture the essence of this great man. I think of John Wooden just about every day, and have for fifty-five years. It would be virtually impossible to put into words what he has meant to Colette and myself."

Chapter Thirteen

❧

If You Want to Be Like Coach: Be as Patient as Possible

Patience is a virtue in preparing for any task of significance. It takes time to create excellence. If it could be done quickly, more people would do it.

—John Wooden

JOHN WOODEN HAS ENCOUNTERED his share of boo-birds. Like any successful coach, he has been verbally assaulted from the stands. But he has almost never given into the temptation to fight back. Somehow, he has been a paragon of patience and virtue.

"I think I learned that [patience] from my mother and dad," he says. "You would find the same trait in my three brothers too. We never had much in the way of material things, but we were always happy. That's the way we were brought up."

* * *

In 1987, I was attending the Super Bowl in Los Angeles and decided to go see a UCLA home game. I bought a ticket and a program and walked over to John Wooden's section to get his autograph. That's the only time I've ever done that, and it was a

*special moment for me to see how gracious, humble and nice
Coach was to everyone.*

—Rick Bozich, columnist
Louisville Courier Journal

* * *

People who have known John Wooden since the early days of his coaching career would probably agree that he has always been a patient man, remarkably under control, even while those all around him were working themselves into a frenzy.

If he said it once, he said it a thousand times, "Be quick, but don't hurry!" In other words, move quickly, but take enough time to do things right. Don't put undue pressure on yourself. Anyone who gets in too much of a hurry is likely to really mess things up! Coach expected his players to know what they were supposed to do and where they were supposed to be at all times. He wanted them to be ready to respond to any game situation that arose, without hesitating for a moment. His teams took the time and patience to plan, think and practice over and over again, and that helped them respond quickly when the game was on the line.

Here's what the John R. Wooden Course says about *"Be quick, but don't hurry":* "This phrase applies not just to sports, but to every phase of your life. It applies to our expectations of anything we hope to accomplish and how quickly we can expect to get there. Impatience and unrealistic goals will sabotage a talented group of individuals in any workplace. Set your sights too high and expect immediate attainment of your goals, and invariably, you will never reach your destination. It is vital to focus on things that you can actually control, like your own effort, as opposed to external controls over which you have no control."

Coach admits that, as is true with most of us, age has brought a new understanding of the importance of patience:

*Youth is a time of impatience. Young people can't understand
why the problems of society can't be solved right now. They*

haven't lived long enough to fully understand human nature and the lack of patience that eventually brings an understanding of the relatively slow nature of change. On the other hand, older people often become set in their ways, fear change, and accept problems that should be addressed and resolved. The young must remember that all good and worthwhile things take time (and that is exactly as it should be). Their elders must remember that although not all change is progress, all progress is the result of change (and to resist or fear change is often to get in the way of progress).

Bill Foster was a sophomore at Mishawaka High School in the 1940s when his team went up against a South Bend Central team coached by John Wooden. "We could never beat them," Foster told me. "He sat there under perfect control while our coaches were jumping up and running around. It was amazing to see him sitting there, legs crossed, holding that rolled-up program, calmly watching his team execute what he had been teaching them all week."

Although patience may be something that comes naturally to Coach, it hasn't always been easy to hold on to it. He says he knew that his decision to retire from coaching was the right one when, after winning the national championship in 1975, an exuberant fan told him, "It was a great victory, John, after you let us down last year." (The Bruins made it to the Final Four in 1974, but lost in the semifinal game.)

In *They Call Me Coach*, Wooden says, "I had been surprised to find out that the more championships you win, the more criticism you receive, the more suspicious people are of you, the less appreciation there is of what has been accomplished, and the less personal satisfaction you have."

Coach also recalls some of the abuse his players endured, especially Kareem Abdul-Jabbar. (Jabbar was Lew Alcindor when he played for UCLA and will be forever remembered by Coach as "Lewis.") "I remember one time when he must have signed thirty or forty autographs before I came out from the dressing room," Coach wrote. "'Lewis,' I said, 'that's enough. We're keeping the rest of the team waiting.' Little kids were running after him trying to get his signature. One of the adults commented, 'Look at that big bleep, too good to sign an autograph.' They didn't know that he had already signed thirty or forty, and I had told him to board the bus.

"On another occasion, when we were walking more or less together, some lady remarked, 'Look at that big black freak.' I heard it. I was two or three feet from Lewis, and I know he heard it."

Coach empathized with his star player. He understood that any human being would have been inclined to strike back when treated that way, but Coach modeled patience and grace in the midst of any difficult situation, and his players tended to follow his example.

Kenny Booker, who played for Wooden during the 1970–71 season, told me that one night during an away game, somebody spit on him as he came out onto the court. "I was really mad," Booker recalls, "and I complained to Coach. He told me to use my anger and energy and channel it into playing basketball." That's exactly what Booker did, contributing spectacularly to yet another one-sided UCLA victory.

Booker smiles at the memory of Wooden's steadying influence on the players he coached. "Coach is a special person because of the effect he has on other people," he says. "He should've run for president. The United States would be a better place if he ran the country the way he ran the UCLA basketball team. Leadership always starts at the top, and Coach is proof of that."

Tommy Lasorda, who earned a spot in the Hall of Fame managing the Los Angeles Dodgers, says, "When God created a basketball coach to be the ideal model, he created John Wooden. He has patience, understanding and was a developer of character. He's a very proud man, but humble. He never pops off or loses his composure."

Bob Bell, who played at UCLA in the late 1960s, says he attempted to follow John Wooden's patient example when he went into coaching. "I learned from John Wooden to be more tolerant of people, to have more patience," he says.

Bell told me that when the Bruins came into the locker room at halftime of a game, Coach "would never rant and rave" no matter what the score was. "He was always pretty much even keel, saying, 'This is what has to be done if we're going to win the game.'" Bell says he's seen other coaches swear at their players, call them names and even throw soda bottles in the locker room. "John was never like that."

Billie Moore, who coached the UCLA women's team for fifteen seasons, says that Coach's patience was demonstrated in the way he treated his players. "He dealt with them as if he was dealing with his family. I never heard him swear or berate a player." She adds, "Time has not diminished the man, because he still has the same values."

Moore, who has participated in summer basketball camps with John Wooden, says, "His patience was amazing. He'd work with those eight- and nine-year-olds and never lose his patience. There would be three hundred of them, and he'd pose for a photo with every one of them." You can bet that each one of those photos is a closely guarded treasure today. She adds, "John Wooden lives up to what you've heard about him. We tend to put people like him on pedestals, and they can't live up to our expectations. John Wooden is everything you hoped he would be. He never disappoints anyone. He's always trying to help someone else."

An old Scandinavian proverb says, "A handful of patience is worth more than a bushel of brains." Smart people, those old Scandinavians.

Here are some specific ways we can all benefit from following Coach's example when it comes to demonstrating patience:

THINK BEFORE YOU ACT

It is better to sleep on things beforehand than to lie awake about them afterward.

—Baltasar Gracian

An ancient proverb says that patience in a moment of anger can prevent one hundred days of sorrow. Coach has often said, "You can't get too high or too low in the course of a contest or season. When the ref makes a bad call, you can't let it throw you off your stride." That reminds me of a letter I received from Bob Overpeck, who played basketball on the UCLA Army team during World War II. Overpeck told me about the time his son Matt attended a basketball camp run by Coach Wooden: "The first day out of the shower, Matt stepped on a broken Coke bottle and they put eight stitches in his big toe. This ended his playing, but it didn't end his camp experience. Wooden had Matt sit beside him the rest of the camp and gave him a copy of his first book. I feel Matt got more out the camp than if he had been playing." Matt went on to earn all-league, first-team honors at Santa Clara Valley High School, and he played college ball as well.

Tom Nakayama was student manager for the UCLA football team from 1957 to 1961, and then went on to serve as head of security for the basketball team from 1963 to 2001. When I asked him for his favorite memory of Coach, he told me about an incident that, to me, perfectly illustrates John Wooden's patience. Nakayama said that at one point during his freshman year in 1957, the Bruins basketball squad had an important game coming up and had closed practices to the public.

"I was guarding the door when a gentleman approached the door and asked to go in. I told him no, and he said, 'I kind of work here. The other coaches know who I am.' At that point, I gulped because I realized it was John Wooden."

Of course, Nakayama immediately stepped aside and let Coach pass through the door. "He didn't huff and puff at me," Nakayama says. "That's a classic story of the kind of man he is."

Over the years, Nakayama got to know Coach very well, and "As high as John Wooden got, he always remained humble, gracious and down-to-earth without a touch of arrogance. He never let his success interfere with his kindness toward others. After all his accomplishments, he's remained a simple, regular human being."

Here's another great story, this one from Brad Wright, who played center for UCLA from 1981 to 1985:

I never played for John Wooden, but I got to know him when he came to watch us practice. At one point I wasn't playing at all, and he asked if I was going to transfer. I said, "No, I'm here to get a UCLA education, and besides, I'm going to graduate in less than four years." Coach said to me, "Brad, if you accomplish that feat, I'll march with you at graduation." That's exactly what happened. We both had caps and gowns on and walked together. I have a photo of us, and it's one of my prized possessions.

BE PATIENT WITH YOURSELF

Have patience with all things but, chiefly, have patience with yourself. Do not lose courage in considering your own imperfections, but instantly set about remedying them. . . . Every day, begin the task anew.

—St. Francis de Sales,
bishop of Geneva

Some people are way too impatient with themselves. No matter what they do, it's not enough. They can't accomplish enough, parent well enough, play golf well enough, cook well enough or do anything else well enough to suit themselves. They think other people are better at everything. But comparing yourself to others is never a good idea, and it can be especially painful if you don't see things as they really are. We are all human beings who struggle and fail in many ways.

* * *

If you can't deal with failure, you can't coach. Because we all fail.

—Mike Krzyzewski, Duke
University basketball coach

* * *

Remember the old poster, "Be patient with me—God isn't finished with me yet." I urge you to be patient with yourself for the same reason. God isn't finished with you yet. If your life isn't going exactly the way you've planned up to this point, you've got plenty of company. Everyone knows about all the failures Abraham Lincoln went through before he finally became president. But perhaps you didn't know:

Albert Einstein dropped out of school for a brief time when he was fifteen years old because he had poor grades in history, geography and language courses.

Thomas Edison was referred to as "addlepated and retarded" by one of his elementary school teachers, who urged his father to take the boy out of school.

Winston Churchill was blamed for two key Allied failures in World War I and forced out of the admiralty. In 1916, Churchill was considered washed up. And yet, a little over two decades later, he led Britain's courageous stand against Adolf Hitler's Nazi war machine.

The list goes on and on and on: **Elvis Presley** was advised to stick to driving a truck; **Lucille Ball** was told she had no acting ability; **Ronald Reagan** was rejected for a role in a movie because he didn't look "presidential." And early in his career, **John Wooden** considered walking away from coaching after getting involved in a fist fight with one of his players (despite his abundant patience). All of the people mentioned above were patient with themselves, and all eventually met with success.

ADOPT A "WAIT AND SEE" ATTITUDE

How poor are they that have not patience. What wound did ever heal, but by degrees.

—William Shakespeare

Some things are beyond your control. You can't do anything about the weather. You can't do anything about a long line at the bank. You can't do anything about a traffic jam on the freeway. And since you can't do anything about it, why get all worked up about it? After all, the one thing you *can* control is your attitude. For all you know, the delay might be God's way of protecting you from some greater danger. I'm sure you've heard the famous story about the church that was destroyed by a gas explosion during choir practice. Many people would have been killed, except for one thing: Every member of the choir experienced unexpected delays that had caused them to be late that evening. Those troubling, stress-inducing, unfortunate events had saved their lives.

Recently, I heard an excellent sermon by David Uth, the newly called pastor of my home church, First Baptist in Orlando. Pastor Uth said that everyone on Earth is in one of three positions: 1) you've just come out of a storm; 2) you're in the middle of a storm; bestseller *The Purpose-Driven Life*, struck a similar note when I heard him speak in Orlando last November. Warren said he used to believe that life was an alternating series of peaks and valleys, of good times and bad times. "I no longer believe that's true," he said. "I've come to see that life is like a set of railroad tracks, with good times and bad times running parallel to each other." He went on to explain, "Within the last year, I've received checks totaling $30 million in royalties for my book. I have influence and affluence I never dreamed of. But at the same time, the woman I love dearly—my wife—was diagnosed with cancer." On the one hand, there is great joy. On the other, tremendous sorrow.

Charles Dickens had it right. The best of times and worst of times often go hand in hand.

No matter what is going on in your life right now, you can be sure that the Bible is right on target when it says that "in all things, God works for the good of those who love him" (Romans 8:28).

There are a couple of common misunderstandings about this promise:

- **It doesn't say that if we love God, everything that happens to us will be good.**

  It says that somehow, God will take everything that happens—bad and good—and somehow work it out for our benefit. John Wooden has a better relationship with God than just about anyone I know. And yet he has endured the bitter pain of seeing his beloved wife, Nell, suffer and die. And although it is a much less severe pain, to be sure, he has known the stinging disappointment of unexpected losses on the basketball court, including the loss to North Carolina State at the Final Four in 1974. Yes, Coach has known many beautiful and special moments in his life, but as is true for all of us, his life has been a mixture of good and bad. But through the worst days, he has kept his faith that God will use *everything* for his ultimate benefit.

• **You cannot understand this promise unless you take a long-range, eternal perspective.**

This life is not all there is. Your reward may or may not come in this life. It may come in heaven. For, as Jesus said, "Blessed are you when people insult you, persecute you and falsely say all kinds of evil things against you because of me. Rejoice and be glad, because great is your reward in heaven, for in the same way they persecuted the prophets who were before you" (Matthew 5:11–12).

If you understand these two things, it becomes much easier to have patience when things don't seem to be going your way, or moving along as quickly as you'd like. The philosopher John Locke said it like this: "If God has taken away all means of seeking remedy, there is nothing left but patience."

* * *

I tell my friends who envy my developing patience that if they truly want patience they should use circumstances to develop it and not pray for it. For tribulation is the modus operandi to increase our patience.

—Fred Smith

* * *

Former UCLA player Bill Johnson told me, "Coach always told us we expected too much too quick. Over and over he would say, 'Faith and patience—whether it's life or coaching—faith and patience.'"

Coach asks, "Why is it so hard for many to realize that winners are usually the ones who work harder, work longer and, as a result, perform better?"

Good question.

I'm sure you've heard of the household cleaner called Formula 409.

Do you know how it got its name?

Because the first 408 formulas didn't work.

READER/CUSTOMER CARE SURVEY

We care about your opinions! Please take a moment to fill out our online Reader Survey at **http://survey.hcibooks.com.**
As a **"THANK YOU"** you will receive a **VALUABLE INSTANT COUPON** towards future book purchases as well as a **SPECIAL GIFT** available only online! Or, you may mail this card back to us and we will send you a copy of our exciting catalog with your valuable coupon inside.

(PLEASE PRINT IN ALL CAPS)

First Name   MI.   Last Name

Address   City

State   Zip   Email

1. Gender
- ☐ Female
- ☐ Male

2. Age
- ☐ 8 or younger
- ☐ 9-12
- ☐ 17-20
- ☐ 31+
- ☐ 13-16
- ☐ 21-30

3. Did you receive this book as a gift?
- ☐ Yes
- ☐ No

4. Annual Household Income
- ☐ under $25,000
- ☐ $25,000 - $34,999
- ☐ $35,000 - $49,999
- ☐ $50,000 - $74,999
- ☐ over $75,000

5. What are the ages of the children living in your house?
- ☐ 0 - 14
- ☐ 15+

6. Marital Status
- ☐ Single
- ☐ Married
- ☐ Divorced
- ☐ Widowed

7. How did you find out about the book?
(please choose one)
- ☐ Recommendation
- ☐ Store Display
- ☐ Online
- ☐ Catalog/Mailing
- ☐ Interview/Review

8. Where do you usually buy books?
(please choose one)
- ☐ Bookstore
- ☐ Online
- ☐ Book Club/Mail Order
- ☐ Price Club (Sam's Club, Costco's, etc.)
- ☐ Retail Store (Target, Wal-Mart, etc.)

9. What subject do you enjoy reading about the most?
(please choose one)
- ☐ Parenting/Family
- ☐ Relationships
- ☐ Recovery/Addictions
- ☐ Health/Nutrition
- ☐ Christianity
- ☐ Spirituality/Inspiration
- ☐ Business Self-help
- ☐ Women's Issues
- ☐ Sports

10. What attracts you most to a book?
(please choose one)
- ☐ Title
- ☐ Cover Design
- ☐ Author
- ☐ Content

BUSINESS REPLY MAIL
FIRST-CLASS MAIL PERMIT NO 45 DEERFIELD BEACH, FL

POSTAGE WILL BE PAID BY ADDRESSEE

Health Communications, Inc., Sports
3201 SW 15th Street
Deerfield Beach FL 33442-9875

FOLD HERE

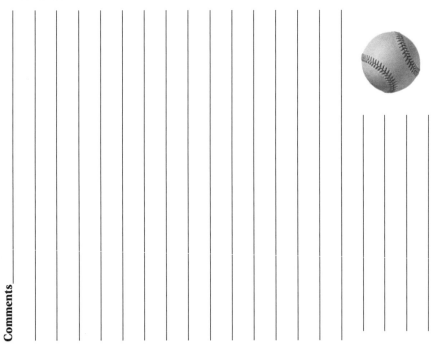

Comments

It wasn't the third time that was the charm, but rather the 409th time. What patience the researchers at the Clorox company must have had! Where I might have given up, they kept on and on and on.

That makes me think of Dick Vermeil. Now coach of the Kansas City Chiefs, Vermeil guided the St. Louis Rams to a Super Bowl victory in 2000. That was quite a turnaround from the way things started out for Vermeil in St. Louis, where he lost his first eight games as head coach.

Now, Vermeil had coached football at UCLA in the mid-seventies, and had an office two doors down from Coach. After that eighth loss in a row, the Rams' coach got a phone call from his old colleague. "He told me, 'What you did in the past worked. It'll work again. Don't worry.'" Vermeil listened, continued to work hard and, sure enough, things changed dramatically.

Coach says, "It has always been my philosophy that patience will win out. By that, I mean patience to follow our game plan."

John Wooden knows firsthand how important it is to have the patience to keep on moving ahead, no matter what. Despite some excellent seasons during his first years at Westwood, it took eleven years for the Bruins to make it into the NCAA tournament. Matt Guokas, a former NBA player and coach, asked me, "Can you imagine that happening today? Why, he'd be fired." Unfortunately, Guokas is probably right. Patience is in short supply. Yet the Bible says, "At the proper time we will reap a harvest if we do not give up" (Galatians 6:9).

Roland Underhill, who played for Coach in the late fifties, reminds me that it took sixteen years for John Wooden to bring a national championship to Los Angeles. "Coach kept at it and never stopped persevering," Underhill says. "He didn't change his style, but he kept honing his craft." All those years, Underhill says, "Coach never compromised his values."

I recently came across an article by Denny Miller, a former screen Tarzan, who played for Coach along with his brother Kent. Miller writes, "Coach, that's what his players still call him, was first of all a teacher. His most important lesson . . . that you are a winner, a success if you do your best . . . a lesson he hoped would stick with you throughout your life. Winning had nothing to do with the score of a game. It was all about how well you played and about that great feeling you got when you knew you had done the best that you could do."

He continues, "Coach was a prince in the gym. The rules of the game were just that, rules not to be broken or bent. That didn't mean he didn't want you to play hard. If you dove on the hardwood floor for the ball and came up with bloody knees, he'd be there to pat you on the back. If you punched someone in the nose, you'd be sitting next to him on the bench. Help your opponent up if he falls, don't stand over him and taunt him while he's down. Coach always kept the ship afloat—the sportsmanship."

Miller writes that he is proud to have served in the United States Army and to be a member of the Past Tarzans Association, the group of men who have played the Edgar Rice Burroughs character in the movies. "But the group of men I'm proudest to be a member of is that bunch of athletes who had the privilege of being coached by John Wooden.

"I love you, Coach!"

PART FOUR

BUILD A SHELTER FOR A RAINY DAY

꘏

Provide yourself money bags which do not grow old,
a treasure in the heavens that does not fail,
where no thief approaches nor moth destroys.

—Luke 12:33

Chapter Fourteen

❧

If You Want to Be Like Coach: Strive for Humility

When I was playing for Coach Wooden, the influence wasn't as strong as now. I learned more after leaving UCLA just by judging the events in my life and comparing them to the examples he set. He set an incredible example, and you don't really realize exactly what he was doing until quite some time later. . . . Wooden was a constant teacher and role model. I really appreciate his morality and what he was able to impart as far as how to live your life, how to enjoy success, and not let fame destroy you. I got that firsthand. Success destroys a lot of people. Fame and glory and money came with the success. It never had a chance with him. That to me says a lot.

Kareem Abdul-Jabbar

I'VE NEVER MET ANYONE who wasn't impressed by John Wooden's accomplishments.

I take that back.

I *have* met one person who remained unmoved.

He wasn't impressed by a thing—not by all the championship banners hanging from the rafters at Pauley Pavilion, not by all the prestigious trophies and medals awarded for coaching prowess, nor by the incredible winning streaks and undefeated season. The only person I have ever met who was not impressed with John Wooden was . . . you guessed it . . . John Wooden himself.

That reminds me of a story I heard from Coach's dentist, Allan Forrest. Forrest told me, "One day a patient in his late sixties, a retired police officer, saw a picture of Coach on a wall in my office. 'Oh, Coach Wooden is your patient?' he asked. 'I respect him so much. I put him right up there with the greatest.' I said, 'You mean with the great coaches like Lombardi and Rockne?'

"'No,' he answered, 'I put him right up there with the pope!' I told him that I'd pass the compliment along the next time Coach came in.

"Coach's next appointment was about a week later, and I proceeded to tell him what the other man had said about him. Coach seemed a little embarrassed and said, 'Just do me a favor. Please don't tell the pope.'"

Coach has always taken his success in stride. He's enjoyed every minute of it, but he's never let it go to his head. He has worked hard to make it all happen, but he's always reacted as if it were a gift from heaven. To those who know him best, it seems that Coach's entire life has been lived out in obedience to the Bible's command, "Humble yourself before the Lord, and he will lift you up" (James 4:10).

Longtime college basketball coach C. M. Newton laughed as he remembered an encounter with John Wooden when Newton was just starting out in his coaching career: "I had gone to Louisville to a Final Four. UCLA was in the middle of one of their winning streaks, and Coach was on the top of his game. I took my wife, Evelyn, to a luncheon for the National Association of Basketball Coaches, and afterwards we got on the hotel elevator to go up to the room. At one of the floors, Coach and Nell got on and everyone kind of parted for them. I wanted Evelyn to meet Coach Wooden so I said, 'Coach, I am C. M. Newton from Transylvania College, and I would like you to meet Evelyn, my wife.' Coach greeted her warmly, at which point Evelyn said, 'Where do you coach?' There was a gasp on the elevator, but Coach smiled and said, 'I teach basketball at the University of California at Los Angeles.'

"About twenty-five years later I introduced Coach at a dinner in Lexington, Kentucky, and told that story. He told the audience that he remembered the incident and said, 'When you are flying high, it is good to have someone to bring you down to Earth.'"

The reality is that Coach has never needed anyone to bring him down to Earth. He's always been "an ordinary guy."

That brings to mind a story I heard from Bill Bertka, longtime assistant coach for the Los Angeles Lakers. Prior to his time in the NBA, Bertka ran a college scouting service, assisted by his wife. One day, when Bertka was out, the phone rang and his wife answered. The voice on the other end asked if Bill was in. "I'm sorry, he's not here right now. Can I take a message?"

"Yes, tell him that John Wooden called. I'm the head coach at UCLA. That's spelled W-O-O-D . . ."

"Coach," she interrupted, "you don't have to spell it for me! I know who you are!"

This was during the peak of the glory days at UCLA, and yet Coach was so humble, he wouldn't take it for granted that anyone would know who he was!

When Coach was at the height of his success, someone asked his brother, Bill, if he was ever jealous of his brother.

Bill's lips twisted into a mirthful smirk at the very idea. "Heavens no!" he exclaimed.

Why not?

"When I'm around him he doesn't act as if he's successful," Bill explained. "He's just my brother. I've never seen him brag."

I recently came across a poignant recollection of John Wooden, penned by a coach named Bruce Brown. Brown writes about an occasion during the early 1970s when he heard Wooden speak at a coaching clinic in Seattle. After the speech, Brown decided he wanted to shake his hero's hand:

> *I found myself last in a long line of coaches. I waited, growing more nervous as the line shortened. When it came my turn to talk to Coach Wooden, I introduced myself as "Bruce Brown, a coach at Hyak Junior High, Bellevue, Washington." In the excitement of the moment, I do not remember much else of what I said, except something about using his Pyramid of Success for our football and basketball players. He seemed genuinely interested and sincere*

*during the short conversation. The entire interaction could not
have lasted more than two minutes, but as I drove home in my
Volkswagen bug, I was about twenty feet off the ground, just
shaking my head thinking I had really talked to John Wooden.*

Brown goes on to say:

*About two weeks later, I received a letter addressed to "Bruce
Brown, Bellevue Junior High, Bellevue, Washington," with a
UCLA return address. Inside the envelope was a copy of the*
Pyramid of Success, *signed, "Best Wishes, John Wooden."
Needless to say, I placed it in a frame and put it in a safe place."*

*As I have thought back over the years, I am amazed at the
many small, but significant lessons that were demonstrated during
that period of time. First of all, Coach Wooden had the courtesy
to stay afterward and personally greet every coach who wanted to
meet him. How different it is today when big-name coaches are
brought in and exit by a side door so that people in attendance
will not bother them. Secondly, the greatest coach of our
generation has listened to what I had to say, remembered what we
talked about, remembered my name and approximately where I
taught. Finally, he took the time to sign a copy of the* Pyramid of
Success *and mail it to me. What a great lesson in humbleness
from the greatest coach of all time. This lesson has stayed with me
through three decades of working with young people.*

I'm sure you've often heard it said that "Power corrupts, and absolute
power corrupts absolutely." So many times, we've seen just how true that is.
In a Third World country, some idealistic rebel ignites a revolution against
a cruel despot. He says he is fighting for the people because he wants freedom and justice. But when he gains control of the government, he becomes
just as ruthless, or even more ruthless, than the tyrant he displaced.

It's the same with fame. I have seen public adulation turn nice young men into arrogant, self-centered jerks almost overnight. One minute, it's "Yes, sir," and "Thank you, sir." And the next minute it's, "Anything you have to say to me, talk to my agent." It does something to you when people are constantly asking you for your autograph, telling you how much they admire you and trying to get close to you. It's got to be hard for anyone who is as famous as John Wooden to stay humble, but somehow he has managed to maintain a proper perspective.

* * *

My grandfather is an extremely humble man.
He's led by example his whole life and stayed true to his beliefs.
He's never asked anyone to do anything he wouldn't do himself.
                                                —Greg Wooden

* * *

Former UCLA player Don Saffer said, "John Wooden is a giant of a man, and yet as humble as humble can be."

When Stan Morrison was coaching at the University of Southern California in the early 1980s, he encountered Coach Wooden at the Final Four tournament. Morrison's team had made it into the NCAA tournament, but lost to Wyoming in an early round game. Coach congratulated him on his successful year, mentioned that he was especially impressed with a couple of the Trojans' young players, and then said, "Just wait until you get your own on-campus arena. Without Pauley Pavilion we would not have gotten Bill [Walton] or Lewis [Alcindor]." Morrison remembers, "It impressed me that he wasn't taking all the credit for UCLA's achievements, but recognized that playing in such a wonderful venue had contributed to their success." (Incidentally, Morrison never got his on-campus arena, which is currently under construction, nearly twenty-five years later.)

Coach's friend Carl Boldt, who played basketball at the University of San Francisco in the 1950s, says, "I have breakfast with John Wooden regularly, and he is always so kind and gracious to everyone. He is such a humble man, and being with him is like a religious experience. He's past being a great coach—he's almost saintly."

John Wooden's humility is especially amazing in light of his astounding popularity. Boldt says, "I've done a Google search from time to time to find out who are the most popular sports figures in the country. One day Tiger Woods had 4 million pops. Magic Johnson had 3 million. Coach had 14 million. He's been as high as 20 million. That's more than the pope."

As I've mentioned several times, Abraham Lincoln has always been one of John Wooden's idols. Coach laughs as he recounts a story of the time an aide came upon Mr. Lincoln in his office, shining his shoes. "Mr. President," the aide gasped, surprised that Lincoln would stoop to such menial labor, "are you shining your own shoes?" The president looked down at the boots in front of him, smiled wryly and asked, "Whose shoes would I shine?"

That's Coach. If something needed to be done, he was willing to do it. He never considered himself to be too important for the smallest, most "insignificant" tasks.

Nearly forty years ago, in January 1966, *Look* magazine ran an article by John Wooden titled, "Shooting Is the Least Important Part of Basketball." (At the time, *Look* was one of the most widely circulated magazines in the United States.) Coach wrote:

> *Psychiatrists tell us that two of the possible symptoms of insanity are delusions of grandeur and delusions of persecution. Since all coaches are subject to delusions of grandeur when their teams on occasion may accomplish what did not seem possible, and subject to delusions of persecution when every close call and every break seems to go against them, they must be philosophically inclined to accept each event with calmness and composure and continue to make decisions in the clear light of common sense.*

Anyone who wants to be like John Wooden needs to know the following:

• Coach has never expected special treatment.

- He's never thrown his weight around.
- He's never snapped at someone, "Do you know who I am?"
- He's never demanded to be picked up at the airport in a limousine.
- He's not the least bit self-important. He's the same decent, polite person in all situations.

Of course, he understands that he is a celebrity, and he hears the praise and the applause that comes his way. But he knows that, as author Robert Montgomery said, "If you achieve success, you will get applause, and if you get applause, you will hear it. My advice to you concerning applause is this: Enjoy it, but never quite believe it."

Sure, John Wooden is proud of his accomplishments. He won't try to tell you it didn't mean anything. "I don't like false modesty," he said. "I'm proud of the fact that I was fortunate to have a lot of wonderful players who brought about national championships. I'm proud of it, but I'm also realistic, and I know that without those players it wouldn't have happened."

When asked about the eighty-eight-game winning streak, Coach smiled and said, "I don't want to belittle it, but that gave me more satisfaction at the time than it does now. My greatest pleasure is seeing the players do well, and I'm not just talking about the ones who played professional basketball. We've got twenty-six ex-players practicing law in California. There are doctors, teachers, businessmen. I find myself reflecting more on how well they are doing rather than the championships."

Young Kylie Puckett, John Wooden's great-great-niece, told me that her "Uncle John" doesn't take credit for his ten national championships, but gives the glory to the players. "Some people are quick to take credit for success and brush failure off on others, but he is the exact opposite," she said. "He has a deep love for family and friends, an unparalleled passion for life and education, and continues to expand his knowledge on a daily basis by reading. He left a legacy at UCLA that coaches will continue to strive to reach and surpass."

Former UCLA assistant coach Ed Powell says, "I've been with Coach Wooden on hundreds of social occasions. He's very unpretentious. He's probably the least impressed with what he's accomplished."

* * *

One year at the coaching clinic I was standing in line with Coach to register—a process that could take as long as two hours. Joe Vancisin, who was running the organization, saw Coach and gestured for him to come around the line. He waved Joe off and said to me, "I'm no better than anyone else."

—Ollie Johnston, longtime coach,
Montclair State University

* * *

Here are four important ways you can be like Coach when it comes to humility:

1) Take your job seriously, but don't take yourself too seriously.
2) Be willing to share the credit when you succeed.
3) When people shout your praises, remember that fame is fleeting.
4) Be willing to listen to criticism.

Let's examine each of these:

1) TAKE YOUR JOB SERIOUSLY, BUT DON'T TAKE YOURSELF TOO SERIOUSLY.

Always take your job seriously . . . never yourself.
—Fox Conner, General John Pershing's chief of staff in Europe,
to a young Dwight Eisenhower

The late Cotton Fitzsimmons had a successful career as a coach in the National Basketball Association. But when he was just starting out at a tiny junior college in Missouri, John Wooden was already winning national championships at UCLA. Fitzsimmons decided he would make a trip to the Final Four and see if he could possibly get a personal audience with Coach. It didn't seem likely because the Bruins were busy trying to win a national championship. Yet, even though Coach was clearly focused on his objective, he still found time for Fitzsimmons.

"John Wooden was generous with his time," Fitzsimmons said. "I was a nobody, but to him I was a somebody. Later on, I used his philosophy more than his Xs and Os. Meeting him was a great thrill for me."

Jack Arnold, who played for Coach Wooden at UCLA in the fifties, nods in agreement when he hears this story. "John Wooden is a truly humble man, even with all the successes he's had," Arnold says. "I've never heard him boast or brag about any of his accomplishments. No coach has ever won ten NCAA titles, and none ever will. Through all of this, John Wooden has always been a gracious man, and that spirit shines through his life."

Steve Jamison, a writer who has often worked with Coach, told me about a book signing earlier this year at a Barnes & Noble in Huntington Beach, California: "People started lining up at 7 A.M. for a 2 P.M. signing," he said. "The publisher had hired a driving service to escort us that day, and after the signing we were driven to Coach's granddaughter's house for dinner. As we were getting out of the car, Coach turned to the driver, a man named Jason, and asked, 'You'll join us for dinner, won't you?' The man was startled—but wound up sitting next to Coach at the table—with a dumbfounded look on his face, as if to ask, 'Is this really happening?' This is how John Wooden thinks: Everyone should be treated properly, with respect and dignity. You don't leave a driver out in the car while everyone else is inside eating. That lesson really hit me; if the greatest coach of the twentieth century acts this way with people at all levels, I can too."

Here is just a small sampling of what people said to me about the humility of John Wooden:

Rick Adelman, coach of the Sacramento Kings: "I was coaching at Chemeketa JC in Salem, Oregon. I heard that John Wooden was coming to town, so I called to ask if he'd come to our campus and talk to my players. We had two hundred people show up and Coach spoke to them for over an hour, and then he answered questions. He was such a gentleman and treated all of us with such respect."

Richie McKay, college basketball coach: "I attended a Fellowship of Christian Athletes function with John Wooden and sat next to him at the head table. The fans mobbed him, but he treated everyone the same, whether it was a waiter or some big shot. When I think of John Wooden, I think of humility."

Writer Mike Sheridan: "I was always impressed with John Wooden's humility. He exuded a special calm, a serenity. You knew he was in charge, but he didn't have to yell and scream to prove it."

Brett Vroman, former UCLA player: "Coach Wooden was very gentle and humble, but he competed hard. I never played for anyone like him."

Broadcaster Billy Packer: "I never met anyone as humble who had that much success in any field."

Coach Dale Brown: "John Wooden goes beyond being humble when it comes to having time for everyone. I don't know how he does it."

Coach Rick Pitino: "He was extremely driven, but he always maintained a dose of dignity and humility. If you want to define a coach for all time, it's John Wooden."

Jason Arragon, John Wooden's great-great-nephew: "When I was in the third grade, I wrote a class report on Uncle John. Later, he sent a note to my family saying he was flattered I had done this. Can you imagine, a man of his greatness being flattered that a seven-year-old kid had written a paper about him?"

Curtis Tong, former coach, athletic director and Coach's longtime friend: "Coach and I first met in Cincinnati where we shared speaker roles at a coach's clinic in the late sixties. At the introductory phase of the session, Coach Wooden was introduced as basketball's 'Coaching God.' After a few more accolades and a big ovation, Coach stood at the lectern and said, 'I am not God. I'm not even close to being God. Yet, I do love God and am inspired by God's example.' I think back often to those words as a reflection of Coach's humble manner."

2) BE WILLING TO SHARE THE CREDIT WHEN YOU SUCCEED.

John Wooden is such a humble person. I think he's almost embarrassed by all the accolades. He always gives credit to everyone else.
—Larry Maxwell, referee

It is human nature to want to be noticed. If I come up with a brilliant plan, I want everyone to know it's *my* brilliant plan. If I devise the solution to a difficult problem, I want everyone to know it's my solution. But the person who is truly humble learns to fight against human nature. He or she is okay about sharing the glory. In a business situation, or a coaching situation, most good ideas are generated by the entire team. This person has the germ of an idea. That person takes the idea and builds on it. The other person refines it further.

Whose idea is it? It belongs to everyone who contributed to it.

Again, because of the selfishness of human nature, we don't always recognize the contributions that other people make. So we hear people say things like, "Hey! That guy is taking credit for my idea!"

But perhaps not. Perhaps it belongs partly to him as well. And besides, as Lao-Tzu said in 565 B.C.:

But of a good leader who talks little,
When his work is done, his aim fulfilled,
They will say, "We did this ourselves."

Sports broadcaster Jim Gray says that John Wooden "never took public credit for Kareem Abdul-Jabbar or Bill Walton's success. You never heard him say what he'd do today or how much money he'd be worth." Gray adds, "He was a humble man who showed that humility matters. There was no conceit in him."

I am reminded of something crusade director Rick Marshall told me about his longtime boss, Billy Graham. "If I were to describe Billy Graham in one word, it would be 'humility,'" he said. "I think God looked down at Billy and said, 'I can give him success, fame and prestige because I can trust him. At the end of the day, I don't want someone taking credit for accomplishments only I can do.'"

3) When Other People Shout Your Praises, Remember That "This Too Shall Pass."

All men are like grass, and their glory is like the flowers of the field; the grass withers and the flowers fall, but the word of the Lord stands forever.

—1 Peter 2:6

At the 2003 Christian Booksellers Association meeting in Orlando, I ran into my old friend Jerry Jenkins. Jenkins, as you probably know, co-authored the *Left Behind* series, which has sold over 55 million copies around the world. He has also written a variety of other bestselling books, both fiction and nonfiction.

He has come a very long way from where he was when I first met him. He was twenty-two then and writing for a little Sunday school paper in the Chicago area. And yet he's the same humble, "nice guy" now that he was back in the early 1970s. When I told him how impressed I was that wealth and fame had not changed him, Jerry told me, "I have a group of men who hold me accountable, and I told them, 'If I ever start acting like a big shot, will one of you hit me in the mouth?'"

I laughed at Jerry's rather effective way to maintain his humility. That made me think about how, in ancient Rome, whenever a general returned from a great victory on the battlefield, he was honored with a parade through the middle of the city. He rode in a chariot of gold and was heralded by trumpeters who marched in front of him. The streets were crowded with people who sang his praises.

Yet, in the midst of all the praise and adulation, there was an added touch to ensure that the conquering hero maintained a humble attitude. A servant rode beside him in the chariot, whispering into his ear, over and over again, "Remember, you are a mortal man. All glory is fleeting."

Andy Hill writes:

> *Coach did clearly understand the need to go out of his way to praise the players who did the little things that make teams win. Getting players to shoot the ball was easy; he knew that the media would invariably focus on the leading scorer or the guy who scored the winning basket, so Coach would go out of his way to single out a player who had made a key steal, grabbed a big rebound, or played strong and consistent defense. Giving credit publicly is the most visible form of positive reinforcement available to any leader; by using it strategically and judiciously, you can encourage the behavior you're trying to bring out in your whole team.*

4) Be Willing to Listen to Criticism.

No leader is exempt from criticism, and his humility will nowhere be seen more clearly than in the manner in which he accepts and reacts to it.

—Oswald Sanders, biblical scholar

Coach says, "You don't want yes-men around you. All they do is inflate your ego. Most leaders already have a pretty big ego, so having people around who inflate it more does you no good at all." He also says that an effective leader not only has to know how to receive criticism, but how to give criticism in such a way that others can receive it and benefit from it. "I have tried hard to be businesslike in delivering criticism and have avoided personal remarks that could create embarrassment or ill will," he says. "But that's not enough. I believe those under your leadership must be taught how to respond properly to your criticism. I did not assume that just because I didn't get personal, the recipient of my critical remarks took them the right way."

He added, "In providing criticism, you must not open wounds that are slow to heal. An individual subjected to personal insults, especially in front of others, can be needlessly impaired."

You may remember the excellent advice given by the *One-Minute Manager* that criticism should always be sandwiched between two compliments. Coach takes it one step further: "Criticism is most effective when made in a positive environment, when something good has occurred—a victory, a well-run play during practice. At those moments, criticism can be given and received with great effect. Likewise, praise is used to great effect when an individual, or the group, has suffered a setback, when they are in need of strong support."

Coach says he also tried his best to combine criticism with a compliment, as in, "I like your aggressiveness on defense. Can I see some of that when you drive to the basket?"

The purpose of a coach, teacher or leader is to build up those he is responsible for, and not to tear them down. Quoting again from Andy Hill:

Far too many managers, insecure in their place on the organizational ladder, only hire people they can intimidate and subjugate. They may give lip service to encouraging people to speak up, but they know that their underlings are so timid that they would never challenge their boss's authority. But a leader who is secure that he alone will ultimately decide what direction to take is never threatened when someone questions his decisions. In fact, a good leader is always open to revising the plan if someone can poke a hole in it or suggest a better alternative. If the boss's door is closed to criticism, you can be sure that criticism will turn up in whispers at the water cooler and behind closed doors. But there's a fine line that must be maintained; employees must understand that they're totally free to challenge and question any decision, but they cannot be allowed to question your authority.

Before we conclude our discussion on this subject, I want to mention that humility and low self-esteem are not the same thing. Self-deprecation is not humility. The person who goes around talking about what a miserable failure he is probably needs some therapy. The humble person is quietly confident. He or she is not loud or boastful. I suppose the best way I could say it is that the humble man or woman is genuine, and thus good to be around. He knows that sometimes, things will go wrong, and when they do, he doesn't get down on himself. He also knows that his talent, his opportunities and his successes are gifts from God—and that keeps him from getting too full of himself when things go right.

The humble person lives as the Apostle Paul urges: "I say to every one of you: Do not think of yourself more highly than you ought, but rather think of yourself with sober judgment, in accordance with the faith God has given you."

Jim Mackin told me about meeting Coach during the Final Four in San Diego in 1975, the year John Wooden retired from coaching. I want to close this chapter with Jim's story because it is such a perfect illustration of John Wooden's humility and grace:

On Sunday morning we got out of bed early (late for us East Coasters) to go to Mass at a small Catholic church up in the hills outside of San Diego. It was a real inspirational time, spent with local people on this glorious morning. After Mass, we returned to the convention hotel to attend the Fellowship of Christian Athletes breakfast. Knowing that Coach Wooden would probably be there, I had put my copy of They Call Me Coach *in my wife's purse in anticipation of getting it autographed.*

Coach Wooden was at the end of a long lobby outside the banquet room talking to one of his granddaughters. No one else was around, so my wife and I stood by waiting for him to finish his conversations. Then we went up to him and introduced ourselves and made my request for his book to be autographed. He signed, "Thanks, Mr. & Mrs. Jim Mackin, for your interest in this coach. Best Wishes. John Wooden." *We stood there with Coach Wooden for the next twenty or so minutes and never talked basketball, but instead about faith and family. I don't remember who spoke at the breakfast or what was said, but I will never forget my twenty minutes with the Coach.*

Later, as I was saving a table for my wife and friends, who were in the serving line, Coach called out to me, "Mr. Mackin." He was standing with Jack Tobin, who had been the writer for They Call Me Coach, *and he wanted Tobin to sign my book, which he did. My wife and friends were amazed that Coach Wooden would remember my name and that he was kind enough to bring Mr. Tobin over to autograph my book.*

On Monday night as the teams were in their final warm-up, I was with another friend of mine from back here in New York. "Snooky" Lee was the father of Syracuse player Jimmy Lee. Snooky had lost both of his legs during World War II. I told him about my meeting with Coach Wooden, and it was easy to say that he was a little choked up. As we continued to talk above the bands and the fans, Coach Wooden entered the arena for the final time as coach of UCLA. We could no longer hear ourselves talk because of the noise and cheering for the Coach. We couldn't talk anyway because we were both wiping away our tears.

Chapter Fifteen

꩜

If You Want to Be Like Coach: Remember That Little Things Mean a Lot

Success all begins with attention to, and perfection of, details. Details. Details. Develop a love for details. They usually accompany success.

—John Wooden

WHENEVER A JOHN WOODEN–coached basketball team got together for their first practice of the year, one of the first things he did was show them how to put on their shoes and socks. The socks had to go onto the feet just so and were then smoothed out so there were no wrinkles or snags. Wrinkles in socks may not seem that important, but Coach knew that in the course of a basketball game—with players running up and down the court as fast as they can go, and then slamming on the brakes and screeching to a stop—even the tiniest wrinkle can cause a great big blister.

That blister, in turn, could result in a player being unable to perform at a high level, and that could lead to a lost game—or even a lost season.

The same could be said for lacing up shoes. You want them to be nice and tight, but not so tight that they hurt your feet.

Dr. Jack Ramsay smiles as he remembers his days as coach of the Portland Trail Blazers: "Bill Walton always pulled his laces tighter just before practice began. He still adhered to Wooden's message: Lace 'em up tight."

Have you ever heard someone say, "Oh, I'm a big-picture person. I don't worry about the details"? I have. But you know what? If you want to be successful, you'd better pay attention to the small details. If you don't, they'll kill you! Sometimes, literally.

We've all read news reports about deadly airplane crashes that were caused by a lack of proper maintenance—by a couple of bolts that weren't tightened properly.

I wonder how many marriages have fallen apart because husbands and wives failed to do the little things, like say "I love you," or show appreciation for each other? Hundreds! Perhaps even thousands—or millions!

How many otherwise successful companies have failed because nobody was paying attention to the real day-to-day expenses of running an office? Or because someone in accounting decided it was okay to fudge on the bottom line, just a little?

Little things really do mean a lot, and one of the reasons John Wooden became a legend was that he always paid close attention to the small details. Here are just a few ways that we could all benefit from being like Coach in the seemingly small matters of life.

LITTLE THING #1: KEEP YOUR WORD

One afternoon in the early 1970s, with the Bruins well on their way to another trip to the Final Four, a television crew from NBC came to Wooden's office to tape an interview. At precisely 2:55 P.M., Coach stood up and announced that the taping was over. One of the producers protested. "We're not through yet," he said. "Practice doesn't start until 3:30."

Coach nodded. "That's right. But every day at 3:00, I go sit in the stands at Pauley and allow my players to come talk to me about anything that's on their minds."

"How many come?" the producer asked.

"That doesn't matter," Wooden replied. "The important thing is that they know I'm there, in case they want to talk with me about anything."

Coach had told his players that he would be available to them at a certain time each day, and he was determined that he would fulfill that promise. Nothing could make him change that. Not even an important interview with a major television network.

LITTLE THING #2: PRACTICE MAKES PERFECT

George Stanich recalls that at UCLA, "The practices were the most important thing. Doing the little things. When we [freshman players] came to UCLA, they figured we didn't know how to play basketball, so they would say, 'This is how we do it here.' They started out by showing us how to run, how to change your pace, to change your direction.

"Coach showed us how we could come together and be like one unit—three ballplayers up above the rim, passing the ball, sliding in between each other, having a cohesive rhythm. Practice was preparing you to be able to take all of those things and put them together in a game. It was so important and so intricate."

Former UCLA student manager George Morgan adds that John Wooden was sometimes criticized for not being a great "game coach." He wasn't quick to call a timeout and switch to a new strategy if things weren't going the way he wanted. But, Morgan says, "He didn't have to be like that because his teams were always so well prepared. His practices were down to the minute."

Every portion of practice was timed out and scheduled on a three-by-five card, and, Morgan told me, "Every drill was built on some element that would relate to the offensive/defensive situation that would happen in the game."

John Wooden believes in the Boy Scouts' motto of "Be prepared." And he knew that the very best way to be prepared for the big things in life is to take care of the little things. If you are well prepared, there is no reason to panic and change things at the first sign of trouble.

Early sixties Bruins standout Pete Blackman says of Coach, "He drove everybody, but within a conception that always had value. Make yourself as good as you can be. Always." Blackman says that Coach stressed, "Focus on yourself, your own values, doing things correctly. Develop a plan for yourself and pursue that plan." Blackman goes on to say that years after his time at UCLA, whenever he had a business presentation to make, he almost always discovered that he was the best prepared person there. Why? Because he learned from John Wooden that "time spent in preparation will pay off."

LITTLE THING #3: LEARN THE FUNDAMENTALS

One of the things that made John Wooden unique is that he never spent much time worrying about his opponents. He didn't spend hours reviewing films or devising special plans to contain the other team's star player. Instead, he concentrated on working on the basic skills his own players needed to develop in order to become as good as they could possibly be. Shooting. Running. Passing. Ball control. Rebounding. Defense. Executing plays to perfection.

"Coach Wooden told us to take care of the little things," remembers former Bruins player Randy Arrillaga. Arrillaga played for Larry Brown at UCLA, after John Wooden had retired, but Coach Brown took advantage of Wooden's wisdom by having him come in to talk to the young Bruins team on a number of occasions.

Arrillaga recalls, "Coach Wooden told us that it was always easy to work on things like shooting, but the little things—like boxing out on a rebound, using the glass when shooting from the side, concentrating on shooting free throws, being in the right offensive and defensive positions—were just as important or more important to a team's success. Many of these little things mastered in practice could make the difference in a close game or in the success of a team over the course of a season."

He adds, "I really believe the words of wisdom we heard from Coach Wooden had a lot to do with the development of our team over the 1979–80 season. It all paid off when the team really came together for a great NCAA tournament run." In the tournament that year, UCLA upset top-ranked DePaul, which featured two of the top players in the country, Mark Aguire and Terry Cummings. Then, on their way to the Final Four, Brown's team also toppled number-three-ranked Ohio State, led by Clark Kellogg. "We made it to the Final Four and beat Purdue in the first game," Arrillaga says, "but we lost in the championship to Darrell Griffith and Louisville."

John MacLeod, longtime NBA coach, calls John Wooden "a teacher of fundamentals and great execution." He told me, "We need more John Woodens, more coaches who teach the fundamentals. It frustrates players when they haven't mastered the fundamentals. When those are missing you can go to a certain level and then you are stymied. You can't go any higher or further. That's a good life lesson."

John Wooden's style matches up with that of baseball managers who win games by playing "small ball." Small ball is the opposite of trying to win games by always swinging for the fences. Those who play small ball know the importance of getting on base any way you can; they understand that a walk really is as good as a hit. Small ball consists of being willing to sacrifice yourself to move the runner over, stealing bases, and scoring one run at a time. It stresses the fundamentals—and it works!

There's a valuable lesson in this strategy. Many people dream about doing something heroic, about swishing the game-winning three-point shot at the buzzer, or smashing a home run to win the game in the bottom of the ninth. But if we pay attention to the little things, and do them well, the last-second buzzer-beater or ninth-inning home run won't be necessary! There will be no need to pull things out of the fire at the last possible moment.

LITTLE THING #4: DO WHAT NEEDS TO BE DONE!

Coach never considered himself to be too big or important to do anything that needed to be done.

Max Shapiro, who for years directed Wooden's summer camps, told me, "Coach is real big on picking up scraps of paper if he sees them on the ground. A lot of very successful CEOs in companies do the same thing and say, 'Hey, if I'm neat and I pick up things out there, everybody else is going to do it. I'm going to set the example.'"

George Stanich recalls that Wooden helped to mop the floor of the men's gymnasium before every practice. Andy Hill adds, "When UCLA played on the road, Coach insisted that we leave the locker room in perfect condition. As we were leaving, many times the janitor would tell Coach how nice the room looked. Coach would beam with pride."

And this from Gail Goodrich: "When I was at UCLA we played in

Arnold Gym on campus. At that time, scholarship players had to do 250 hours a year of work. Every day before practice we had to sweep the gymnasium floor. Every day, John Wooden was out there helping with the sweeping."

LITTLE THING #5: WALK YOUR TALK

Coach also took care of the "little things" in his daily life. On those occasions when he discovered lapses of character in his life—or thought he did—he was quick to take steps to make things right. Writer Mike Waldner remembers when Coach became angry with a reporter over a question asked during a weekly media luncheon. "He was very angry," Waldner remembers. "That night I was at a reception that also included John Wooden. He came right over to me and was very contrite that he'd lost his cool at the luncheon. He was upset with himself and quick to admit it. It was the first thing on his mind."

Bruins center Swen Nater wrote the following poem after watching Coach Wooden prove faithful in "the little things" day after day after day:

> I met a man the other day,
> Who thought he knew you well.
> "What was the greatest thing Coach gave?"
> He wanted me to tell.
> "Was it the things of which he spoke?
> I know that man can talk."
> "Not even close," was my reply.
> "He simply walked the walk."
> "What's most important," he then asked,
> "The way to pull the sock?"
> "No, not at all," I answered back,
> "He simply walked the walk."
> "I know the key. He passed it on,
> Because he was a jock."
> "You're getting closer, sir," I said,
> "He simply walked the walk."

"I have it now!" then said the man,
"He used to be a rock."
"You're almost there, but here's a clue.
He simply walked the walk."
I said, "For me he has done much.
Agreeing with his talk.
But the greatest gift he ever gave,
He simply walked the walk."

LITTLE THING #6: BE GOOD TO OTHERS

Sometimes, what might seem like a little thing to you or me is a great big thing for someone else. For instance, coach Brad Holland, who played his college basketball at UCLA, told me about a letter he received from Coach, two years after Wooden had retired. "I'll never forget it," Holland said. "My career wasn't going the way I wanted it to. I wasn't playing a lot, and when I did get into a game, I would force it a little bit. He [Coach Wooden] was on an airplane, and he took the time to write me a letter."

Coach wrote, "Brad, you're an excellent player. I think you have a chance to be an All-American. Just keep working hard and stay positive." Holland recalls, "I still have the letter, and I keep it in a very special place. It really helped me that he thought enough of me and of my situation to do that."

It didn't take Coach Wooden very long to write that letter. Five or ten minutes at most. But it was a very big deal to the young man who received it. And that makes me wonder: When was the last time I took a few minutes to write a letter of encouragement to someone? In the future, I'm going to do that type of thing a whole lot more often!

In fact, during the writing of this book on John Wooden, I've come up with a whole list of "little things" that I am determined to do with more frequency in the future:

- **Offer** an encouraging word whenever I can.
- **Extend** a helping hand when I see someone in need.
- **Let** the people I care about know that I love them.
- **Look** for opportunities to compliment people.

- **Send** e-mails and notes and make phone calls to stay in touch with old friends.
- **Really listen** to what people are saying to me.
- **Take the time** to show that relationships are more important than accomplishments and that people are more valuable than things.

You never can tell. Doing something "little" like writing a note might have a huge impact on someone's life.

Brad Holland wasn't the only person to receive encouraging notes from John Wooden. Ex-UCLA coach Steve Lavin received encouraging notes from his predecessor when he was at the helm of the Bruins basketball team. "When I was having trouble at UCLA, Coach Wooden would write me the most thoughtful letters," Lavin told me. "Sometimes he'd write me about the importance of integrity. When we lost a tough game, he wrote me about the criticism he received whenever he would lose a game."

ESPN radio announcer Bob Valvano recalls a letter his late brother Jimmy received after his 1983 North Carolina State team won the NCAA championship. "Wooden wrote, 'This was one of the two finest coaching jobs in NCAA history (Don Haskins at UTEP in 1966 was the other). Don't ever change. You're good for the game.'" Valvano had that letter framed and hung it on a wall in his office, where it remained until his premature death from cancer.

Rod Dedeaux, whose USC teams were a fixture in the College World Series, says that whenever his team won a big game, "John Wooden would send me a handwritten note of congratulations." That simple, encouraging act becomes even more amazing when you consider that UCLA and USC are bitter crosstown rivals. But despite the intense rivalry between the two schools, Coach took the time to write—not one letter—but several letters to congratulate a fellow coach on a job well done.

Jason Rabedeaux, who went on to become head basketball coach at University of Texas at El Paso, told me that he read *They Call Me Coach* for a book report when he was a seventh-grader in Wisconsin. He then wrote Wooden to tell him how much he had enjoyed the book. "About a week later I heard back from him. He sent me his *Pyramid of Success* and signed it, 'To Jason, Best wishes for continued success.' I still have it."

I'm not surprised by any of these stories. Coach does his best to return every phone call or answer every letter he ever receives. These are just two more of the "little things" Coach does that can produce huge results in the lives of those who benefit from them.

Chapter Sixteen

꩜

If You Want to Be Like Coach: Keep It Simple

Keep things as simple as you can, and you have a chance to do them better. I'd always rather do a few things well.

—John Wooden

TRICK PLAYS DON'T WIN BALL GAMES. The old razzle-dazzle may catch an opponent off guard for a moment. But in the end, it is persistence and skill that pay off—in all aspects of life.

During his coaching career, John Wooden's teams were sometimes criticized for their style of play. They were called "predictable" and "simplistic" in their approach to the game.

But if they were so predictable, why couldn't anyone beat them?

That is because they did all of the simple things so well.

Coach says, "Our UCLA teams kept it simple. Our opponents always said we were easy to scout, but difficult to play because we executed well. We weren't complicated. Now, I know some great coaches in the game who were very complicated, but we kept things simple."

Attorney Len Elmore, who enjoyed a long career in the NBA, told me, "John Wooden is the most remarkable, uncomplicated genius ever. Everything he teaches and does is so basic. It just comes down to using common sense. That phrase of his, 'Be quick, but don't hurry,' I refer to that all the time."

What does Elmore mean when he calls Wooden an "uncomplicated" genius? "His accomplishments remain uncluttered by the complexity of personality. He came from humble beginnings and still won't toot his own horn. He is a man without ego, and all that he has done in life has been done without the trappings of entertainment. His mission has always been to get the job done, not to put on a show." Elmore says he is a firm believer in the power of Coach's Pyramid of Success. "John Wooden teaches us there is no substitute for paying attention to the smallest detail. Then, when you stack one detail on top of the other, you are building a strong foundation that will allow you to get the maximum out of your abilities."

"John Wooden knows the value of simplicity." That's the opinion expressed by John Dudeck, a businessman and author who knows Coach well. "He still lives in the same two-bedroom condo with the same furniture," Dudeck explains. "He's always lived within his means. He's a simple man, and what you see with him is what you get."

To explain what he means when he says that Coach is "a simple man," Dudeck adds, "Coach has a special kind of wisdom, which comes from being a teacher, and he is someone who is always striving to improve himself." Wooden, he says, "always seems to do the right things, in the right ways, for the right people, at the right times, for the right reasons."

Coach hasn't always done the right thing in the right way in the right time, but he has come closer to that ideal than just about anyone else I've had the pleasure of knowing—and I've known some great men and women. He is one of those people who can be counted on to offer encouragement whenever it's needed—he's quick to offer a kind word, a smile, a shoulder to cry on. Diane Ridgeway Cloud remembers how devastated she was when her first husband, former UCLA player Dick Ridgeway, died at the age of thirty-nine, leaving two young boys behind. She told me, "We had a very small, private service in Claremont, California. Out of nowhere, John Wooden showed up. At one point, he took my two boys by the hand and took them on a thirty-minute walk around the cemetery. To this day I have no idea what he said to them, but I do know they have never forgotten the experience."

I had the privilege of talking to Bill Eblen, who played basketball at UCLA in the mid-fifties. Eblen went on to be a successful food distributor, and UCLA was one of his accounts. He told me, "On at least six or seven occasions, I'd be in the cafeteria and see Coach Wooden at a table with a bunch of students. They'd be talking about their lives, the courses they were taking and their future plans. Even during those years when UCLA was going undefeated and winning national championships, Coach was still taking time to chat with 'regular' students, and he was enjoying it, too."

When I asked Eblen about his own years at UCLA, he said, "John Wooden is a brilliant man, but so simple. As players, we didn't know how good we could become until we plugged into his simple system. His approach to basketball was never flashy. It was always about consistency." He went on to say that he took the principles he learned from John Wooden and applied them to his business life. "They worked there, too," he said.

* * *

In studying John Wooden, I learned the importance of sticking to the fundamentals and keeping it simple every day in your teaching and instruction.
                                        —Clem Haskins, former college coach

* * *

In 1962, two years before the UCLA Bruins won their first national title, they fell just short, losing by two points to Cincinnati in the first round of the Final Four. In the aftermath of that loss, Coach felt that he had done some things wrong.

"I added new plays and piled on more information. Instead of staying with what had worked during the regular season—a clear and uncomplicated strategy—I unintentionally made things complicated. I resolved that in the future I would keep it simple going into postseason play."

"Simple" is a word that many apply to John Wooden's philosophy about basketball . . . and life. College coaching great Abe Lemmons once said, "I think people try to read something complicated into John Wooden's life, but I think it's so simple that people can't believe it. He has a personal character like so many other great men in history. I think he would have been a success in anything, a general in the army or the head of a great business empire. We're lucky he chose the coaching profession."

Lemmons said that he had seen Coach "get emotional, tough and demanding with his team. I have seen him fight for his club when he thinks an injustice has been done. But this is not a fault. He is a rare man." Coach's willingness to fight for what he thinks is right is also attested to by Bill Bennett, UCLA's sports information director. Bennett says, "Today, Coach is correctly viewed as a sweet, gentle grandfather figure. Don't be fooled, however. He didn't get to where he is in life without being a fiercely competitive man who has an intense desire to win."

Pete Blackman, who played for UCLA from 1958 to 1962, says, "Don't be fooled into thinking Coach was this soft, cupcake kind of man. He always demanded absolute excellence from all of us, and he was a tough cookie. He was a take-no-prisoners guy, but his life values system was always in place. All great coaches have that quality."

Kenneth Washington, another former UCLA basketball star, calls Coach "a warrior who teaches that one should respect everyone and fear no one."

* * *

A thorough proficiency in the fundamentals enables each player to adjust quickly and counteract whatever the opposing player might throw at him. That way, we can execute something without thinking too long about how we're going to do it.

—John Wooden

* * *

When I asked former Bruins standout Ralph Drollinger for some thoughts on his experience as a UCLA player, he sent me this wonderful story concerning Coach's attention to the fundamentals of the game:

In my first year at UCLA in 1972, freshmen were deemed eligible to play on the varsity team. I therefore found myself practicing with the Walton gang; and for reasons more to do with timing than ability, I would become the first player to go to the NCAA Final Four tournament four years in a row. It was during one of those first practices that I learned a huge lesson I will never forget—a lesson that would shape my life for years to come.

After grabbing a defensive rebound, I turned to make my outlet pass to the awaiting guard near the sideline, just this side of the half court. In an irresponsible fashion, I threw away the outlet pass (it was intercepted). Coach Wooden blew his whistle, stopped practice and kindly instructed me in front of my championship-winning teammates, "Ralph, you are not to throw away the outlet pass."

"Yes sir!" I replied, standing somewhat at attention, with my tennis shoes properly laced and my jersey neatly tucked into my seemingly tailored all-white, all-cotton practice gear.

About a half hour later, I threw away another outlet pass. This time, in stopping the practice, Coach questioned me in a now more distinguishable tone of admonition. "Ralph, do you know why you are not to throw away the outlet pass?" In brevity of words, I knew enough to know this was my clue to recite the philosophy of a fast-break offense and the numerical advantage that is either gained or lost depending upon the successful completion of the outlet pass. Coach seemed to buy my respect-laden response, and the ballet-like practice continued under the careful, scrutinizing eye of the master choreographer.

Near the end of practice, guess what happened? I threw away another outlet pass. With an unmistakable sense of sternness, the coach thrice blasted his whistle in halt, much like the final, powerful notes of a grand symphony. Coach sat me down on the half-court paint and, with teammates overshadowing the impromptu meeting, he exhorted me with furled brow and pointed finger, "Ralph, if you ever throw away one more outlet pass, you will be denied the privilege of practice with your teammates." I was beginning to get the message.

He went on:

Every profession has its inviolate fundamentals that need to be rigorously adhered to. The success of Coach Wooden's career serves to vividly illuminate this important truth. As a matter of fact, ten national championships in twelve years should act as underscores and exclamation marks to this insight! Those Pauley Pavilion banners lend indisputable testimony to this truth and serve to indelibly etch the incredibly important need for one to master the fundamentals throughout his life and career.

Drollinger writes that it was during his years at UCLA that he became a Christian and first felt God calling him into full-time ministry. Today, as a Bible-believing minister, he says he is sometimes referred to as "a fundamentalist." Then he adds:

I attribute Coach Wooden's tutoring of me via basketball to having made me into a fundamentalist. And I am proud of that title, because it is only in properly conveying the fundamental nature of the Scripture I teach that will ultimately lead to the best outcome in the heart of a listener.

As I look back over the lives of those whom I have had the blessed opportunity to lead to a saving faith in Christ or disciple in the truths of Scripture, I am thankful that Coach Wooden modeled and kindled such an emphasis on fundamentals in my heart. Even though Coach might not have bought it back then . . . God had a reason for me throwing away those outlet passes! (Mind you, Bill Walton often made up excuses that were much, much more outrageous than that!)

But even more importantly, it is on that basis of one's

faithfulness to the text of Scripture that will determine if or not the Master in Heaven will one day state of his follower in the day of judgment, "Well done, good and faithful servant" (Matthew 25:23). Thank you for instilling in me a passion for the fundamentals, Coach; it is one that promises both present and eternal benefits.

Former Bruins standout Lynn Shackleford says, "I get questioned about Coach Wooden every day. People ask what made him special. My unusual answer is because he kept things simple. He didn't overcomplicate it. Basketball is a simple game. It's not meant to be complicated. It's a game of reaction. By the time you think, the guy has gone by you."

Shackleford says, "We never put plays on chalkboards. You have these NBA teams who use chalk every day. Keith Erickson and I used to laugh because we've got guys on our teams who don't even know our plays." He adds that one of the things that made Coach so good as a coach was that "he had a master's degree in English, and he could say in one or two sentences what it takes most coaches five minutes to say."

Asked to give an example of Coach's "simple" style of basketball, Shackleford says, "A great example of simplicity to me is when I was a 75 percent free-throw shooter in high school, and my talent was shooting. One day after my freshman year, Coach comes up to me and says that I should be a much better free-throw shooter because I could make every jump shot from the same spot. He told me not to take too much time bouncing and dribbling and all that, but just do it. If I did, I would probably make every one. I was over 80 percent for most of the next year and finished up making 83 percent of my free throws."

THE GREAT TRUTHS ARE THE SIMPLE ONES

Big things are accomplished only through the perfection of minor details.

—John Wooden

According to Dr. Steve Franklin, a college professor at Emory University, "The great truths in life are the simple ones." He explains, "You don't need three moving parts or four syllables for something to be significant. There are only three pure colors, but look at what Michelangelo did with those three colors! There are only seven notes, but look what Chopin, Beethoven and Vivaldi did with those seven notes! Lincoln's Gettysburg Address contained only 272 words, and 202 of them were one syllable. Think of the impact those simple, direct words have had on our society!"

Gail Goodrich went from UCLA to the Los Angeles Lakers and an outstanding NBA career lasting fourteen years. Goodrich admits that when he was in college, Coach Wooden's Pyramid of Success didn't mean that much to him. "It was introduced, but the impression wasn't there." But as the years went by, and Goodrich played for a number of different coaches, he says he came to appreciate the Pyramid more and more. "When you teach—and that's what John Wooden is, a teacher—you break the fundamentals down. I was able to shoot the basketball, but I could never figure out why I was a good shooter. Then, when I was teaching youngsters myself, I'd break it down and understand the fundamentals. That's the Pyramid—understanding the fundamentals."

If you understand all the simple things, and do them well, you're going to come out on top.

Coach is not a "simple" man—far from it. But he has lived by a simple and straightforward philosophy. As former referee Jim Tunney told me, "You can summarize his life in just one statement: 'Just be good, to yourself and others.'"

Dick Glucksman, who played for the UCLA freshman team in 1966–67, told me, "John Wooden's success is miraculous—seven in a row, nine out of ten and ten out of twelve. But he's remained an excellent person through all of it and is not a fallen hero like so many. Anyone can get in touch with him, and he shares with everybody. Basically, he's an ordinary guy and has remained a warm, wonderful human being who lives his principles."

Another former UCLA player, Henry Bibby—who went on to become head coach at USC—said, "Coach never changed his beliefs for his players, the media or anyone else. He's a man who didn't change with the times—and that is a great compliment."

Jim Nielsen, who played for the Bruins in the late sixties, agrees. "We're all looking for role models, and we'll never find a better one than John Wooden. I wish there were more like him."

Sometimes, following seemingly "ordinary" rules can lead to extraordinary success. Swen Nater, who was never a starter at UCLA but was a good enough player to have a successful professional career, told John Akers of *The Basketball Times*, "He [Coach] was a very simple person. He didn't overbook any schedule. He didn't go to speak everywhere. He wasn't on the road all the time. He was at home at five o'clock or after practice because he enjoyed being home more than anything else. He was married for umpteen years. His priorities were right. He kept getting smarter and smarter and smarter. I think everyone wants to be like that."

Akers gives his own list of some of the seemingly "simple" things John Wooden lived by that helped to make him such a great coach and human being:

Explanation. Demonstration. Correction. Repetition. Failure to prepare is preparing to fail. Two-hour practice limits. The journey is better than the end. Save running for drills, not laps or wind sprints. Be quick, but don't hurry. Three-by-five note cards. Things turn out the best for those who make the best of the way things turn out. Scouting by composite reports from other coaches. Build a shelter for a rainy day. Use a seven-man rotation, yet involve the bench. Don't mistake activity for achievement. Expect your players to test you and don't back down when they do. Make each day your masterpiece. Spend nights at home with Nellie and your two kids. Explanation. Demonstration. Correction. Repetition.

How I wish everyone could experience the inner peace and contentment that comes from paying attention to the simple matters of life—it's about finding joy in daily experience instead of always looking for something bigger and better.

Despite his fame and success in the game he loved, John Wooden's true happiness came from spending time with his wife and children, from hours spent reading poetry, from his active involvement in his church, and from his dogged adherence to positive moral values.

A man named Will Mosselle told me that when he was seven years old—in 1977—he attended John Wooden's summer basketball camp at Pepperdine University in Malibu. Early one morning, before the camp opened, young Mosselle was practicing his shot on one of the basketball courts on campus, "even though I could barely get the ball to the hoop." As he was out there on the court, Coach Wooden happened to pass by on his early morning walk. "He came over and spent several minutes with me, working on my shooting form." Mosselle shakes his head, "It was amazing. The greatest coach ever taking that time to help a little kid."

Moselle went on to serve as student manager for the UCLA basketball team under Jim Harrick, where he discovered that Coach's simple, unassuming friendly attitude had not changed.

"I was standing in the office when Coach popped in. He engaged me in conversation about school, sports, etc., for about ten minutes. At that point, Coach Harrick came out of his office and said, 'Coach Wooden, come on in!'

"Coach smiled and said, 'Just a minute. Let me finish my conversation with Will.' By doing that, he put me on a par with the UCLA basketball coach. Talking with me was just as valuable to Coach Wooden."

Another story, this one from Coach's nephew Kim Puckett, made me chuckle as it reminded me of John Wooden's appreciation of the simpler things in life. Puckett told me that once, when he was visiting his uncle in Encino, Coach had a meeting with some officials from a basketball tournament on the East Coast. "They made it clear that, once the meeting was done, they wanted to take Coach out to a nice, expensive restaurant," Puckett says. "And, just because I was there, they included me in their invitation."

Coach politely declined, and Puckett tried not to let his disappointment show. He could almost taste that juicy steak—and now he wasn't going to get it! But after the men had left, Puckett says, "As excited as I have ever seen him, Coach told me he had two free passes to Sizzler and wondered if

I would like to go." Puckett says he and his uncle had a wonderful time at Sizzler. In fact, "Of all the times I have had with Coach, that was my favorite. It reminded me of my home and family in Indiana, of the simple pleasures that were part of the framework of a Hoosier. Here was this man who had met presidents and movie stars—and the greatest of basketball players ever to step on a court—as excited as he could be about a couple of free passes to Sizzler. In that one moment, he reminded me that no matter how long I live in Los Angeles, I will first and foremost always be a Hoosier—and very proud of it."

Brad Holland, former head coach at the University of San Diego, told me about the time his school decided to invite John Wooden to be the featured speaker at a fundraising dinner. "Our athletic director set aside fifteen thousand dollars to pay Coach for speaking at our event. I called and made the offer. Coach replied, 'I will come on one condition. You take that fifteen thousand dollars and tell them to put it back into your program.' That's Coach—always giving back."

Holland pauses for a moment, reflecting on that experience. Then he says quietly, "John Wooden is such a giver with a servant's heart. He is the most successful coach ever, and yet it is never about him. It is always, 'What can I give back? How can I be of service to you?' In a world full of takers, Coach proves that nice guys can finish first."

Before we move on, here's a look at some of the simple truths around which John Wooden has built his life. Simple words of wisdom for those who desire to be like Coach.

- **I will get ready,** and then, perhaps my chance will come.
- **If I am through** learning, I am through.
- **Goals achieved** with little effort are seldom worthwhile or lasting.
- **Tell the truth.** That way you don't have to remember a story.
- **Never make excuses.** Your friends don't need them, and your foes won't believe them.
- **Be more concerned** with what you can do for others than what others can do for you. You'll be surprised at the results.
- **The time to make friends** is before you need them.
- **Don't permit** fear of failure to prevent effort. We are all imperfect and will fail on occasion, but fear of failure is the greatest failure of all.

- **You cannot live** a perfect day without doing something for another without thought of something in return.
- **Treat all people** with dignity and respect.
- **Acquire peace of mind** by making the effort to become the best of which you are capable.

Chapter Seventeen

❦

If You Want to Be Like Coach: Be Yourself

What I am is God's gift to me. What I do with it is my gift to him.

—Pastor/author Warren Wiersbe

In 1974, the UCLA Bruins were stunned by the North Carolina State Wolfpack in the opening round of the Final Four. It was a shocking loss because, by that time, everyone had come to expect that UCLA would win. As Oklahoma City coach Abe Lemmons put it, "We had all come to look at the NCAA tournament as the UCLA Invitational." But 1974 was State's year.

Early the following summer, Wooden was summoned to the office of UCLA athletic director J.D. Morgan. His assistant coaches, Gary Cunningham and Frank Arnold, were also there. Arnold remembers, "J.D. explained that he had just received a telephone call from one of the television networks. They had offered UCLA a 'whole lot of money' to play a rematch against North Carolina State as the first game of the 1974–75 season on national television."

But there was a catch. The game was to be played on a Sunday afternoon. Arnold says, "To the best of our group's recollection, no college basketball game had ever been televised nationally on a Sunday to that date.

J.D. first asked me what I thought, and I said something to the effect that I would prefer not to, but if we had to, we had to.

"Then he asked Gary about his feelings, and Gary gave a similar response. But frankly, I got the feeling that Morgan didn't really care what either one of us thought about the situation. Then he turned to Coach, and asked, 'John, what do you think?'

"Coach said, 'J.D., if you want to schedule that game on Sunday afternoon, you go right ahead—but I will not be there.'"

That was the end of the discussion. The game was never scheduled.

Looking back on that moment, Arnold says, "John Wooden is a man of great moral values. One of the values very high on his list was his love for and loyalty to UCLA and its basketball program. But another value, much higher on his list, was his love for and loyalty to God, his church and his family.

"Every Sunday morning for years, he and Nell would attend their church in Santa Monica. Then, that afternoon, their children and grandchildren would meet with them for dinner in their home."

Coach wasn't about to set that aside for anything, even for a high-paid appearance on national television. He was a family man at heart, and he wouldn't even pretend to be anything else. He has always been true to his core values, and that's one reason he is so esteemed and loved.

Coach's longtime friend Jim Collins put it like this:

"Coach has lived a consistent life. He doesn't change. You can bet on him. His words of wisdom have permeated our society. Coach is a great guy. He never disappoints." Collins also told me, "Coach's basic philosophy teaches us that how you conduct yourself is the key to being a successful human being."

When you are content to be simply yourself and don't compare or compete, everybody will respect you.

—Lao-Tzu

William Shakespeare gave some excellent and timeless advice, when he penned these lines from *Hamlet*:

This above all: to thine own self be true,
And it must follow, as night the day,
Thou canst not then be false to any man.

In his book *Wooden on Leadership*, Coach says, "I cannot improve on Shakespeare, but I will expand just slightly. First, do not betray yourself. Second, do not betray those you lead. This is loyalty."

The building block titled "loyalty" makes up the center of Coach's Pyramid of Success, and Wooden says he placed it in that central space for an important reason. First of all, because it is important to be loyal to yourself and to the values and standards you truly believe in. And because "It is impossible to be a good leader without loyalty to your organization—your team—just as it is impossible to be a good citizen without loyalty to your country. You must, of course, have the courage to be loyal to those you lead. Doing so is not always easy."

John Wooden never patterned his style after any other basketball coach. He was always his own man. "Whatever coaching and leadership skills I possess were learned through listening, observation, study, and then trial and error along the way," he says.

Among the important coaching skills he learned during his career:

"Positive acknowledgments have impact only when offered by someone who is held in esteem. Even then, however, positive words become meaningless when offered habitually and excessively.

"Frequent and gratuitous praise removes the great value of a sincere compliment. Leaders who dole it out with little thought sacrifice a most powerful motivational ally—the pat on the back. . . . For example, I avoided the phrase, 'That's great!' Instead, I would say, 'Good, very good. That's getting better.' Or, 'That's the idea. Now you're getting it. Good.' I kept in mind that how I conveyed information was often as important as the information itself. My tone was measured and my demeanor controlled. And I was honest." He was also unmistakably himself in every situation.

And that's the best thing anyone can be.

If you want to be like Coach, you must never forget that you are completely unique. No one else has ever had your fingerprints, and no one else ever will. No one has looked out at the world through your eyes. No one has had your voice, your smile, your blend of talents and experiences or touched the world in the same way you've touched it. God doesn't want you to wish you were somebody else, or to try to be like somebody else. He wants you to be completely you, fulfilling the role that was designed for you from the very beginning of time.

Jack Arnold, who went into the ministry after playing basketball for UCLA in the mid-fifties, told me, "Coach Wooden is a faithful and steady Christian who walks the walk for Christ without the trappings of professional religion. . . . Coach's life of faith has been an example for me and has challenged me to live the same way."

Arnold wrote, "I can count on one hand the people who have influenced my life in a big way, and John Wooden is one of them. The other four are ordained ministers."

Arnold quit the basketball team during his senior year at UCLA. He had become a Christian and said later that, "Everything in life paled into insignificance compared to the new life I found in Christ." Recalling the day he went to Coach's office to announce that he was quitting the team, Arnold said, "He listened patiently, was very gracious and encouraged me to do whatever God had put on my heart to do. He sensed that whatever decision I made, even if it resulted in failure, would somehow work out for me." Arnold said that during his years in ministry, he often modeled the boldness and strength he saw modeled in his college basketball coach. "Sometimes I find myself the only one who feels a certain way, and I often have to stand alone and be true to myself and my God," he says. Whenever that happened, he always remembered the example set by his old coach, who has always been true to himself and the values he believed in.

* * *

Do not be too concerned about what others may think of you. Be very concerned about what you think of yourself.

—John Wooden

* * *

As I was writing this book, ABC newsman Peter Jennings lost his battle with lung cancer. Shortly after Jennings passed away, I saw this quote from Brian Zippin, manager of Café des Artistes, one of the broadcaster's favorite restaurants in New York. Said Zippin, "He was very real and not full of himself." What a tribute—and a reminder of the importance of just being yourself.

John Wooden never tried to copy anybody else. He didn't try to coach like Piggy Lambert or Red Auerbach or Adolph Rupp or any of the other legendary coaches of his day. He was the one and only John Wooden, and that turned out just fine.

Never forget that you don't have to be like anyone else. You don't have to sing like Sarah Brightman or Josh Groban. You don't have to stand at the plate like Barry Bonds. You don't have to throw the football like Peyton Manning, hit a long jumper like Kobe Bryant or swing a golf club like Tiger Woods. Just be yourself, and in the process you'll be very much like Coach.

As writer John Mason said, "You were born an original. Don't die a copy." The late Judy Garland said something very similar: "Be a first-rate version of yourself; not a second-rate version of someone else."

Every so often, you have to call a time-out, step away from the rat race and ask yourself some important questions. If you can, I recommend getting away to a quiet place for a few days so you'll really have the time to think. And when you do, ask yourself how you really feel about things—in matters of faith, politics and other areas of life. I'm not suggesting that you should decide to jettison your faith in God, embrace radical politics or take up a hedonistic lifestyle. But it is important to decide for yourself what you believe and why. Don't let others do your thinking for you. You are entitled to your own point of view.

Ralph Drollinger, who was a member of those great UCLA basketball teams in the early 1970s, now serves as a leader of Capitol Ministries in Sacramento, California. He says, "Coach insisted that we concentrate on our own behavior (which we could control) and not focus on what the other team might do. He virtually never showed us scouting reports on our opponents." In other words, don't pattern your own behavior after what the other guy does, says or thinks. Be yourself.

Says Drollinger, "The importance of holding oneself accountable is a lesson I haven't forgotten. It is not only true in basketball, it is also true in life."

Former UCLA star Walt Hazzard said, "Coach's pre-game speech was not 'You have to run over them. . . .' It was, 'At the end of the game, everyone should be capable of walking to the mirror and looking at themselves, and saying to themselves, 'I did the best I could.'"

ASK YOURSELF WHAT YOU REALLY WANT OUT OF LIFE

Do you really know what you want, or have you let others make up your mind for you? Are you happy with the path your life has taken, or do you need to make some substantial changes? Do you find joy and satisfaction in your daily life, or is it an unfulfilling grind? If you find that you spend Monday through Friday just waiting for the weekend to arrive, and then spend the weekend dreading Monday's arrival, then it's probably time to make some major repairs.

* * *

Set your compass in a chosen direction and then focus your attention and efforts completely on the journey of preparation. A successful journey becomes your destination and is where your real accomplishment lies.

—John Wooden

* * *

TAKE A LOOK AT YOUR SKILLS AND ABILITIES

It's important to stop and reassess whether you are using your innate skills, strengths, knowledge and experience. If you are not using the skills God gave you, then you probably won't feel a great deal of satisfaction about the life you're living. Now, of course, it's important to have a realistic view of your skills—and that's part of knowing who you are. There are several ways to assess your skills: through your own experience, what others tell you, by thinking about what you really enjoy, and so on.

Dr. Doug McIntosh, senior pastor of Cornerstone Bible Church in Lilburn, Georgia, played for John Wooden from 1964 to 1966. He says, "Every UCLA basketball player who spent time under Coach Wooden's tutelage received more than improved skills. He received a way of thinking about solving problems and overcoming obstacles. If you paid attention and believed in what he said, you not only became a better basketball player, you also became a much more competent person. He was as much a philosopher as he was a coach, and he was equally proficient at both activities. My basketball skills I lost long ago, but the life principles he left with me are more valuable today than they were when I first heard them."

He gives this illustration: "One of the building blocks of Coach Wooden's Pyramid of Success is self-control, exchanging short-term comforts for long-term excellence. During the years I was at UCLA, we played against many excellent teams, some of which had better athletes. Yet we lost to very few of them, in large measure because we were in better condition than any team we played. . . . Coach insisted that we had to push ourselves beyond what we thought we could. It was a valuable lesson that has stayed with me: You can usually do more than you think you can. It takes a good coach to make that lesson penetrate skulls that were inclined toward personal comforts."

SET GOALS FOR THE FUTURE

Ask yourself what you really want out of life. Are you moving in the right direction? It's important to figure out where you want to be next week, next month, next year, and five or ten years from now—and then set specific goals to help you get there. Goals are like mileposts on a highway. If you don't have any clear, concrete goals, you probably won't know where you are in life.

REARRANGE YOUR PRIORITIES

Take a look at your daily activities and ask yourself how many of them are really necessary. Are you spending a lot of time doing things you don't really need, or want, to do? Are you held so captive by "the tyranny of the urgent" that you don't have time for things you'd really like to do? If so, then it's time to rearrange your priorities. Stop involving yourself in time-wasting activities that are a detriment to your quality of life. Make a list of all the things you do, and cross off those activities that have taken you off track. Make first things first. Concentrate on what's really important to you!

REASSESS YOUR PROGRESS AND MAKE ADJUSTMENTS

I believe it's important to stop at regular intervals—every year or so—to reevaluate your life. Are you keeping a clear image of what you really want in life? Are you moving toward your goals? Do you have your priorities straight? Do you have a clear understanding of why you're doing what you do?

One other important thing to remember:

TAKE TIME TO ENJOY LIFE

Here are some words of wisdom from eighty-six-year-old Nadine Stair:

If I had my life to live over again, I'd dare to make more mistakes next time. I'd relax. I'd limber up. I'd be sillier than I've been this trip. I would take fewer things seriously. I would take more chances. I would take more trips. I would climb more mountains and swim more rivers. . . . Oh, I've had my moments. If I had it to do over again, I would have more of them.

Chapter Eighteen

✤

If You Want to Be Like Coach: Grow Old Gracefully

Over thirty years have passed since I left UCLA, and it amazes me how smart Coach Wooden has become in those years.

—Bill Walton

MICHELANGELO WAS STILL designing cathedrals when he was nearly ninety.

Ben Franklin helped in the writing of the United States Constitution when he was eighty-one.

Claude Monet finished his famous water lily series of paintings when he was eighty-five.

Thomas Edison was still spending most of his time in his laboratory, coming up with new inventions, when he was eighty-four.

And **Count Leo Tolstoy** was nearly seventy when he learned how to ride a bicycle.

Obviously, it is possible to stay "sharp" well into what might be referred to as "old age."

And yet, when the UCLA Bruins failed to win the NCAA championship in 1974, the school received a handful of letters from alumni suggesting that John Wooden should retire.

"He's out of touch," they said.

"It's time to turn the reins over to a younger man."

The following season, Coach went out and proved that his critics didn't know what they were talking about. In 1975, he led the Bruins to their tenth national championship in twelve years.

And then he retired. Not because people were criticizing him, but because he was sixty-four years old, he had been the Bruins head coach for twenty-seven years, and he felt that it was time to hang up the old sneakers. He didn't decide to retire because he couldn't keep up with changes in the game or because he no longer had the ability to motivate young college players. It was because John Wooden knew it was time for a change. He was determined not to make the mistake so many star coaches and athletes have made and hang around way too long. Coach went out on top, with his skills and his reputation intact.

Today, John Wooden is ninety-five years old. He's a long, long way from his playing days at Purdue. As was true when he was sixty-five, Coach doesn't try to be what he's not. He's ninety-five, and he knows it. And yet I have the feeling he could still give some of today's best college coaches a run for their money.

I like the way Roland Underhill put it. Underhill, who played for UCLA from 1957 to 1959, told me, "Coach Wooden always stressed conditioning so we would be strong in the fourth quarter. Now in the fourth quarter of his life, he is finishing strong."

Coach's daughter, Nan, laughingly says, "At Daddy's condo, I keep looking for a special charger he plugs into each morning, but I haven't found it yet. At age ninety-five he wants to give life everything he's got. He's told me he's ready to go and see Mother, but until then he's more driven than ever."

Coach's friend Carl Boldt tells me that in 2002, the Angels invited Wooden to throw out the first ball for a World Series game at Anaheim. Boldt says Coach was trying to make up his mind whether he should accept the Angels' invitation. "Finally, his daughter, Nan, said, 'Go ahead, Dad. It'll look good on your resume.' We all cracked up."

When Coach was a younger man, there weren't too many hotshots who could beat him in a game of one-on-one. Some of the old-time UCLA players remember what happened on the first day of practice in 1948. After watching an intrasquad scrimmage, Coach announced that he and his assistant coach, Eddie Powell, would take on the winners—two against five. It wasn't fair. Wooden and Powell dominated the contest. From that moment on, Coach had the full attention of his basketball team.

I've heard dozens of similar stories. Sidney Wicks and Keith Wilkes both remember times when Coach stepped onto the court and showed his NCAA champions that he could still teach them a thing or two about the game of basketball.

These days, Coach *might* not be such a formidable foe on the basketball court. (Notice that I said *might*. He still has that old competitive twinkle in his eye, and I wouldn't be surprised to see that he could still sink a long set shot.) But I still wouldn't want to take him on in a battle of wits. Coach is still as sharp as ever. He has the presence of mind of a man half his age. He's alert, and he pays attention to what's going on around him.

* * *

John Wooden is an American treasure. When the world loses him, his brain should be preserved in the American Historical Museum. His mind is so sharp and perceptive even in his midnineties.

—Julius Erving

* * *

Coach's dentist, Allan Forrest, told me about the time his wife, Carole, presented Coach with this baseball trivia question: "What are the seven ways a batter can reach first base?" Says Forrest, "He came up with six of the correct answers before he left the office, and we gave him until his next appointment to get the last one. The next morning at 8 A.M. our phone rang, and it was Coach. 'Can I speak to Carole? I have the seventh answer.' It turned out he had started calling everyone he knew until someone gave him the right answer. I guess you never really lose those competitive fires."

How does Coach manage to stay so sharp? "The key is my desire to stay busy," he says. "I've stayed interested in things. The people in my life keep me engaged, as well as my thirteen great-grandchildren."

Coach was ninety-two when the new Wooden floor was dedicated at Pauley Pavilion. Craig Shermon, an announcer for Fox Sports, told me that a number of former Bruins players were on hand for the occasion, and Coach was given some typed-up notes to help him introduce them to the crowd. He never even looked at them. He knew every one of their names, recalled the years they played for him, and talked about each one of them in detail—all from memory!

A similar story came from James Washington, another Fox announcer who played football at UCLA from 1983 to 1986. Washington told me that one night, following his freshman season at the university, he spotted Coach at a Bruins basketball game. "I nervously slipped down the aisle to introduce myself. He said, 'Oh, I know who you are,' and proceeded to recite all my freshman stats."

Author John Feinstein told me about seeing Coach Wooden at the 2003 Final Four in New Orleans. "I went over and introduced myself, and he replied, 'Oh, John, I know you. Tell me what you are working on.' I told him I was writing a book with Red Auerbach, who was eighty-five at the time. 'Red?' he said. 'Oh, he is such a nice young man.' I about cracked up."

As longtime friend Dick Enberg says, "He doesn't age. His body may be a little slower, but it almost seems as if his mind is quicker."

Bill Walton agrees: "There is a reason Coach Wooden has aged so well. He takes great care of himself. He stays physically and mentally active. His memory is meticulous. He can still recite long poems word for word." What are some of the reasons that Coach has aged with such grace?

1) HE MAKES EVERY DAY HIS MASTERPIECE.

Coach came to UCLA in June of 2002, at the age of ninety-one, and spoke to all the coaches. He got there thirty minutes early and spoke for two hours straight. After that he had a photo taken with everyone there and then had lunch. At the end, he told me he had intestinal flu and hadn't slept much.

—Al Skates, UCLA volleyball coach

John Wooden is amazing. He never grabs hold of an excuse to take it easy or to bail out of a commitment. If Coach doesn't show up when he's supposed to, then you'd better believe something is seriously wrong.

He is always striving to grow and become better than he was yesterday. Ann Myers Drysdale is one of the most enduring stars of women's basketball and the widow of Hall of Fame pitcher Don Drysdale. She told me about an occasion when Coach was ninety-two and someone asked him what he would do if he could have his life to live over again. He replied, "I would like to be a better, kinder person."

Those words take on extra meaning when you realize what a caring, kind and giving man he is. And yet he has never thought of himself as having achieved everything he wanted to accomplish in life.

As former Bruin Brandon Loyd told me, "John Wooden is a classic, an American treasure. He's like apple pie or a 1955 Chevy. Nothing but class and charm. You can't ask for a better role model no matter what your age." He added, "Coach has done the right thing so much and so long, it's become a habit."

Andy Hill admits that he and Coach had a "troubled" relationship during his playing days at UCLA. Hill wasn't a first-stringer, and his lack of playing time and what he perceived as a lack of attention from Coach left him somewhat embittered by the time he graduated from the university.

He told me, "After I left the school, I had no contact with him for twenty-five years."

Then they renewed acquaintances and wound up working together on their book. Hill said, "We're driving to do a 'Power Lunch' radio show with Bill Griffith. We're on the 134 Freeway going from Coach's home to Burbank. Out of the blue John says, 'Andy, have I ever told you how much this book means to me and how much our relationship means to me? I've loved spending all this time with you.'"

Andy went on, "My first reaction was that I was going to cry. I have so much respect for this man, and I've waited all my life to hear that from a man who I admired. . . . It was so emotional for me. I can't tell you how incredible those words made me feel."

When Coach saw the impact his words had, he explained, "I've been working at getting better at saying what's inside of me.'"

Hill says, "This was an example of Coach not just talking about making each day your masterpiece, but living it as well. No one has any expectations of a ninety-something-year-old man trying to improve or changing at that age. But he was still working on being better each day."

Sportswriter Alexander Wolff asks and answers his own rhetorical question: "Why does John Wooden continue to meet with people—some total strangers—and spend countless hours with them? Yes, he likes to counsel and advise, but he believes there is something he can learn from everyone."

2) He refuses to "act old."

I was the NBC broadcaster for nine of UCLA's ten title games. John Wooden won them all when he was past fifty.

—Curt Gowdy

What does "aging gracefully" mean? In John Wooden's case, it certainly doesn't mean that he acts like an old man. He doesn't. His attitude about life reminds me of a quote from late bandleader Artie Shaw: "I haven't practiced being old. I don't know how to act that way. People say, 'You talk and think like a young man.' Well, what other kind of man is there? You have to be young; every day is new."

* * *

John Wooden continues to strive to get better at age ninety-five. That pursuit and desire he has is amazing. What John Wooden did at UCLA seems impossible now, but it was impossible then, too.

—John Akers, editor,
Basketball Times

* * *

Former NBA coach Jack Ramsay told me about a basketball clinic in 1999, when Coach was eighty-eight. "There were 750 coaches there, the place was packed. John Wooden did ninety minutes and sat on a stool the whole time. No notes, no pauses. The crowd was mesmerized. He was quoting poetry. It was spellbinding."

(Incidentally, Dr. Ramsay, who hired me for my first NBA job in 1968, is another who refuses to let his age determine his outlook on life. He started participating in triathlons when he was fifty-five, and when I interviewed him for my radio show, seventeen years later, he was still doing them. He told me he's not as fast as he used to be, but that he thinks he can get his speed back with some harder training. I loved it! What an outlook on life!)

Announcer Bob Costas has also seen this side of Coach. "He will recite a little poem from his youth at the drop of a hat. You can't fake this stuff—it's who John Wooden really is. There is so much artifice in public life today. That's why we are amazed with someone that authentic."

Coach says that he has always wanted to be the best he could possibly be. "I still do, so I work at it. My knees and hips make it difficult to walk very far or stand very long, but I keep a full speaking and traveling schedule. I continue to meet with individuals during the week. And I still answer every letter and return every phone call."

He admits that some things have changed:

"I used to read more than I do now. I don't remember quite as well as I used to. My memory is going too." But still, "I will continue to do the best I can with what I have. Although I don't know any other ninety-five-year-olds who work as hard as I do, that is not the point. The only competition I have is with me. Even at ninety-five, I want to be the best I can be, and hard work is the only way to make it happen."

* * *

Children listen to him because they have the innate sense that he's genuinely interested in them. He loves them so much, and you can feel it all over the room.

—Michael Wooden, Coach's grandson

* * *

3) HE HAS LEARNED THE MEANING OF CONTENTMENT.

As Coach Wooden aged, he didn't get bitter that life was passing him by. That happens with so many older people, but not him.

—Bill Walton

We all know people who light up a room by their presence. Paul Ma, who owns VIPs, the small coffee shop where Coach has breakfast just about every day, says, "When the door to the restaurant opens and Coach walks in, we all feel better."

In the fourth chapter of Philippians, the Apostle Paul writes about the importance of learning to be content in any and all circumstances. "I know what it is to be in need, and I know what it is to have plenty. I have learned the secret of being content in any and every situation, whether well fed or hungry, whether living in plenty or in want. I can do everything through him who gives me the strength" (Philippians 4:11–13).

Coach is content to be ninety-five years of age. He doesn't sit around wishing he could be forty again. He is content with his cozy and comfortable condominium in Encino. He doesn't spend his time wishing that he lived in a multimillion-dollar estate in Beverly Hills or Bel Air. He doesn't brood about the fact that the most money he ever made at UCLA was less than thirty-five thousand dollars a year. He is content with every aspect of his life, and that is a primary reason that he has been able to age so gracefully.

Peter Trgovich, who played for Coach from 1971 to 1975, told me, "When my son, Pete III, was about ten years old, we visited Coach at his condo in Encino. Pete whispered to me, 'Coach Wooden lives here?' I think he was expecting Shaq's home. Later, I said, 'Pete, you don't have to live in a mansion to be a superstar.'" Coach has never needed money and possessions to make him content.

That doesn't mean he has no sorrows. He misses Nell terribly. When he looks back on his coaching career, he sees decisions he wishes he had made differently. For example, when he was a high school coach, he kicked a player off the team when the boy was caught smoking. Later on, the young man dropped out of school. Coach now feels that if he had allowed the boy a second chance, he might have completed school and gone on to a better life.

Sure Coach has regrets. We all do. He says, "There was a game in high school when four of my five starters came down with measles and could not play in a road game. The opposing coach ran up the score on us. So I waited for an opportune time and got back at him. I told him later that I was sorry, I hadn't been true to my values.

"There was also a time at UCLA when an opposing coach got away with putting the wrong free-throw shooter up to the line. He had done it in previous games and got away with it, so I did it too. I got caught, but I did try, and that's just as bad as if I'd gotten away with it. I regret having given in to temptation."

But he is content with himself because he has come to terms with his mistakes, and he knows that he has always tried to do the best he could. Coach says, "I had peace with myself before we ever won a national championship. I didn't have any more peace with myself or feel more successful after we started winning than I had beforehand."

Coach told author Steve Bisheff, "I could have been very happy if I had stayed in Indiana and taught English and been a high school coach." Bisheff's response: "And with almost anyone else, you'd laugh and say, 'Sure you could.' But with him, you believe it. All you have to do is join him one morning at his regular breakfast stop a few minutes from his home. It is a small, old-fashioned coffee shop that could easily be transported back to Martinsville, Indiana, complete with all the regulars sitting in the tiny booths and at the nearby counter.

"Wooden knows them all, but only by their first names. They, in turn, shout their greetings as he arrives, usually with his son-in-law or Tony Spino, the UCLA trainer who spends two or three mornings a week working with him, or a former Bruins player."

4) COACH STAYS BUSY PHYSICALLY AND MENTALLY.

When we named the gymnasium after John, he came back [to Martinsville, Indiana] and put on a clinic for the high school boys. Coach got them started running drills, and he lit up like a lightbulb—and he was already getting up in years at the time.

—Hubert Bastin,
Coach's boyhood friend

"John Wooden has the body of a ninety-five-year-old, but the mind of a twenty-five-year-old." That's the view of Gary Cunningham, the former UCLA assistant coach who now serves as athletic director at UC Santa Barbara. "It's hard to get on his calendar these days," Cunningham told me. "I'm amazed at his energy level and the active life he continues to lead."

Coach says, "I am still independent, and I want to stay that way. I want to continue to live where I shared my life with my dear Nellie." He adds, "It is not my way to count my awards. . . . I know that people still want to hear me speak. I am honored by their requests. Folks still want to meet with me, and they come from all over the world to do so. It is a privilege to be able to continue to help others. My hectic schedule has probably done much to keep my mind as lucent as it is, even though it's not as sharp as it once was. All of my family has been around me all these years. What a blessing that has been! I am blessed beyond belief . . . but am I a success?

"Believe me when I say, none of the above are part of the criteria. I am not saying I don't appreciate the blessings that have come my way. I am not saying that at all. But if none of the things of which I have spoken had happened, I would not be any less successful."

He concludes, "I can tell you about the blessings in my life, but blessings aren't success. Did I make the effort to do my best? That is the only criteria, and I am the only one who knows. Am I a success? I have peace of mind."

So many of the people I interviewed for this book told me that what amazes them most about Coach is the sharpness and agility of his mind. Boston sportswriter Bob Ryan told me, "Bill Walton and I went to visit Coach Wooden in Los Angeles when he was eighty-nine years old. He was so sharp. He recited the 1931 Martinsville High School baseball lineup and batting order. All the names sounded Polish (meaning they were long and difficult to pronounce), but he got all of them."

A similar comment came from Morgan Wootten, former head basketball coach at Maryland's DeMatha High. "Coach is so sharp," he says. "There might be six or eight of us having dinner together, and he'll hear what we're saying at the other end of the table."

Tom Desotell, who worked with Coach at his summer basketball camps for years, told me, "Recently, I was visiting Coach at his condo, and he gave me a beautiful pair of new basketball shoes in my exact size, a ten. I asked, 'Coach, how did you know my size?' He said, 'Tom, thirty years ago when you started working at our summer camps, you wore a ten. Your feet haven't grown have they?'" What a memory!

Dave Yanai, who is now head coach at Cal State University, Los Angeles, first met Coach Wooden when he was twenty-two years old, a student at Cal State, Long Beach, and writing a research paper on pressure defenses. The year was 1966, and John Wooden's UCLA Bruins were just hitting their stride. "He had already won two national championships, and here he was taking the time to speak with me. Up until that point I had an interest in coaching and teaching, but with that small gesture and the subsequent meeting," Yanai says, "I was sold on making a career of coaching basketball and teaching young people."

Yanai did just that, coaching both high school and college basketball in the Los Angeles area. One of his favorite stories concerns the time Coach agreed to appear at a fundraiser for Cal State, Los Angeles. "He arrived at 3:30 P.M. and stayed until 10:30 P.M.—until the last autograph was signed and that last person got to spend just a brief quality moment with a true legend."

He went on, "I am sixty-one years old now, and when I feel just a step slower or a little tired going into practice, or when I am watching tape, I think about ninety-five-year-old Coach Wooden with all that energy, and it gives me that extra motivation to give my all to help my team and my players get better."

Former UCLA coach Steve Lavin agrees: "John Wooden continues to learn. He has an openness to diverse beliefs and backgrounds. He has a real curiosity about life and is still a student of life."

When he was thirteen years old, the great Michelangelo applied for an art apprenticeship. When asked if he could draw, the future master replied, "I have the capacity to learn." Seventy-one years later, near the end of his life, someone asked Michelangelo to summarize his life's philosophy. *"Ancora imparo,"* he replied. "And I still learn."

I read that the Roman scholar Cato started to learn Greek when he was in his eighties. When someone asked him why he would tackle such a difficult task at his age, he answered, "It's the only age I have left." As Regis Philbin might say, "Good answer."

5) COACH UNDERSTANDS THE MEANING OF LIFE.

Everything about John Wooden is unique because he is true to himself in his quiet, quiet way. Everything around him can be totally negative, but he will never say anything negative. He lives his pyramid.

—Barbara Traylor

Barbara Traylor got to know Coach Wooden at the coffee shop in Encino where he eats breakfast just about every day. She told me that from the first day they met, she has marveled at his kindness and his concern for others. She said, "He'll be eating his breakfast when someone asks for an autograph, and he'll sign and never complain. He will never turn anyone down because he is a good person inside and out. He's a beautiful man."

Traylor is not the only one who feels that way about Coach. Last year, *Philadelphia Daily News* sportswriter Dick Jerardi called Coach and asked if he could come to Encino for an interview. Naturally, Coach said, "Come on over."

Jerardi had never met John Wooden before, but he says, "Within five minutes, he made me feel comfortable and acted as if I was his best friend. He does that with everyone." Jerardi also told me, "He's a teacher at heart, and you feel like a student absorbing all of his wisdom from the ages. At ninety-five, he senses everything going on around him better than most forty-five-year-olds."

As Dr. James Dobson of Focus on the Family told me, "John Wooden gives respect to people and is so kind to everyone. He's still very sharp. He won with dignity and he still has that, along with great personal charm. He knows what he thinks and believes and has never wavered."

*   *   *

I'm in awe of my dad. His name is still out there because he's practiced everything he's taught others. People can't get enough of his message because it's timeless. He believes in God, family and work, and that never changes with him.

—Jim Wooden

* * *

Dal Shealy, former president of the Fellowship of Christian Athletes, said, "Coach built his life on Scripture and prayer, and that's brought a consistency to his life. People meet him and feel they can depend on him because he's trustworthy. His countenance says to people, 'Follow me. I won't let you down.'" Shealy went on, "Despite his unbelievable success, he's remained an unassuming man without a self-serving bone in his body. People look at him and wonder, 'What makes him tick?' The answer is his humble spirit. He's never bragged about what he's accomplished."

Shealy's words were echoed by Greg Johnson, who played JV basketball at UCLA in the early seventies. Johnson told me, "Coach is special because of his consistency of purpose to his moral beliefs. He gives all of us a blueprint for a successful life, a centering point to go back to. It's important to be consistent like Coach."

Len Miller, who spent four years playing for Coach in the 1950s, told me about a recent conversation in which several people started debating about the identity of the greatest American who ever lived. Several people chose Abraham Lincoln, somebody else suggested Helen Keller, and then Miller said, "The greatest American might be John Wooden."

"Oh, come on," someone replied. "He's just a coach."

Lenny shook his head. "No, he's far more than that. He's a man who's set an example for millions with his values and principles. There's not a life he hasn't left his imprint on in some positive way. Yes, if I had one vote, I'd vote for him."

Miller went on to say, "John Wooden is just a shining light. Think of the world today if everyone lived by his values. If all of us loved our fellow man and our God like Coach, it would be a perfect world. He's never strayed from his principles, values or priorities. He sets an example every day of his life because of the consistency of his thoughts and deeds."

Another who shares that view is Jack Hirsch, who was a tough young kid from Brooklyn when he first put on a UCLA basketball uniform more than forty years ago. Hirsch is quick to admit that he and Coach didn't always see eye to eye—on basketball or anything else. But now Hirsch says, "John Wooden is an American icon. We won't see the likes of him ever again."

Hirsch told me, "I was not an easy player to coach. I'm sixty-three now, and all these years, Coach was a mentor to me and he instilled his values in me. So many times, I'd make a good decision about something or other, and I'd ask myself, *Where did I learn that?* Then I'd remember—I learned it from Coach."

John Vallely, who graduated from UCLA in 1970 and was the Atlanta Hawks' number-one draft choice that year, says, "Coach's foundation in life is very solid, and he's maintained a consistency throughout his ninety-five years. You don't see changes in Coach. He's totally committed to his faith."

Vallely recalls, "Coach taught us that life is not going to be easy, but there's a prize at the end if you live the right way. We will have wins and losses, but the main thing is to achieve peace of mind by doing your best. He's a wise old friend to his former players, and to Coach, we are all extended family."

6) COACH HAS NEVER TAKEN HIMSELF TOO SERIOUSLY.

John Wooden is not a pretentious man. He's never let his fame affect him. Nobody will ever do what he did at UCLA, but he's still a real nice guy. It's good to know there are still some nice people out there.

—Mike Hehr, a customer
at VIPs Restaurant

Brian Burmeister recalls a recent occasion when Coach locked himself out of his condo. Seems a group of friends were involved in an animated discussion when Burmeister realized they were running late for a meeting at VIPs, Coach's favorite restaurant. Says Burmeister, "As soon as Coach closes the door, a sheepish grin crosses that marvelous face. 'Oh my!' he says. 'I locked my keys in the condo.'"

The solution was to call Coach's daughter, Nan, who had an extra key. Burmeister told me, "We all know that Coach is really on the ball," and that it was only the excitement of the conversation that caused him to forget his keys. It's the sort of thing that could have happened to anyone. Nevertheless, "We are all listening to the one-sided phone call, which consists of Coach's many 'Yes, dears,' in response to Nan's comments. Finally Coach says, 'Well, after all, I *am* ninety-five,' to obtain a little forgiveness, and we all erupt in laughter. What a guy!"

When Coach was sixty-eight years old, and UCLA trainer Bill Cowdrey was twenty-three, Cowdrey asked him a question: "Coach, I thought that at twenty-three and a college graduate I would feel grown up, but I don't. When will I feel grown up?"

Coach just smiled and said, "Bill, I'm not old enough yet to know the answer to that question."

Cowdrey says, "He meant that he was still learning, growing and maturing. As longtime UCLA track coach Ducky Drake once said, 'You learn something every day if you live long enough.'"

Former Coach Stan Morrison, who I've mentioned several times before, believes that Coach became one of the all-time greats when he changed his coaching strategy to concentrate more on defense, installing the 1-2-1-1 press. Morrison said, "I cannot admire anything more than change in men, change for the better. Coaches are notoriously conservative and reluctant to change. They get in a comfort zone and stick with what they know. To venture into the unknown is daunting . . . because the changes will be 'live and in living color' on ESPN for everyone to see and criticize." Regarding the switching to an emphasis on defense, Morrison told me, "I believe the magnitude of that philosophical change cannot be overstated."

Hall of Fame broadcaster Dick Enberg, longtime announcer for John Wooden's UCLA basketball teams, tells this story: "I asked Coach once what he remembered most about his first national championship back in 1964.

"'It was in Kansas City, as all the championships were in those days,' he answered. 'We won the championship on Saturday night, and the next day was Easter Sunday, so my wife, Nell, and I were on our way to church. We had taken no more than two steps out of the hotel when a pigeon dropped a perfect hit right on my head. I said to myself, "Johnny, maybe you're not as important as you think you are."'"

Despite his success, Enberg says, "which seems more unbelievable as each year passes, he remains modest and self-effacing." Here's more of what Enberg has to say about Coach:

As I've spent time with John Wooden since his retirement from coaching many years ago, my appreciation for him has continued to grow. His interests are so much wider than just basketball. Besides his love for poetry—he was a high school English teacher—I think he could quote from every book ever written on Abraham Lincoln. As his players will tell you, he was a brilliant teacher and certainly an inspiration. I found him to be the ultimate example of not only greatness, but also goodness. Wooden is ninety-five and continues to lead an active life, making speeches, doing interviews, meeting with other coaches who seek his advice and spending time with many of his former players.

The record will tell you that John Wooden retired after the 1974–75 basketball season. But the record is wrong. Coach never really retired. And that reminds me of something George Burns said when he was in his nineties: "Retirement at sixty-five is ridiculous. When I was sixty-five, I still had pimples."

Dan Guerrero, who was named UCLA's athletic director in 2000, says he has often turned to John Wooden for wisdom and guidance. He wrote:

In a job like mine, there are precious few people with the experience and perspective to turn to for counsel and discussion. I have been truly blessed because I have had the opportunity to consult regularly with John Wooden. By the time I started at UCLA, Coach had already completed six decades of college athletics experience, but I have learned that his grasp of contemporary issues remains up to date. Coach Wooden possesses a wisdom and an approachability that assures a dependable and steady sounding board. While there has been no single revolutionary concept or revelation from Coach, the accumulated exposure to his principles in inspiration, ambition and humility has been profoundly helpful to me. His stellar moral fiber is ingrained in his every thought, his every action. He continues to be the proof that reserve, integrity and class are always in style.

7) COACH LIVES IN THE MOMENT.

Therefore, do not worry about tomorrow, for tomorrow will take care of itself. Each day has enough trouble of its own.
—Matthew 6:34

Who could blame Coach if he spent a lot of time thinking about the past, paging through his scrapbook, reliving all those important victories? By the time a person reaches ninety-five years of age, it makes sense to think that the past would be a more comfortable and hospitable place than the present. After all, the passage of time takes its toll on all of us. It steals our parents, our friends, our spouses—in fact, if we live long enough, it takes just about all of the people we love—and it erodes our strength and vitality.

But Coach just doesn't go there. Not long ago he got a call from an old classmate from Martinsville High School. She told him that she was the head of the reunion committee for their class. In fact, she was not only the head of the committee, she *was* the committee.

"It's just you and me now, Johnny," she told him. "What should we do?"

Coach responded, "Well, you can't come here . . . and I can't come there. Why don't we just chat on the phone for awhile?"

So that's what they did—enjoying their time together, reminiscing and laughing about all the good times they had together over seventy-five years ago. John treasures the memories of a life well spent. But he doesn't live in the past.

Kent Taylor, founder and chairman of Texas Roadhouse Grille, told me that in April 2004, his company invited John Wooden to speak at their annual convention in Cabo San Lucas, Mexico.

"One night we were sitting at a Mexican restaurant when a strolling guitarist came by," he told me. "Coach requested that he play a song that was a favorite of his wife, Nell. When the music started, Coach closed his eyes and just focused on that music. He had a little smile on his face as he thought about his wife. After the song, he reengaged with our dinner—but for those few minutes, he was totally enjoying the moment."

Taylor added, "Coach acts today the same way he did before UCLA won its first NCAA title in 1964. He's like Sam Walton [founder of Wal-Mart] that way. Sam was still driving his pickup truck and seeing the same barber after he became a billionaire. The essence of John Wooden's life is to live life in the present and be happy every day."

In his outstanding book *My Personal Best*, written with Steve Jamison, Coach explains that one reason for his calm spirit is his belief that when his life is over, he will be reunited with Nell in heaven. He writes:

> *Mind you, I'm in no hurry to leave, but I have no fear of leaving. When the time comes, it will be a very good day—Nell and I will be together again. In the meantime, each day of the journey is precious, yours and mine—we must strive to make it a masterpiece. Each day, once gone, is gone forever.*
>
> *My father's words and deeds, his wisdom, taught me that and more. He gave me a direction I continue to try to live up to. His advice was good, and his example even better. My mentors, Earl Warriner, Glenn Curtis and Ward "Piggy" Lambert, shared their knowledge and wisdom as all great teachers do. Their interest in students went beyond the basketball court or even the classroom. They wanted to help us have good lives.*
>
> *I've tried to live up to my mentors' examples in teaching those young people who've made my life so rich along the way. My goal has always been to help them become not only better basketball players or English students, but better people. That's the most important thing a coach or teacher can do, and I have given it my personal best.*
>
> *And as I hope you find in your own life, none of it amounts to a hill of beans without the love of family and friends. I'm a very fortunate man who has much to be thankful for. 'Love' is the most important word in the English language, and my journey*

has been filled with so much love. I pray that yours is too—that your own journey is full of love. And that along the way you never cease trying to be the best you can be—that you always strive for your personal best.

That is success. And don't let anybody tell you otherwise.

Chapter Nineteen

❧

Epilogue

I'M FRUSTRATED. As I read back over what I've written so far, I realize that it barely scratches the surface of John Wooden's life. It's so hard to capture the essence of the man in a single book. Every morning, my mail brings letters from people who have played for, worked with or been acquainted with John Wooden in some way, and they all have great stories to tell. Every time I check my e-mail, I have several messages from people saying, "Here's another story about Coach you might want to put in your book." Although there are hundreds of stories, the facts they tell about John Wooden tend to be the same: Coach is wise. He is kind. He genuinely cares about people. He is very well organized.

Nobody has written to say, "Coach Wooden was mean to me once." Or, "Coach isn't really the nice guy you think he is." Everyone seems to agree, Coach's public image is in total agreement with his private life. He is the genuine article.

This morning, I'm looking over some comments sent to me by Neville Johnson, a Los Angeles attorney who wrote the book *The John Wooden Pyramid of Success.* Johnson says, "Coach Wooden is a model of a man who has gained extraordinary achievement in his profession, but done it with exceptional grace and style. John Wooden shows us that we can have an extraordinary impact on the world without being vociferous, boisterous and boastful. I am a trained litigator, and my life is spent finding the flaws in people. I started researching John Wooden in 1982 and have kept up my 'labor of love' for over twenty years. I have found virtually no fault in the man. He is poised, calm, dignified, intelligent, courteous, friendly, disciplined. He's astonishing."

A few days ago, I received this from Duke University basketball coach **Mike Krzyzewski:** "Coach Wooden was always teaching. I have loved listening to him and reading the many books which have been written by him or about him. Any time spent with Coach is time well spent."

As I go through the other letters and e-mails I've received, I can't help but think, *So many good stories . . . so little space.* But there are some I just can't leave out:

Like this one from **Jerry West,** NBA Hall of Famer and general manager of the Memphis Grizzlies: "When I was with the Lakers, John Wooden and I would have lunch together from time to time. He is a down-to-earth man who has time for everyone. In a quiet, humble way, he is a real leader. I have always admired John Wooden's wisdom. I ask the question, 'Is it better to be wise or smart?' I would take wise, but Wooden is both. He draws people to hear him and still has a twinkle in his eye at ninety-five."

Brendan Suhr, a former NBA assistant coach, wrote that he attended a number of coaching clinics where Coach was one of the instructors. "His philosophy and teaching style were superb," Suhr says. "He was so organized. I was more interested in that than the Xs and Os. You have got to get the foundation of the house in place before you put on the roof."

Similar comments came from **Mike Hibler,** who played basketball at UCLA from 1950 to 1954: "Coach Wooden was a master of detail," he said. "He was organized to the second and the master of utilizing time well. He was also the first person I heard talking about being all that you can be. He stressed the importance of maximizing your potential. At UCLA we all learned each other's positions. We were interchangeable and practiced Coach's drills over and over. We then played the games by instinct."

Broadcaster Merle Harmon: "I worked with Coach Wooden after he retired from coaching. He was like a father or grandfather that every young man should have. He never demanded special treatment and was a humble and caring person."

Attorney Gary Stern: "John Wooden gets it. He has his priorities in order, and people sense that and gravitate to him. His life's motto is very simple: Treat people like you would like to be treated. He was never in the news for the wrong reasons. He lived his life the right way—with utter class."

Gene Keady was the longtime and highly successful basketball coach at Purdue University, John Wooden's alma mater. Keady told me, "John Wooden still comes to some of our games and alumni meetings. He kids me, 'You shouldn't get so many technical fouls. I might stop sending in my alumni dues.' He's a down-to-earth person with a terrific sense of humor. He has always been a man of integrity and showed respect for others."

Former Stanford coach **Mike Montgomery,** who now coaches the Golden State Warriors, says, "Coach always has time for people. It is incredible how he will sit for hours, talking and signing. He has unbelievable energy at his age to be able to do that. With his age, wisdom and life perspective, it is as if Coach is looking out at all coaches and saying, 'Now, don't take yourselves too seriously. You are just a basketball coach, and your main responsibility is to the young men who you are leading.' He puts the whole thing in perspective."

Dr. John MacArthur, pastor and author: "John Wooden has fixed principles that govern all he does. Players came and went, but his principles never changed. I love people like that, who have strong principles and are loyal to them, because you always know how they will respond—no matter what the situation or the circumstances."

Mike Waldner, a columnist for the *South Bay Daily Breeze* newspaper in Southern California, told me: "As serious as he was about coaching, he never took himself that seriously. His players trusted him. Some tested him. But with rare exception they trusted him. Parents trusted him. We still trust him because he is so wise. When you talk to him you walk away wondering how someone so old can remain so sharp. You figure that if you remain even half that sharp if you reach his age, you'll be in pretty good shape."

Bruins standout and NBA player **Keith Erickson** told me, "I was fortunate enough to play for some great coaches in my long NBA career—including several Hall of Famers—but as I look back now, I realize just how special Coach Wooden was." Erickson went on to say, "Coach has an aura about him and is a true national treasure. People he doesn't know will call and ask if they can fly in from around the country just to spend time with him. Coach doesn't know these people, but he always says yes. One of my friends visited Coach and came away saying, 'That's the most profound day of my life.'"

Fred Claire, former general manager of the Los Angeles Dodgers, said something similar about Coach: "The more time I spend with him, the more I am awed by the vastness of his knowledge—not knowledge about basketball but about life. We all know people who look good under the glare of the spotlight. But not many end up as good as their reputations. John Wooden is one of those rare ones who is better than his reputation."

Other coaches are lavish in their praise for Coach Wooden:

Hugh Durham, former head coach at the University of Jacksonville: "John Wooden lives that pyramid he teaches. He is consistent and true to himself and his beliefs."

Jim Forkum, a college coach for thirty-three years who also taught at Coach Wooden's summer basketball camps: "John Wooden is as close to perfect as any human I have ever met. All that he stands for is still with me: treating people with respect, being humble and so forth."

Tubby Smith, head coach at the University of Kentucky: "I read John Wooden's book *They Call Me Coach* and used it as a textbook. That is where I developed my coaching and life philosophy. Years later I got Coach Wooden to sign it for me."

Bill Foster, former Clemson coach: "I was a young nobody coach and would go to the summer clinic at Stetson University. I was just a punk, but Coach treated me as an equal. I have never forgotten that."

Jim Calhoun, University of Connecticut coach: "I called Coach up in 1990 and asked if I could come visit him because I wanted to go over some pressing defensive ideas. He was gracious enough to spend several hours with me. We went on to have a great pressing team that year, averaging twelve steals a game. At the end of the season, Coach told me, 'Your team this year reminded me so much of my 1964 UCLA team.' That was incredibly high praise for him." Calhoun went on to say, "When you meet famous people, they oftentimes don't measure up to what you have been told. Whatever you have been told about Coach, he is sharper, more intelligent and more gracious than you expected."

Lute Olson, University of Arizona head coach: "John Wooden sees value in every person. It doesn't matter if you walk off the street or are the top coach in the NBA, Coach will treat you just the same. At ninety-five, he has an amazing mind. When we go over to play UCLA, I'll see him sitting at the games, smiling and signing autographs. What an exceptional person!"

Mark Gottfried, University of Alabama head coach: "John Wooden is the best leader I have ever been around. He is a man of character, wisdom and graciousness."

Bobby Pounds, longtime coach and UCLA player from 1950 to 1952: "I was the first black player John Wooden ever recruited, and I love the guy. I spent my whole career as a coach because I wanted to help kids just like he helped me. John Wooden was a great leader because his subjects were willing to jump over a wall for him. You didn't question what he told you because you had confidence in him. You knew that everything he asked you to do was for your benefit and not his."

Homer Drew, basketball coach, Valparaiso University: "The centerpiece of John Wooden's life is his faith in Jesus Christ. He has always had such a humble spirit. He always has time for you, and he listens. He is never in a rush with people."

George Terzian, former college coach: "Our Pasadena City College team was invited to play the UCLA junior varsity team in a preliminary game. Before our game began, I felt a tap on my shoulder. It was Coach Wooden, who had worked his way down to the court to greet and bring encouragement to a nervous junior college coach."

Tom Wasdin, longtime college coach: "I was a high school coach when I attended a coaching clinic at Stetson University where Coach Wooden was one of the keynote speakers. This was the summer after he had won his first national championship. After his speech, I introduced myself to him, and even though I was only a high school coach, he treated me with great respect and made me feel that he was sincerely interested in helping me with my chosen career."

Billy Gillispie, Texas A&M head coach: "I have always been impressed with how humble John Wooden is. He is just comfortable being himself. He has never assumed he was a star. Coach lives by the Golden Rule and models it for the rest of us."

Ricardo Patton, University of Colorado head coach: "The thing that distinguishes Coach Wooden from most is his high level of intelligence, coupled with his clear understanding of priorities."

Steve Alford, University of Iowa head coach: "I grew up in Coach's hometown of Martinsville, Indiana. As a gym rat, I spent some time in the gym almost every day, beginning when I was a first-grader, and saw his picture hanging on the wall. As I learned more about Coach Wooden, the more I realized he was a man who truly had life figured out. He has taught me to serve God daily and strive to make each day a masterpiece."

George Raveling, longtime college head coach: "John Wooden will not be remembered just for his ten titles at UCLA, but for the everlasting lessons he taught all of us. Coach Wooden is basketball's version of Gandhi, Martin Luther King Jr. and Nelson Mandela. He mentors all of us in a vast variety of fields well beyond basketball."

Ben Howland, UCLA head coach: "Coach has lived his life by a standard that very few have. The man is so giving and unselfish. He teaches us to reach for our dreams because anything is possible, to live by the Golden Rule and to be willing to stand up for what is right. He is the greatest coach ever and such a great role model for all of us."

Jim Harley, longtime coach at Eckerd College in St. Petersburg, Florida: "John Wooden is a humble giant. At the 1975 Final Four, I saw him sitting by himself one morning, getting some sun. I walked over, sat down next to him and we talked for thirty minutes. What an awesome time it was for me as we talked about recruiting, practices and other things coaches discuss. Here he was going for his tenth national title, and he had time for an unknown coach from a small school in Florida."

Dave Buss, former college coach: "One year, the Final Four was in Indianapolis. I walked into the McDonald's at the Hyatt hotel to get breakfast. It was early, and there were two people sitting there. One of them was John Wooden. I'd never met Coach, but he asked me, 'Would you like to join me?' We sat there for thirty minutes like two old friends. That was one of the highlights of my coaching career."

Gene Smithson, former coach at Wichita State and Illinois State: "In the spring of 1977 I was at the Dapper Dan High School Tournament in Pittsburgh. I got on the hotel elevator, and Coach Wooden was there. The first words out of his mouth were, 'I know you. You're Gene Smithson of Illinois State.' I was startled he knew who I was."

Charlie Woollum, former college coach: "In 1963, I was a young coach just starting out. John Wooden was doing a clinic outside of Philadelphia, and I went armed with pads and pens to write down all his Xs and Os. Coach spent about 70 percent of his time talking about relationships, and I left kind of disappointed. As I got older, I realized Coach Wooden had nailed it. Coaching is at least 70 percent about relationships with people, and probably more."

Roger Goodling, longtime basketball coach at Shippensburg University in Pennsylvania: "One year at the Final Four, John Wooden conducted a coaches clinic that I attended. Afterwards, at lunch, I sat down by myself at one of the tables. The next thing I knew, I felt a tap on my shoulder. It was John Wooden. He said, 'Would you mind if we joined you for lunch?'" Of course, Goodling didn't mind. "So Coach and his staff sat down and talked basketball. For some reason, I was the fortunate one that day."

Larry Farmer, who played at UCLA, and then coached there, told me that he'll never forget the recruiting trip he made to UCLA when he was eighteen years old. "We sat in his office for several hours, and all he did was ask questions about me as a person. No basketball talk at all. Thirty-five years later, I was at the Final Four in New Orleans with my wife and two children. We all went up to Coach Wooden's hotel room to visit. He put my eight-year-old daughter on his lap, recited poetry, told stories and encouraged my children to be good citizens. No basketball talk this time either. Coach is a kind man who loves people of all races, ages and classes. He wants to make a difference in people's lives, and basketball has given him a bigger platform. I think basketball was God's way of letting him impact more of the Lord's children."

Says **Tay Baker, former head coach at the University of Cincinnati:** "Coach Wooden is the epitome of the word 'coach.'"

A FINAL WORD

A few days ago, my mail brought a letter from Jim Spillane, who, as a sophomore in 1975, was an occasional starter at guard for Coach Wooden's last team at UCLA. Spillane brought tears to my eyes as he wrote of the profound impact Coach has had on his life. With his permission, I want to share his story with you:

I had lost track of Coach in my years after I was out of school, running into him occasionally at certain events. This was probably due to the fact that I felt I had underachieved in my professional career and was somewhat embarrassed by it.

I had become a commercial real estate broker and lived the ups and down of a commission-based life. I was never satisfied with that profession. While I also went through a divorce, I always felt that I was still a good person and the values that had been important to me growing up, and reinforced by Coach, were still within me. My daughter, Kelly, was four when her mother and I split up, but my little girl was always the most important thing in my life. In addition to being able to see her regularly and be a part of her life, I spoke to her every day, and I am happy to say that we have a very close relationship as she reaches her twenty-second birthday this month.

About ten years ago, I attended an event to honor Coach at the Jonathan Club in downtown Los Angeles. I was with my new wife, Lori, and this was the first time she had met Coach. He is always so gracious and welcoming and made Lori feel extra special. Lori knew about Coach but had not fully understood or appreciated him until that night. As Coach spoke so eloquently and from the heart we were both crying—as I am right now— when he spoke about Nell and the relationship he had with her. Lori suggested that I reach out to Coach, as she knew I did not feel good about being over forty and was unhappy with my career—or lack thereof.

I had decided that I needed to change my direction but was not really sure where to begin. I lacked confidence, something I feel held me back as a player as well. I started making an effort to attend functions that involved Coach because he always made me feel good. When he saw me, it was like walking into a practice back in my playing days. On one of those days I was in the middle of an interview process for two positions. One was safer and would require less of a change in my lifestyle, and the other was more exciting but would take a total commitment and involved a daily commute of over an hour. I was also not completely confident of my ability to be successful in the second position.

Coach asked me how I was doing, and I told him I was having a difficult time making a decision on some potential career changes and was actually considering staying where I was. Coach said, "You know, Jimmy, there is no progress without change." Now, this is something I had heard Coach say before, but it had never sunk in until that day. I quickly made a decision that I needed to go after the "change of life" position, although I was still not sure I could handle it. As it turns out, I got the position as a development manager for Starbucks Coffee Company, and it was the start of a whole new life for me. I was responsible for finding the sites and opening the company-owned stores in the Los Angeles market.

What I quickly discovered at Starbucks was what had been missing in my professional life. I was now part of a "team"—a team built on treating each other with respect and dignity. As a broker, I had been an individual out there on my own without a support system. Teamwork, dedication, enthusiasm, industriousness, all building blocks in Coach's Pyramid of Success, were starting to make their way back into my life.

After two and a half years, I was promoted to director of development and had a greater responsibility. While I had inherited some great Partners (all Starbucks employees are considered Partners), I set out to mold the group into a team based on many of these same values. Most important to me are integrity (my personal favorite), loyalty, commitment, dedication, honesty, determination and teamwork. I hired only Partners who I felt would buy in and thrive in this philosophy. The team has done some incredible things over the last four and a half years. We have opened more than five hundred stores: stores that have the highest new store sales and profits in the history of the company. However, what makes me most proud is how we have done it and that we are recognized within the entire company as one of the best teams, always committed to being the best we are capable of being (Coach's ultimate goal) and always treating everyone with respect and dignity.

Spillane went on to write that, for Christmas of 2003, his wife, Lori, surprised him with the special gift of a "Breakfast with Coach" scheduled for Saturday, January 3. The entire family went, including Jim, Lori, Kelly, her boyfriend, Jeff, and Jim and Lori's sons, Jake and Luke, who were four and two years old.

"What a wonderful day," Jim writes. "We spent about an hour at the condo, and he was great with the boys. He had them doing little chores like bringing in his mail that the mailman leaves on his balcony so he doesn't have to walk down to the mailbox. Lori took a peek in Coach's bedroom and was brought to tears when she saw Nell's nightgown, her pictures, and the bundle of letters that Coach writes to her. Coach signed a poster and books for us, including his children's book. Just the other day Luke asked me, 'Daddy, was Coach Wooden your coach when you played basketball?' I answered, 'Yes, he was,' and a big smile spread across his face.

"This past year I have had a chance to spend more time with Coach, as he was asked to be a guest speaker at a Starbucks function in Rancho Bernardo, California. Howard Shultz, founder of Starbucks and owner of the Seattle Supersonics, is a big fan of John Wooden. When he heard Coach was speaking, he made a special trip down to meet him, along with Jim Donald, our CEO. It was a very special day for all of us as we visited together for about forty-five minutes before the event. Howard and Jim were like two little kids meeting their hero for the first time. They were amazed at how sharp he is, how humble, and by his extraordinary message.

"Coach's speech that day was so special that Starbucks decided to bring him back to speak to a larger audience. This time, I was able to request that my entire team attend and was able to have all of them meet Coach. It was extremely meaningful for me to share Coach with my team and have them experience firsthand one of the greatest influences in my life.

"On a personal level, the last few years of having Coach back in my life have been remarkable. I have never been more appreciative of his message and what he stands for. I also recognize the importance of having mentors in your life. How I wish I had reached out to him sooner. I know he would have been there for me at any time. Now I am closer to him than ever before. The last time I saw Coach, as I hugged him goodbye he told me that he loved me, and I told him, 'I love you, too, Coach.'

"Pat, just two weeks ago I was promoted to vice president, store development, West Division. While it is a big job, I have more confidence than ever. As long as I keep Coach's message and the principles of the Pyramid with me, I will be fine. I am now blessed with a loving family and a great job and company to work with. I wonder where I would be if I did not take Coach to heart when he said, 'There is no progress without change.'

"I know Coach does not think of himself as a great person. He is just Coach, doing the best he can and being respectful to others, keeping his priorities of God and family first. What I think makes for a great person is the positive influence they have on other people's lives. There is no doubt in my mind that Coach is a great person.

"Thanks for letting me share this. I have never written anything like this before, and it was very emotional for me."

Thank you, Jim, for sharing this powerful story with all of us. Your letter about Coach Wooden's impact on your life concludes this book in perfect fashion.

Stan Jacobs, student manager of high school and college teams coached by Coach Wooden: "I came out of a rather disturbed home life. . . . Whatever good values and standards of ethics that I might have today I attribute to my association with John Wooden, and looking at his values and learning from him, the standards he set, the character he acted out. What he not only spoke about, but acted and lived, has held me in very good stead."

Lynn Schackelford, coached by Coach Wooden at UCLA: "UCLA is a really tough place to play basketball, and that makes what John Wooden did even more amazing when you consider all the people he had to keep happy—if not happy, at least satisfied, and if not satisfied, at least still on the team or in the school. . . . What I learned from John Wooden about life is the basic faith that things in the long run will work out. If you have principles, stick to them even if they cost you some in the short run. They will help you in the long run, and it will be for the best."

Pete Blackman, coached by Coach Wooden at UCLA: "I learned from his extraordinarily detailed organization. He was fantastically prepared, literally every practice was planned down to the minute. You don't lose track of lessons like that. When you are preparing for a major business presentation fifteen years later, you look around and you're probably the best prepared person there. Well, why is that true? Because people like [Coach Wooden] proved to you at an early stage of development that the time spent in preparation will pay off."

Sebastian Nowicki, coached by Coach Wooden in high school: "I played for Wooden in 1937 and 1938. . . . He had a tremendous effect on me. . . . [Once we drove down to southern Indiana] and stopped at Logansport. We were supposed to have a meal there. Pete Donaldson, a black man on our team, sat down, but they went to Coach and told him [Pete] had to eat in the kitchen. That's fifty years ago. And [Coach] says, 'Let's go somewhere else.' And we did."

Lucius Allen, coached by Coach Wooden at UCLA: "It's hard to put into words all the different ways Coach Wooden has had an impact on me. He is a shining example of what you can do if you keep yourself in shape and treat everyone well around you—good things will happen."

Paul Silas, former NBA coach: "I heard John Wooden lecture at Michael Jordan's Summer Camp in 2003. Coach said, 'The key to being a good athlete is physical, mental and emotional balance. You can't get too high or too low, in the course of a contest or the season. When the ref makes a bad call, you can't let it throw you off stride.'"

Bill Walton said to John Wooden during his UCLA days while suffering with great pain in his knees: "Coach, I've heard that smoking marijuana will reduce the pain in my knees. Is it okay with you if I use it?" Coach Wooden replied, "Bill, I haven't heard that it is a pain reliever, but I have heard that it's illegal."

Andy Hill, former UCLA player: "No one's perfect and, of all people, I know he's not, but he's closer than anyone else I know and, by that, I mean Coach really does live in congruence with the philosophy he espouses."

I'll let Coach Wooden have the final word on his successful life: "I have peace with myself."

A SPECIAL MESSAGE FOR COACHES

Can you imagine what it must have been like to attend a practice session at UCLA when Coach was at the peak of his career? What a wonderful experience for a coach in any sport! Imagine the lessons you could learn from just a few minutes of watching John Wooden put one of his championship teams through its paces.

Unfortunately, there are no time machines to take us back to one of those magnificent moments in basketball history. But recently, I came across the next best thing: a brand-new book by Bruins standout Swen Nater. Nater does a masterful job of telling exactly what it was like to be present at one of those practices. As I read his words, I almost felt as if I were there in person. I know that you'll feel the same way. Please read the next few paragraphs carefully. This is the closest you'll ever come to seeing Coach preparing his troops for battle:

Each one of Coach Wooden's practice sessions was planned to the minute. Every activity lasted a predetermined amount of time, and time was never compromised, for any activity or for the duration of the session. Not a moment was wasted. When the whistle blew, signaling the end of a drill, players, coaches, and managers moved purposefully and quickly to the next drill in a machine-like manner. But there was quickness, not hurrying. Even before we were in place for the next activity, Coach was already shouting instructions. Seniors and experienced team members echoed his instructions to the rest of us. Efficiency, intensity, industriousness and purpose dominated and controlled our effort and concentration.

He never let up. From the beginning to the end of practice, Coach commanded, exhorted and demanded our best. He moved with us, around us, before us, and paced, stopped, and started, always setting the pace of practice and constantly increasing the tempo. Although off the court he was a mild-mannered man, when he stepped into his basketball classroom, he was an intense, very verbal and possessed teacher who had three things on his mind—improvement, improvement, improvement. And off the court, that meant planning, planning, planning.

I also remember that each practice session had a purpose and was related to the one before, the one yet to come, and to some future goal. What we learned was cumulative, like a well-planned math curriculum where prior information was needed to solve future problems.

From the moment he stepped on the practice floor, he set the tone for the intensity; the meter was always pegged high, and he worked our tails off for the entire two hours. He demanded our best effort, every minute of practice. He corrected every mistake, became disgusted and impatient often, and sparingly distributed praises. Mentally, emotionally and physically, he drove us to the brink of collapse. It seemed like nothing was ever good enough. Perfection was what he was after. He was like a drill sergeant.

And he didn't stop there. He demanded impeccable class attendance, never condoned inconsiderate treatment of others, strongly addressed waste, despised the mistreatment of animals and would not put up with inappropriate language. If he found one piece of trash in our locker room after a practice, we would hear about it at his next opportunity. He was a stickler for proper dress; even our practice shirts were to be tucked in with a minimum degree of slack allowed. Any player who tried to get away with anything was immediately spotted and received a lecture.

Here's what Coach himself has to say about the way he ran practice at UCLA:

> I thought my basketball practices were well-organized and efficient. After observing Coach Frank Leahy's football practice at Notre Dame, I realized more work was needed. There was not one minute wasted. Even the transitions from drill to drill were done with no wasted second. Players seemed to enjoy the work, and everyone worked hard for the entire two hours. I was impressed and after meeting with Frank Leahy for answers to questions I had, I immediately applied what I had learned to my own situation.
>
> After witnessing Leahy conduct practice so efficiently, I raised the

bar for myself and was determined to jump over it. I continued to learn and to improve my planning. I deeply believe that the teacher and coach who has the ability to properly plan . . . from both the daily and the long-range point of view together with the ability to devise the necessary drills to meet his particular needs for maximum efficiency, has tremendously increased his possibility of success.

Coach also writes:

I would spend almost as much time planning a practice as conducting it. Everything was planned out each day. In fact, in my later years at UCLA I would spend two hours every morning with my assistants organizing that day's practice sessions (even though the practice itself might be less than two hours long). I kept a record of every practice session in a loose-leaf notebook for future reference. Prior to practice time, the secretary would type the entire daily plan onto 3 x 5 index cards, give them to me, and I distributed them to all coaches and managers. Those cards informed every staff member of all activities and the exact time each would start and finish. As a result, coaches and managers were prepared to quickly transition from activity to activity without any wasted time. Every second is important. . . .

I could go back to the [19]48–49 year and tell you what we did on November the 15th—minute by minute what we did—and I think that helped me tremendously by doing those (plans).

Perhaps you were born too late to see Coach in action. But now, thanks to Swen Nater—and Coach himself—you know what it was like to see one of sport's great geniuses at work.

A Heartfelt Thanks

❧

I sincerely wish to thank the men and women listed below who responded to my request to share their insights, reflections and feelings about Coach Wooden. Included below are family members and friends, coaching colleagues, sportswriters, admirers and just plain fans from all over America. If I have omitted any names, I sincerely apologize. I conducted 837 interviews, and my only regret is that I didn't get to talk to thousands more who have been impacted by Coach Wooden's life.

FRAN ABBOTT
KAREEM ABDUL-JABBAR
ERNIE ACCORSI
DICK ACKERMAN
MIKE ADAMLE
CARROLL ADAMS
GARY ADAMS
DR. MEL ADELMAN
RICK ADELMAN
FRANKLIN ADLER
DANNY AINGE
DON AINGE
JOHN AKERS
RICK ALBERTSON
BOBBY ALEJO
STEVE ALFORD
SONNY ALLEN
ARTHUR J. ALPER
BOB ALSHULER
DR. HARLAN AMSTUTZ
MRS. LLOYD G. ANDERSON
JASON ARAGON
FRANK ARNOLD

JACK ARNOLD
MURRAY ARNOLD
RANDY ARRILLAGA
JEFF ASHER
RED AUERBACH
RANDY AYERS
PETE BABCOCK
KEITH BAILEY
TOBY BAILEY
TAY BAKER
GREG BALLARD
RICHARD BANTON
DR. GREGORY BARNETT
JIM BARNETT
JIM BARON
JIM BARON JR.
RAY W. BARTLETT
GENE BARTOW
TOM BARTOW
HERBERT BASTIN
RALPH BAUER
GARY BEBAN
BILL BENNETT

DICK BERG
CARYN BERNSTEIN
ERIC BERNSTEIN
GARY BERNSTEIN
BILL BERRY
BILL BERTKA
RICK BETCHLEY
HENRY BIBBY
ED BILIK
LARRY BIRD
DOUG BIRNIE
STEVE BISHEFF
FURMAN BISHER
PETE BLACKMAN
MARTY BLAKE
DARRON BOATRIGHT
HAL BOCK
CARL BOLDT
KENNY BOOKER
KEVIN BORG
VINCE BORYLA
WAYNE BOULDING
RICK BOZICH
BILL BRADLEY
CLIFF BRANDON
PETE BREY
BEAU BRIDGES
JOEL BRILES
CHARD BROCK
BORIS BRODETSKY
SOPHIA BRODETSKY
GARY BROKAW
BRUCE BROWN
DALE BROWN
HERB BROWN
HUBIE BROWN
JAMES BROWN
JEFF BROWN
JOE BROWN
LARRY BROWN
RENEE BROWN

STEPHEN BRUCKER
DALE BRUDVIG
STEVE BRUMBACH
HALLIE BRYANT
VIC BUBAS
ANELIDA BUCCOLA
GUY BUCCOLA
QUINN BUCKNER
BOB BURKE
JIM BUSH
DAVE BUSS
BILL BUSSENIUS
MITCHELL BUTLER
JIM CALHOUN
JOHN CALIPARI
AL CAMARILLO
P. J. CARLESIMO
CHRIS CARLSON
GENE CARMICHEAL
LOU CARNESECCA
PETE CARRIL
ROBERT CARSON
VINCENT CARSON
BILL CARTWRIGHT
JAY CARTY
BOB CASE
DON CASEY
GALE CATLETT
DEAN CHANCE
VAN CHANCELLOR
JOHN CHANEY
DWIGHT CHAPIN
JONATHAN E. CHAMPAN
GORDON CHIESA
FRED CLAIRE
JERRY COLANGELO
JIM COLCLOUGH
DONALD A. COLEMAN
BARRY COLLIER
DOUG COLLINS
JIM COLLINS

GARY COLSON
GENE CONLEY
CURT CONRAD
MICHAEL COOPER
BOB COSTAS
BOB COUSY
BILL COWDREY
DAVE COWENS
JOE CRAVENS
BOBBY CREMINS
DAVE CRIDER
RANDY CROSS
DENNY CRUM
BILLY CUNNINGHAM
GARY CUNNINGHAM
DON CURRIN
DENISE CURRY
BOB CURTIS
LIN CURTIS
MIKE CURTIS
RENE CURTIS
TOMMY CURTIS
DONNY DANIELS
ADRIAN DANTLEY
TOM DAVIES
BARON DAVIS
BRAD DAVIS
TOM DAVIS
CARROLL DAWSON
DARREN DAYE
JOE DEAN
BOB DEANO
ROD DEDEAUX
FRANK DEFORD
JOE DEGREGORIO
TOM DESOTELL
BILL DETRICK
DON DEVOE
DENNIS DEXTER
LARRY DIAMOND
ROGER DICKINSON

JAMIE DIXON
DR. JAMES DOBSON
JOHN DOLEVA
MARC DOLLINS
JIM DONALD
MICHAEL DONAHUE
DON DONOHER
SONIA DONOHER
ED DONOHUE
BILLY DONOVAN
EDDIE DOUCETTE
ROSE DRAKE
HOMER DREW
LEFTY DRIESELL
RALPH DROLLINGER
ANN MEYERS DRYSDALE
JOHN DUDECK
JEFF DUNLAP
MIKE DUNLEAVY
FRAN DUNPHY
MARV DUNPHY
BRICE DURBIN
HUGH DURHAM
MELVIN DURSLAG
BILL DWYER
MAL EATON
MARK EATON
BILL EBLIN
TYUS EDNY
BOB EHRLICH
ED EHLERS
EDDIE EINHORN
RON EKKER
NORM ELLENBERG
LEN ELMORE
DR. CHARLES ELSWICK
WAYNE EMBRY
DICK ENBERG
DOUG ERICKSON
KEITH ERICKSON
CARL ERSKINE

JULIUS ERVING
BOB ESKEW
FRANCIS ESSIC
LT. COLONEL GERALD C. EVANS
LARRY FARMER
GENE FAUST
DUTCH FEHRING
JEFF FELLENZER
DENNIS FELTON
LISA FERNANDEZ
ARNIE FERRIN
MARK FEW
VALERIE KONDOS FIELD
CHUCK FIELDSON
GARY FILBERT
MYRON FINKBEINER
STEVE FISHER
BILL FITCH
COTTON FITZSIMMONS
JASON FLOWERS
TIM FLOYD
KEVIN FOLEY
JIM FORKUM
DR. ALLAN FORREST
CAROLE FOREST
CHERYL FORSATZ
BILL FOSTER
JIM FOULK
GARY FRANKLIN
MIKE FRATELLO
JERRY FRIEDMAN
BUD FURILLO
DAN GADZURIC
JOHN GALBRAITH
CLARENCE GAINES
MARY GARBER
RICH GARON
CLIFF GARRISON
JOHN GASSENSMITH
OLLIE GELSTON
BOB GEOGHAN

RAY GIACOLETTI
BILLY GILLESPIE
LARRY GITTLER
BILL GLEASON
DICK GLUCKSMAN
DAN GODWIN
MITCH GOLD
DONALD GOODENOUGH
ROGER GOODLING
GAIL GOODRICH
MARK GOTTFRIED
BOB GOTTLIEB
CURT GOWDY
LARRY GOWER
JIM GRAY
STEWART GRAY
BRETT GREENBERG
SETH GREENBERG
STEVEN GROOTHUIS
MARVIN GROSS
DAN GUERRERO
MATTY GUOKAS
TIM GURGRICH
BILL GUTHRIDGE
PAT HAGGERTY
FRANK HAITH
JOE B. HALL
JOHN HALL
JIM HANEY
MEL HANKINSON
GUY HANSEN
BILL HANZLICK
JIM HARLEY
MERLE HARMON
JIM HARRICK
DEL HARRIS
KEITH HARRISON
MARV HARSHMAN
GJ HART
DICK HARTER
CLEM HASKINS

DON HASKINS
TOMMY HAWKINS
JALEESA HAZZARD
WALT HAZZARD
JUD HEATHCOTE
MIKE HEHR
ROLAND HEMOND
LOU HENSON
RICH HERRIN
GARY HESS
PAUL HEWITT
CHRIS HIBLER
J. MICHAEL HIBLER
MIKE HIBLER
BILL HICKS
ANDY HILL
BOB HILL
BRIAN HILL
CALVIN HILL
GRANT HILL
RICO HINES
JACK HIRSCH
STAN HOCHMAN
VAUGHN HOFFMAN
BRAD HOLLAND
TERRY HOLLAND
DAVE HOLLANDER
MICHAEL HOLTON
DR. RICK HOWE
BEN HOWLAND
LARRY HUEBNER
BILL HUEGELE
JERRY HUESER
ROD HUNDLEY
BOBBY HUSSEY
DAVE IMMEL
CHRISTY IMPELMAN
CRAIG IMPELMAN
JOHN IMPELMAN
KYLE IMPELMAN
MRS. RICHARD INGRAM

STU INMAN
RALPH IRVIN
TOM IZZO
KEITH JACKSON
PHIL JACKSON
STANLEY JACOBS
STEVE JACOBSEN
BRIAN JAMES
STEVE JAMISON
BILL JAUSS
JOHN JAY
DICK JERARDI
RALPH JOECKEL
BILL JOHNSON
DON JOHNSON
DR. DUNCAN JOHNSON
ERNIE JOHNSON
GREG JOHNSON
MARQUES JOHNSON
NEVILLE JOHNSON
PHIL JOHNSON
BILL JOHNSTON
OLLIE JOHNSTON
STEPHANIE JOSEPHSEN
E. THAYNE KAING
JOHN KALIN
JASON KAPONO
GEORGE KARL
JIM KARVELLAS
VYTAS J. KATILIUS
DR. JERRY KAY
GENE KEADY
DUSTIN KEARNS
DR. H. LINDY KELL
TED KELLNER
STEVE KELLY
YVAN KELLY
ERNIE KENT
JOHN KERR
DIXIE KILLGORE
DALE KINDRED

JEFF KING
STAN KING
DR. KEN KLEINMAN
BILL KNAPTON
ANDREW KNOX
JACK KRAFT
CARL KRAUSHAAR
DOUG KRIKORIAN
DENNIS KRUSE
MIKE KRZYZEWSKI
STEVE KURASCH
CRAIG KUSHEN
LON KRUGER
MIKE KUNSTADT
HANK KUZMA
ALAN KYBER
TONY LA SCALA
DR. MALCOLM LAING
DON LANDRY
DR. RICHARD LAPCHICK
STANLEY LAPPEN
TOMMY LASORDA
BUD LATHROP
STEVE LAVIN
FRANK LAYDEN
JEFF LEBO
GREG LEE
NEIL LEIFER
FRANK LENTZ
GLENN LENTZ
BOB LEONARD
MICHAEL LEVI
BUZZ LEVICK
RICH LEVIN
RANDY LEVINE
BEN LEVOIS
MARV LEVY
BEN LEWIS
GUY LEWIS
HARRY LINDEN
RON LIVINGSTON

DUKE LLEWELLYN
JOHN LOTZ
BRANDON LOYD
JOHN LUCAS
BOB LUKSTA
JIM LYNAM
TONY LUFTMAN
DICK LYNN
BILL LYON
PAUL MA
DR. JOHN MACARTHUR
GIL MACGREGOR
CLAUDIE MACKEY
JIM MACKIN
DON MACLEAN
JOHN MACLEOD
KYLE MACY
RICK MAJERUS
GENE MAKO
LARRY MALANCON
BRENDAN MALONE
TIM MALONEY
BOB MARCUS
MICHAEL MARIENTHAL
JOHN B. MASTERSON
THAD MATTA
JOHN MAXWELL
LARRY MAXWELL
ALBERT MAZZA
BOB MAZZA
ANGELO MAZZONE
CARL MCBAIN
JACK MCCLOSKEY
CAREY E. MCDONALD
JIM MCFERSON
THAD MCGREW
DOUG MCINTOSH
FRANK MCINTYRE
RITCHIE MCKAY
FRANK MCLAUGHLIN
GENE MEHAFFEY

EDDIE MERRINS
ED MESSBARGER
DON MEYER
JOEY MEYER
RAY MEYER
BOB MEYERS
DAVID MIELKE
NIGEL MIGUEL
JIM MILHORN
ALAN B. MILLER
CHERYL MILLER
DENNY MILLER
LEN MILLER
RENE J. MILLER
WILLIAM MILLS
DAVID MILNE
MICHAEL MINK
DENNIS MISHKO
TOM MITCHELL
HUBERT MIZELL
DOUG MOE
CHARLES MOIR
SAM MOIR
PAUL MOKESKI
BRUCE MONFETTE
DAN MONSON
MIKE MONTGOMERY
RANDY MONTGOMERY
PALMER MOODY
JOHN MOON
BETH MOORE
BILL MOORE
CYNTHIA MORGAN
GEORGE MORGAN
JIM MORRIS
ROGER MORRISON
STAN MORRISON
WILL MOSSELLE
DICK MOTTA
DICK MUEHLHAUSEN
NAN MUEHLHAUSEN

MARK MULHALL
CHARLES MURPHY
TRACY MURRAY
BOB MURREY
BRENT MUSBURGER
ERIC MUSSELMAN
TOM NAKAYAMA
SWEN NATER
WILLIE NAULS
JAMEER NELSON
ERNIE NESTER
PETE NEWELL
C. M. NEWTON
AB NICHOLAS
BOB NICHOLS SR.
HANK NICHOLS
CORI NICHOLSON
DAVID NIELSEN
JIM NIELSEN
TOM NISSALKE
NORM NIXON
CHUCK NOE
AL NORDQUIST
CHRIS NORDQUIST
BILL OATES
BOB OATES
CHARLES O'BANNON
ED O'BANNON JR.
ED O'BANNON SR.
JIM O'BRIEN
JIM O'CONNELL
KEVIN O'CONNER
DAVE ODOM
KEN OLSON
LUTE OLSON
ALEX OMALEV
SHAQUILLE O'NEAL
BRUCE O'NEIL
JOHN ORR
BOB ORTEGEL
R. K. OVERPECK

KEITH OWENS

TED OWENS

BILLY PACKER

ROD PALMER

DAVE PARKER

LOUIS PATLER

STEVE PATTERSON

RICARDO PATTON

BARRY PAVLOVICH

BOB PAYNTER

RON PEARSON

CAROLYN PECK

DICK PERRY

CARL PETERSON

NEAL PETERSON

LEE PFUND

RANDY PFUND

JIM PHELAN

DAWSON PIKEY

ROBYN PIKEY

JERRY PIMM

RICK PITINO

BOBBIE POE

ED POPE

TOM POPE

BARRY PORTER

BOB POSER

ERIC POSER

JOHN POSER

LOIS POTENCA

BOBBY POUNDS

EDDIE POWELL

SHAUN POWELL

JIM POWERS

SKIP PROSSER

JEFF PRUGH

KIM PUCKETT

DAVE PUMP

DANA PUMP

JASON RABEDEAUX

DR. JACK RAMSAY

TODD RAMSUER

BILL RANKIN

DENNIS RASMUSSEN

GEORGE RAVELING

HANK RAYMONDS

MARK REICHSLING

MATT REISCHLING

WIL RENKEN

ELMER REYNOLDS

MIKE RICE

BOBBY RICHARDSON

DOT RICHARDSON

POOH RICHARDSON

DIANE RIDGEWAY

RICH RIDGEWAY

PAT RILEY

MICHAEL J. ROANE JR.

CLAIRE ROBBINS

COLE ROBBINS

DAVID ROBBINS

GAILEND ROBBINS

KIM ROBBINS

CHRIS ROBERTS

DANNY ROBERTS

MIKE ROBERTS

OSCAR ROBERTSON

GLEN ROBINSON

LES ROBINSON

PEPPER RODGERS

BEN ROGERS

LORENZO ROMAR

DAVE ROSE

LEE ROSE

JOEL ROSS

DEE ROWE

SAUL ROWEN

JEFF RULAND

BILL RUSSELL

DON RUTLEDGE

BO RYAN

BOB RYAN

BUTCH RYAN
MATT RYAN
LENNY RZESZEWSKI
JOHN SAINTIGNON
DON SAFFER
HERB SALBERG
DOUG SALE
KELVIN SAMPSON
GRETCHEN SAMUELS
MIKE SAMUELS
MICHAEL SANDERS
WIMP SANDERSON
NEVILLE SANER
PAUL R. SAUNDERS
BONNIE SAWYER
CRAIG SCALISE
FRED SCHAUS
DOLPH SCHAYES
SHARM SCHEURMAN
HOWARD SCHULTZ
DOUG SCHWAB
JIM SCHWEITZER
CHARLES "BUD" SCOTT
DON SEIDEL
FRED SHABEL
MAX SHAPIRO
BILL SHARMAN
DAN SHAUGHNESSY
DAL SHEALY
EDDIE SHELDRAKE
JUDY SHERBERT
RON SHERBERT
MIKE SHERIDEN
CRAIG SHERMON
DON SHOWALTER
WALT SHUBLOM
LARRY SHYATT
PAUL SILAS
SANDY SILVER
JIM SINEGAL
VICTOR SISON

AL SKATES
ROY SKINNER
FRED SLAUGHTER
JERRY SLOAN
NORM SLOAN
LEE SMELSER
BILL SMITH
BRIAN SMITH
CHRIS SMITH
DEAN SMITH
GAVIN SMITH
MICHAEL SMITH
SONNY SMITH
STEPHEN A. SMITH
TUBBY SMITH
GENE SMITHSON
QUIN SNYDER
DON SODERQUIST
MICHAEL SONDHEIMER
JIM SPILLANE
TONY SPINO
CHARLIE SPOONHOUR
GEORGE STANICH
RICK STANSBURY
DICK STARMANN
HARRY STATHAM
GORDON STAUFFER
JERRY STEELE
JIM STEFFEN
WAYNE STEPHANOFF
GARY STERN
JOHN STEVENSON
LARRY STEWART
NORM STEWART
SCOTTY STIRLING
TERRY STOTTS
DAVE STRACK
BEN STULL
BRENDAN SUHR
PAT SUMMITT
EDDIE SUTTON

BILL SWEEK
CARL TACY
MORRIS TAFT
GEORGE TALBOT
JERRY TARKANIAN
KENT TAYLOR
TOM TAYLOR
CLAUDE TERRY
GEORGE TERZIAN
BOB THAU
HUGH THIMLAR
DOUG THOMSON
FRED THORNLEY
DICK TOMEY
CURTIS W. TONG
GENE TORMOHLEN
EMORY TOTH
CAMERON TRAPANI
CATHLEEN TRAPANI
PAUL TRAPANI
TYLER TRAPANI
BARBARA TRAYLOR
JAY TRIANO
PETE TRGOVICH
MIKE TSCHIRRET
JIM TUNNEY
ROLAND UNDERHILL
SONNY VACARRO
JOHN VALLELY
BOB VALVANO
JAN VAN BREDA KOFF
LANNY VAN EMAN
CHARLIE VAN SLYKE
BOB VANATTA
JOE VANCISIN
DR. ERNIE VANDEWEGHE
KIKI VANDEWEGHE
BILL VAN GUNDY
JEFF VAN GUNDY
STAN VAN GUNDY
ROBERT L. "BOBBY" VAUGHAN

DAVID VENA
DICK VERMEIL
DICK VERSACE
PETE VESCEY
GENE VICTOR
DICK VITALE
BRETT VROMAN
ROY VUJOVICH
GARY WACKER
MIKE WALDEN
MIKE WALDNER
KEN WALES
CHET WALKER
DR. LEROY WALKER
WALLY WALKER
CHRIS WALLACE
JUDY WALLACE
DONNIE WALSH
BILL WALTON
LUKE WALTON
MAY LEE WANG
MIKE WARREN
TOM WASDIN
JAMES WASHINGTON
KENNETH WASHINGTON
KERMIT WASHINGTON
BRUCE WATANABE
BUCKY WATERS
EARL WATSON
BOB WEBB
CHRIS WEBBER
BRUCE WEBER
KEN WEINER
BOB WEISS
DICK WEISS
JERRY WELSH
JERRY WEST
PAUL WESTHEAD
PAUL WESTPHAL
RALPH WHITLEY
LEWIS J. WHITNEY JR.

SIDNEY WICKS
GEORGE WIGTON
MORLON WILEY
LENNY WILKENS
GLEN WILKES
JAMES WILLIAMS
JIM WILLIAMS
JIMMY WILLIAMS
JOE WILLIAMS
KAY WILLIAMS
PAT WILLIAMS
ROY WILLIAMS
SANDRA WILLIAMS
SPENCER WILLIAMS
TOM WILLIAMS
TOMMY WILLIAMS
KEN WILSON
TREVOR WILSON
IRVIN WISNIEWSKI
HAL WISSELL
RALPH WITT
DARYL WIZELMAN
ALEXANDER WOLFF
BOB WOLFF
DUANE "MOOSE" WOLTZEN
MAE LEE WONG

ASHLYN WOODEN
AVERY WOODEN
BRIDGET WOODEN
CARLEEN WOODEN
GREG WOODEN
JIM WOODEN
JOHN WOODEN
JOHN WOODEN
JOSHUA WOODEN
KATHY WOODEN
KIM WOODEN
LACEY WOODEN
MICHAEL WOODEN
RUTH HARRIETTE WOODEN
WILLIAM WOODEN
JOE WOOTTEN
MORGAN WOOTTEN
PATRICIA WOOTTEN
BRAD WRIGHT
JAY WRIGHT
DAVE YANAI
CHARLES YENDORK
DR. CHARLES YOUNG
ZIG ZIGLAR
RODNEY ZIMMERMAN
SCOTT ZUFFELATO

Bibliography

Abdul-Jabbar, Kareem. *Kareem.* New York: Random House, 1990.

Bisheff, Steve. *John Wooden. An American Treasure.* Nashville: Cumberland House, 2004.

Chapin, Dwight, and Jeff Prugh. *The Wizard of Westwood.* Boston: Houghton Mifflin Company, 1973.

Enberg, Dick. *Oh My!* Chicago: Sports Publishing, LLC, 2005.

Hill, Andrew. *Be Quick—But Don't Hurry!* New York: Simon & Schuster, 2001.

Hollander, Dave. *52 Weeks.* Guilford, CT: The Lyons Press, 2005.

Johnson, Neville, C. *The John Wooden Pyramid of Success.* Los Angeles, 2000.

Johnson, Neville, C. *The John Wooden Pyramid of Success.* Los Angeles, 2003.

Johnson, Neville, C. *The John Wooden Pyramid of Success.* Los Angeles, 2004.

Nater, Swen, and Ronald, Gallimore. *You Haven't Taught Until They Have Learned.* Morgan, WV: Fitness Information Technology, 2006.

Naulls, Willie. *Levitation's View 2: The Wooden Years.* Laguna Niguel, CA: Willie Naulls Ministries, 2005.

Reger, John. *Quotable Wooden.* Nashville: Towlehouse Publishing, 2002.

Wooden, John. *My Personal Best.* New York: McGraw-Hill, 2004.

Wooden, John. *Practical Modern Basketball.* New York: John Wiley & Sons, 1966, 1980.

Wooden, John. *They Call Me Coach.* Chicago: Contemporary Books, 1988.

Wooden, John. *Wooden on Leadership.* New York: McGraw-Hill, 2005.

Wooden, John and Jay Carty. *Coach Wooden One-on-One.* Ventura, CA: Regal Books, 2003.

Wooden, John, and Jay Carty. *Coach Wooden's Pyramid of Success.* Ventura, CA: Regal Books, 2005.

Wooden, John, and Steve Jamison. *Wooden: A Lifetime of Observations On and Off the Court.* Lincolnwood, IL: Contemporary Books, 1997

Acknowledgments

❧

WITH DEEP APPRECIATION I acknowledge the support and guidance of the following people who helped make this book possible:

Special thanks to Bob Vander Weide and Rich DeVos of the Orlando Magic.

I'm grateful to my assistant, Diana Connery, who managed so many details that made this book possible.

Many thanks to Doug Connery and Katie Radkewich, for all of their hard work in helping to coordinate the research for this book.

Hats off to four dependable associates: my colleague Andrew Herdliska, my adviser Ken Hussar, Vince Pileggi of the Orlando Magic mail/copy room and my ace typist Fran Thomas.

Special thanks to Nan Muehlhausen, Bill Bennett and Eddie Sheldrake, for making significant contributions to this book in the area of research and interviews.

Hearty thanks are also due to Peter Vegso and his fine staff at Health Communications, Inc., and to my partner in writing this book, Dave Wimbish. Thank you all for believing that we had something important to share about Coach Wooden and for providing the support and the forum to say it.

And finally, special thanks and appreciation go to my wife, Ruth, and to my wonderful and supportive family. They are truly the backbone of my life.

—*Pat Williams*

You can contact Pat Williams directly at:
Mr. Pat Williams
c/o Orlando Magic
8701 Maitland Summit Blvd.
Orlando, FL 32810
(407) 916-2404 (private line)
pwilliams@orlandomagic.com
Please visit Pat Williams's website at:
www.patwilliamsmotivate.com

Pat Williams is one of America's leading motivational and inspirational speakers. He speaks about 150 times a year on a wide range of topics, including teamwork, leadership and personal improvement. He tailors every presentation for the particular audience. Visit Pat's Web site at *www.patwilliamsmotivate.com*.

If you would like to set up a speaking engagement for Pat Williams, please write his assistant, Diana Connery, at the above address or call her at (407) 916-2454. Requests can also be faxed to (407) 916-2986 or e-mailed to *dconnery@orlandomagic.com*.